STRATFORD-UPON-AVON STUDIES 14

General Editors

MALCOLM BRADBURY
& DAVID PALMER

Already published in this series

★ *Under the general editorship of John Russell Brown and Bernard Harris*

STRATFORD-UPON-AVON STUDIES 14

SHAKESPEARIAN COMEDY

CRANE, RUSSAK & COMPANY, INC.
New York

© EDWARD ARNOLD (PUBLISHERS) LTD 1972

First published 1972 by
Edward Arnold (Publishers) Ltd

Published in the United States by:
Crane, Russak & Company, Inc.
52 Vanderbilt Avenue
New York, N.Y. 10017

Library of Congress Catalog No. 72–83715

ISBN 0 8448 0067 8

Printed in Great Britain by
Butler & Tanner Ltd, Frome and London

Contents

Preface

THE time is past when Shakespearian comedy could be regarded simply as light entertainment; in its own way it is an art as 'serious', as much concerned with human values, as the art of tragedy. Informed by a critical awareness of the limitations as well as the possibilities of different attitudes to life, the comedies achieve an increasingly subtle equilibrium between romance and reality, reason and imagination, wisdom and folly, restraint and licence, and they are consequently both rich in meaning and complex in dramatic effect. These are the qualities that have attracted particular attention from the contributors to this volume. The approach through form and structure is made by John Russell Brown, who examines Shakespeare's skill in manipulating the dramatic interest between tension and relaxation; by Stanley Wells, who analyses and compares the patterning of *Love's Labour's Lost*, *A Midsummer Night's Dream* and *The Tempest*, three plays in which Shakespeare is free to organize his material without following a narrative source; and by Anne Barton, who argues that the conclusions of *As You Like It* and *Twelfth Night*, far from being hurried and careless (as Dr. Johnson thought), are highly wrought and finely balanced resolutions. Three other chapters deal with character-types whose presence in the plays to which they belong deepens yet sustains the comic tone: R. A. Foakes considers the moralists and spokesmen of reason, including Duke Theseus, Jaques and Malvolio, in terms of the contrapuntal structure of Shakespearian comedy; Gareth Lloyd Evans explores Shakespeare's conception of the wise fool as a result of his collaboration with Robert Armin; and Tony Nuttall traces the literary genealogy that illuminates the kinship of Jaques and Caliban. Each of the other four chapters in the volume is focused on a particular play: Inga-Stina Ewbank reconsiders the problems of interpretation and critical evaluation in *The Two Gentlemen of Verona*, from the point of view of poetic style; John Dixon Hunt discusses the courtly values embodied in *Love's Labour's Lost*; David Palmer distinguishes between different kinds of seriousness in *The Merchant of Venice*; and Jocelyn Powell studies the dramatic method of *Measure for Measure*. Of the ten comedies which belong to the first half of Shakespeare's career, only *The Comedy of Errors*, *The Taming of the Shrew* and *The Merry Wives of Windsor* are not given detailed consideration here: an omission which reflects less on their merits than on the volume's prevailing interest in the more 'romantic' plays. On the other hand, the reader will find in the volume a ubiquitous sense of the continuity and development which leads from the comedies to the problem plays and forward into the last plays: the unity of Shakespearian comedy cannot be reduced to a formula, but it is as discernible as its versatility.

DAVID PALMER

December 1971   MALCOLM BRADBURY

The Presentation of Comedy:
The First Ten Plays

JOHN RUSSELL BROWN

I

THE dominant focus of Shakespeare's comedies is wide. Their very titles proclaim it, for these plays are not named after their main characters like the tragedies. *The Merchant of Venice* sounds like an exception: but who is the 'Merchant'? Antonio, Shylock, the venturer Bassanio, Lorenzo and Jessica who exchange a turquoise for a monkey, or Portia who tries to buy Antonio's life and encounters Shylock's bond? The audience of a Shakespearian comedy is not led towards an intimate knowledge of a single character, but towards a wide view of the whole stage. It will sympathize with several of the characters in turn; it will be excited, charmed, interested, enlivened, surprised, but when all has been experienced in the due sequence of performance and is thus truly summed up, then the audience must sit back and be aware of the whole effect, must 'take it all in', the relation of character to character, the contrasts in attitudes, words and silences. Shakespeare's comedies lead towards such a wide focus.

This accords with much that has been said about the comic spirit in general. A wide view of the stage can ensure an experience in keeping with Bergson's notion of comedy:

Step aside, look upon life as a disinterested spectator: many a drama will turn into a comedy.[1]

It provides the appropriate view for comic acting, as described by Athene Seyler in the light of her accomplished stage-career:

Comedy is simply a point of view. It is a comment on life *from outside*, an observation on human nature.[2]

---

[1] Henri Bergson, *Laughter*, translated by F. Rothwell (1900); quoted in *Comedy: Meaning and Form*, edited by R. W. Corrigan (San Francisco, 1965), p. 473.

[2] Athene Seyler and S. Haggard, *The Craft of Comedy* (London, 1943), p. 8 (the italics are mine).

A wide focus permits an audience to make the comparisons or contrasts which are often held to be the source of comic pleasure. The opposite, intense focus would involve an audience too directly and minutely to allow laughter: to take an example from every-day life, the teacher of dancing does not laugh at the movements of his pupils as a disinterested person entering the room is free to do. No matter how serious a playwright's intention may be, to raise laughter from his audience he must relax each auditor so that, in one sense, he becomes 'disinterested'. Freud put this point in other terms when he said that:

> The pleasure in jokes has seemed to us to arise from an economy in expenditure upon inhibition, the pleasure in the comic from an economy in expenditure upon ideation and the pleasure in humour from an economy in expenditure upon feeling. All those are agreed in representing methods of regaining from mental activity a pleasure which has in fact been lost through the development of that activity.[3]

'Economy', in this sense, implies the opposite of intent and close involvement. Whether we explain the comic spirit in Freud's terms, or in an actor's, or by observing how we laugh in everyday life, we may believe that, if a comedy is to provoke laughter in a theatre, it must gain our interest but must also induce a width of view and ease of reception. It needs the range and relaxation of a predominantly wide dramatic focus.

A Shakespearian comedy is not, of course, 'laughs all the way'. A romantic, fantastic or ideal strain runs through each of them. Often this is quantitatively the greater part, and always it provides the dominant mood of the concluding scene. But then, for romance, a somewhat similar width of focus is required as for comedy. Numerous authors have described the kind of relaxation that is called for by their romantic fictions: so Sir Philip Sidney told his sister to read *The Arcadia* in her 'idle times' (and its style and narrative method clearly presuppose a leisured reader); and Edmund Spenser has confessed that his own delight in the 'spacious and wyde' ways of 'the land of Faery' often caused him to forget his detailed and 'tedious' work, even as he was writing *The Faerie Queene* (Book VI, Proem i). Shakespeare himself

---

[3] S. Freud, *Jokes and Their Relation to the Unconscious*, translated by J. Strachey, *Works*, VIII (London, 1960), p. 236.

has caused Puck, in his epilogue, to liken *A Midsummer Night's Dream* to a 'weak and idle' dream; and John Lyly presented his earlier romantic and witty comedies on the same condition: 'Remember all is but a Poet's dream,' advises the Prologue to *The Woman in the Moon,* and 'imagine yourself to be in a deep dream,' the Prologue to *Sapho and Phao.* Such instructions were intended to excuse improbabilities to the censorious, and they do so by invoking a relaxation of precise and close concerns. Viewing a romantic comedy is like enjoying an idle dream.

Some modern critics have argued that Shakespeare encountered difficulties in linking the comic elements with the romantic, but such problems often disappear when we view the plays in the theatre, in the relaxed, wide focus which is suitable to both elements. Indeed, Shakespeare's comparison of his play to a dream may be more apt than he could have known. It may be true of both the romantic and the comic elements, for Freud has argued that the mental processes which he called 'wit-work' are very similar to those he called 'dream-work'. Both involve displacement of normal experience, illogical sequences, exaggerations, condensations, substitutions and indirections. Freud concluded that jokes and dreams alike provide a release of reactions which are normally censored by the alerted ego. Perhaps Shakespeare sensed that the relaxation of a wide focus was required both for comedy and for romance. Christopher Sly calls for relaxation from immediate concerns as the players enter:

> Come, madam wife, sit by my side and let the world slip:
> we shall ne'er be younger.
>
> (*The Taming of the Shrew*, Induction. ii. 139–40)

II

Some of the basic decisions that Shakespeare made in planning his comedies helped to ensure a predominantly wide dramatic focus. When he chose to present, not one pair of lovers, but two, three or four, and to develop their stories simultaneously rather than successively, he was deciding for range rather than for concentration. As the intertwining actions of the plays cause solemn lovers to follow close upon lighthearted ones, hesitant upon confident, selfish upon generous, the audience is invited to compare and contrast, to remember, as one character stands pleading, how another had done so earlier, in the same place and with the same gesture. Often three or four pairs of lovers are on stage at the same time, and often all in similar predicaments. And likewise, when Shakespeare chose to present stories which involve disguise and the over-hearing of plots and counter-plots, he often provided for two or three centres of interest on the stage at one time, a dispersal of interest and a wide dramatic focus.

These effects can be illustrated abundantly from any of the comedies. In *As You Like It*, for instance, Rosalind disguised as a country youth over-hears the talk of two shepherds, one of whom is as hopelessly in love as she thinks herself. At the same time Touchstone, the clown from court, listens to the wisdom of a country clown, and Celia who is free of love-thoughts listens, with impatience, to the two shepherds and then to Rosalind and Touchstone. Later in the play, Celia talks to Oliver, not knowing he is Orlando's brother, and then Oliver speaks to Rosalind as if she were the youth she appears to be, not knowing that she is the woman his brother loves: here the audience's attention is claimed by the unlooked-for arrival of a changed Oliver, by Celia's growing concern for him, and by Rosalind's inward concern for Orlando's danger. While each centre of interest is here subtly presented, in other comedies—*The Comedy of Errors*, *The Shrew* and *The Merry Wives*—the misunderstandings have greater exaggeration and vigour, and are in the mood and tempo of farce rather than that of fine or 'high' comedy. But one effect they have in common—the view of the audience tends to encompass the whole stage: Petruchio finally wins his shrew on a crowded stage, Falstaff is discomforted as the whole *dramatis personae* assemble at Herne's Oak.

Not every scene is thus complicated, and in the more straightforward ones we may often observe how Shakespeare has used verse and prose, humour and plot-development in ways that ensure a wide focus. The opening of *A Midsummer Night's Dream*, for example, presents young Hermia strenuously defying her father and then being threatened with death by her sovereign. With a sudden action or command, a prolonged or unexpected silence, a soliloquy, or a single speech in a more spontaneous style than the others, Shakespeare could easily have focused attention closely on the Duke's predicament, or on the father's, or on the girl's. But for this comedy he did not use these devices which he had used already in other plays. Here the verse is consistently full-phrased, varied only by the simplest commands and appeals; the scene flows with but one interruption, and then all four parties in the dispute enter together, each claiming attention. Emphasis is given by repetition, not by sudden immediacy:

> Therefore, fair Hermia, question your desires,
> Know of your youth, examine well your blood. . .
>
> (I. I. 67–8)

or in young Lysander's vein:

> Demetrius, I'll avouch it to his head,
> Made love to Nedar's daughter, Helena,
> And won her soul; and she, sweet lady, dotes,
> Devoutly dotes, dotes in idolatry,
> Upon this spotted and inconstant man.
>
> (I. i. 106–10)

The Duke leaves the stage among a peaceful concourse and the next movement of the play begins with Hermia and Lysander alone. But the focus remains wide: although their situation is desperate, they speak in close metrical, as well as verbal, harmony; their plight is impressed by repetition, and by images relating to 'roses' and 'tempests', and comparisons involving the 'lightning in the collied night'. As they plan to escape from Athens, Hermia's resolution is robbed of the audience's most intent interest by chiming rhymes, a jest at Lysander's expense, and the immediate entrance of Helena, the fourth in the quartet of young lovers. At the end of the scene, Lysander and Hermia depart busily and happily, and this new character bids for her full share of interest with a concluding soliloquy about herself and her love, Demetrius—and once more each line of verse is full-phrased and rhymed.

 Much Ado about Nothing can provide many examples of this persistent dispersal of dramatic interest. In its first scene, Claudio's avowal of love could have afforded a poignant moment of intense focus, for he is hesitant and inexperienced, and yet entirely filled with desire. But Shakespeare has presented it in three stages: first Claudio speaks in modest prose accompanied by the mocking, dominating comments of Benedick, then more shortly as Benedick tells the secret to Don Pedro, and then, when he is alone with Pedro and his purpose already known, he speaks fully in clear and flowing verse, to be dominated now by Pedro in similar style. Claudio's shyness and passion have both been presented, and in lively manner, but he has not drawn attention wholly to himself for more than the briefest, undeveloped moment.

Shakespeare's technique in the larger problems of structure and development—matters of great importance for the comedies with multiple plots which were then in fashion—shows the same concern. A brilliant example is Act II of *The Merchant of Venice*, which speedily forwards the narrative and establishes characters, places and moods, yet without sustaining the development of any single interest or state of feeling, and without allowing any character to draw all interest to himself consistently. Shylock's grief at the loss of gold and daughter and Antonio's at parting with Bassanio are both wittily reported by others. Portia is presented in exotic and somewhat comic company. Shylock parts with Launcelot as he instructs his daughter to lock up all treasures. Jessica elopes dressed as a boy amid preparations for a masque and, possibly, accompanied with fifes and drums. Despite excitement, pathos and lyrical utterance, the dramatic focus is kept predominantly wide.

Music, song and dance can fill the stage with uniform movement or with stillness, and the air with patterned and completed sounds, and thus they are particularly useful for maintaining a wide focus. Before the last scene of *Much Ado* there are music and formal solemnities at Hero's supposed tomb, and towards the end of *As You Like It*, as the affairs of Rosalind and Orlando grow to a crisis, an anonymous forester sings at the death of a deer and others bear the burden of his bawdy song and lead the victor to the Duke, dressed as an animal in deer-skin and horns. Either of these episodes could be (and often has been) removed from its play without loss to the plot-development or characterizations. One of their main justifications is that they relax the quickening pulse of the action with the measure of their music and widen the focus visually with formal movement or celebration. Intellectually they are a reminder of the timeless or the general. They take a considerable time to perform but pay their way theatrically by their influence over tempo and focus.

Music, song, dance and processions are especially common at the very end of these comedies, when almost all the characters meet together in new or tried relationships. Each conclusion is, indeed, a general resolution, a full close which occupies the whole stage. So Benedick and Beatrice make but one pair in a dance with Hero and Claudio, and probably Margaret and Balthazar, Ursula and Antonio. Viola walks with Orsino, while Sebastian walks with Olivia. *Love's Labour's Lost* closes with two songs with no direct reference to the personages of the play but listened to by them—songs which tell of Spring and Winter, all married men and Dick, Tom, Joan and Marian.

Such general conclusions, involving the whole stage, make a great impression, for they answer lengthy preparations, the final dispositions having been suggested as soon as the lovers exchanged looks. Shakespeare's plots are often complicated—lovers are separated by distance or misunderstandings, parents at odds with children, men struggling with ill-understood duty—yet the disorder will always seem eminently tidiable. Each of the comedies is viewed within the frame of an expectation of ordered resolution so that, as the stage fills at the end of the performance, the audience observes it all gratefully, with a sense of completion and satisfaction. Even when the audience is concerned with the most precarious moments in the unfolding of the comedy, a deeper and timeless consciousness may still keep its members aware of the incipient balance, the final stability. (So in looking at a detail of a fully-balanced picture—a Poussin or a Cézanne—one may be simultaneously half-conscious of its complete reference.) Certainly, after a performance the momentary excitements are all but forgotten, being satisfied in the wider, almost static, perception of the whole consort of the comedy.

III

Any writer of comedy, and especially one who mingles several plot-interests, runs the danger of superficiality. The focus of a comedy can be so wide that it is also unsteady and indistinct. By avoiding a consistent growth in the audience's knowledge of a character, the dramatist may destroy all sense of its particular identity, by providing laughs he may introduce trivial irrelevances, and by contriving a general conclusion he may invent one that is slick and mechanical.

Of course, the enduring popularity of Shakespeare's comedies has shown beyond doubt that he avoided superficiality. In the first place, we may say that he did this by submitting the material for each play to a governing theme or idea, and by selecting, shaping and emphasizing every detail of his writing in accordance with that idea. So one comedy may present generous and possessive loves, another deep and shallow loves, another the privacy and precariousness of all human idealisms. But this puts the matter in a way that sounds routine and intellectual. We might prefer to say that each comedy is an image of a world—with idealisms, wit, humour, tensions and resolutions—in which the audience can see what Shakespeare's Hamlet called the feature of virtue, the image of scorn and the form and pressure of the very age and body of the time. Or we might say that the stage-action and speech of each of the comedies is a world which Shakespeare accepted as true to his imagination. The mood of these plays is, for the most part, easy and light (Shakespeare is concerned more with the happiness of events than with their inevitable cost and seeds of sorrow), but his essential artistry ensures that they have a unifying conception as little superficial as the judgements which so obviously underlie the histories and tragedies. In short, the comedies are great and enduring because they are shaped by Shakespeare's full imagination.[4]

But such a general assertion can bring us little closer to an understanding of these plays in performance. A play which is laden with significance for its author might communicate to its audience nothing that was not disordered and trivial. More practically, we may say that Shakespeare avoided superficiality by writing dialogue that is vital, musical and varied, that attracts attention. He also imagined his characters in close detail, so that small parts, and large, have individual voices and are realized in a precise environment. This is a matter of detail, and needs to be considered in detail, by choosing one character or one passage of dialogue, and discussing that at length, rather than by engaging in a roll-call of Shakespeare's obvious successes in this kind.

Dogberry, the clown's part in *Much Ado*, will serve as an example. We know that this character was written for William Kemp to perform (we learn this from speech-prefixes in the first quarto edition of the play), and Shakespeare might have been excused if he had written it with little study, leaving the actor to embellish it with his own individualizing tricks. The author and playwright Thomas Nashe called this actor, the 'most comical and conceited Cavaliere Monsieur du Kemp, Jestmonger and Vice-gerent General to the ghost of Dick Tarleton'.[5] The role of Dogberry is marked out for such an entertainer: he makes relatively few appearances but all, effectively enough, rather late in the play; and most of the time he is obviously intended to hold the centre of the stage. He has been given a wealth of professional

---

[4] In *Shakespeare and his Comedies* (London, 1957) I have tried to trace the main ideas underlying the comedies.

[5] *An Almond for a Parrott* (1590); *Works*, edited by R. B. McKerrow (Oxford, 1904–10), iii, 341.

(and now famous) malapropisms, and he is provided with a 'stooge' or 'feed' in Verges (a part originally played by the experienced actor, Richard Cowley). Yet Shakespeare has made even these old conventions illuminate a consistent character. We can say that Dogberry has kindliness, vanity and an absurd inability to know what his words or actions mean to other people: so a malapropism—'If I were as tedious as a king, I could find it in my heart to bestow it all of your worship'—is benignly pronounced to the busied Leonato; so Dogberry treats his 'feed' with kindness, flattering him from the eminence of his own greatness while pretending not to need him. Yet Dogberry is more than a characterized clown; he is a Constable of the Watch as well, and Shakespeare has also taken care with his performance of this office. About 1681, John Aubrey, the collector of gossip and facts concerning the great, reported of Shakespeare that:

> The humour of the Constable in *A Midsummer Night's Dream*, he happened to take at Grendon (I think it was midsummer night that he happened to lie there) in Bucks., which is the road from London to Stratford, and there was living that Constable about 1642 when I first came to Oxon. Mr. Jos. Howe is of that parish and knew him. Ben Jonson and he did gather humours of men daily wherever they came.

Even if this tale is untrue—and only the name of the play is unbelievable[6]—Shakespeare might have 'gathered' some notion of Dogberry nearer home, for his own father had been a Constable and later had been acquainted with magisterial procedures as Alderman.

Lambard's *Duties of Constables . . . and such other low Ministers of the Peace* (1583) tells how Dogberries must 'see their watches duely set and kept' and may arrest a

> suspected person and . . . carry him to a Justice of the Peace together with him that doth suspect him, . . . to the end that they both may be examined.[7]

All this Dogberry enacts, and in a way that makes him the epitome of one kind of volunteer, unpaid, public servant which, in Volunteer Corps of various kinds, is not unrecognizable today. He is obviously

---

[6] It would imply that Shakespeare saw Dogberry as a young, upstart Constable, rather than the old buffoon that is usually seen on the stage today; Aubrey's Constable could hardly have been above 30 years of age in 1596.

[7] *Op. cit.* (1594 edition), A7 and A8.

pleased with himself and with the dignity of his office, and he cannot help saying so:

> I knew it would be your answer . . . Five shillings to one on't, with any man that knows the statues . . . an there be any matter of weight chances, call up me.

(III. iii. 16–79)

—Dogberry allows himself no leisure for uncertain, long words here. But truly the Constable is little better than his watchmen: he probably can't read or write; he takes sleep on duty as a normal course. Characteristically he is much concerned with those pieces of equipment that were probably chargeable to himself, making a great fuss about trusting the head-watchman with his lantern and charging, strictly, 'have a care that your bills be not stolen'. The humour is further developed when Dogberry is given a job far above his proper status, when the local JP—that is, Leonato—tells him to take the 'examination' of the suspected persons himself. Now the Constable's pleasure and dignity have no bounds: he departs alone on his mission, sending Verges off on an errand with a dramatic 'meet me at the gaol'. He starts the enquiry (IV. ii) in his own highest style—'Is our whole dissembly appeared?' —and he attempts a superior sarcasm—'A marvellous witty fellow, I assure you'. But, really, he cannot handle his 'malefactors', and the sexton who is clerk-of-court has to guide, and finally control, proceedings. And, then, his hour of greatness over, the way to Dogberry's heart is still through a tip, the sign of dependence for which he cries 'God save the foundation!' (V. i. 328).

The more one knows about Elizabethan Constables and JPs, the funnier and the livelier Dogberry appears. When he defends his wounded dignity by asserting that he has 'two gowns and every thing handsome about him', he may have put on the Constable's gown (a purple one was provided by the Corporation at Stratford-upon-Avon) and on top of that put another, to represent his second temporary office. When he insists that he should be 'written down an ass' he is clutching, perhaps somewhat pathetically, to his official dignity—for Lambard rules:

> if any such officer, . . . do take hurt, he shall have good remedy by action against him that did the hurt.[8]

Here Shakespeare may have been developing an old family story dating

8 *Op. cit.*, A8.

from 14 April 1559, when his father was Constable and the Stratford Court Leet had to deal with a case of assault, and fined a certain butcher on two counts. As the Corporation Account Book records it:

gryffyn the bochar (ij^d) for makynge a sawt & gevynge obprobryous [words] to the constabulles.[9]

Dogberry is watched by the audience with an unattached mind, for he does not involve them in his puzzlement. His most dominating and personal speech, which is almost a soliloquy, is an expression of what he knows ('O that I had been writ down an ass'), not of what he wants to know or is striving to understand and express. But his character is not superficial, not merely the jesting of a comedian with his 'feed'; it is individualized, and within the wide focus of the comedy a lively imitation—with exaggeration and special emphasis—of life itself, perhaps of daily life at Grendon or Stratford.

Not every character in the comedies is created with the same close study, but many are; so that, by catching such traces of their own world, the audience will watch the dreamlike mirror-world of the stage with attention, even though the predominant focus is wide and far-ranging.

IV

We may say that the audience observes Dogberry 'with an unattached mind', but this needs qualification, for when Dogberry dominates the stage with personal utterance there is a *tendency* towards a more intense focus. The audience's view is never very close or deep, and this moment, coming at the very end of a scene, can have no immediate development; yet in watching a performance the alteration of focus will surely be felt. This is, in fact, a recurrent experience in all the comedies: the wide view of the stage is maintained against a series of momentarily narrowing and intensifying elements.

Such a tension must have been consciously devised, for it accomplishes several essential tasks: it keeps the audience attentive and encourages a greater regard for detail, and it emphasizes particular points in the narrative or characterizations. This is, in short, another means whereby Shakespeare avoided superficiality in his romantic comedies,

[9] *Minutes and Accounts of the Corporation of Stratford-upon-Avon*, ed. R. Savage and E. I. Fripp for the Dugdale Society, vol. i (Stratford-upon-Avon, 1921), p. 94.

and prevented their predominantly wide focus from being imprecise or unsteady.

The soliloquy is an obvious device for introducing such a tendency towards an intense focus, and Shakespeare used it frequently. In one of his earliest comedies, *The Two Gentlemen of Verona*, Launce, the servant of Proteus, soliloquizes three times, speaking directly to the audience. In one way these scenes serve the overall wide focus, for Launce's talk of parting from his family and of loving a milkmaid compares obviously with the affairs of his master. His last tale, of how he allowed himself to be whipped in the place of his offending dog and then offered to give that dog away to serve his master, is a preparation for Valentine's suffering and his generous, rapid and inadequate offer to give away 'all that is his in Silvia' to satisfy his friend. The emphasis derived from the more intense focus is not wasted in the larger issues of the play, but neither is the change of focus allowed to be too strong. Despite Launce's painstaking efforts to be correct, his utterance is not fully immediate. He makes emendations and adds new detail in too leisured and balanced a way for his soliloquies to represent thought and feeling directly: his style is picturesque, not nervous or truly sentimental. What appears at first to be a personal utterance is really a 'turn', a 'personality' performance. Nevertheless, intimate soliloquy of any kind—especially in a play where much of the dialogue is easily fluent—is bound to intensify the dramatic focus to some degree, and if he wished to maintain the predominantly wide focus, Shakespeare had good reason for banishing Launce from the play in the fourth act.

Most of the soliloquies in the comedies stop short of full intimacy. Those of Proteus, Valentine, Helena and others in the earlier plays are written in sleek and, sometimes, rhyming verse which sharpens the presentation of their dilemmas without permitting the audience to recognize the inner movement of thought and feeling: such, from *The Two Gentlemen*, is:

> I cannot leave to love and yet I do;
> But there I leave to love where I should love . . .
>
> (II. vi. 17–18)

or

> I am my master's true confirmed love,
> But cannot be true servant to my master
> Unless I prove false traitor to myself.
>
> (IV. iv. 99–101)

At other times a soliloquy is, like Launce's, more truly a performance: such are most of Benedick's in *Much Ado*. But any of these can become immediate or revealing. So after Benedick hears that Beatrice loves him, and before he begins to enjoy his new role, he has a few abrupt, unwitty sentences that offer a deeper view (II. iii. 201–10).

Among the comedies written before *Twelfth Night*, *The Merchant of Venice* has the strongest tendency towards an intense focus. Shylock's passionate and reasoned resentment against the Christians in III. i— 'Hath not a Jew eyes? . . . If you prick us, do we not bleed? . . . if you wrong us, shall we not revenge?'—brings the dramatic focus to bear intensely on himself. But Shakespeare has carefully avoided soliloquy here by bringing first Salerio and Solanio, and then Tubal, to fill the stage. Moreover, if Shylock is played fully in this scene, the horror aroused by his callous talk of desiring Antonio's flesh will repulse the audience's sympathy even as the presentation of his suffering draws it. Later in the same scene, Shylock's rapid alternations between greedy hope and despair, as Tubal tells the news point by point, may even bring the relaxing—and therefore the widening—influence of humour; certainly there is no occasion for a single emotional response or identification to develop. Shylock's strongest bid for an intense focus is in his defeat, when he draws attention away from Gratiano's easily blood-thirsty gibe by a silent exit across the crowded and attentive stage. For such an important character, the absence of an 'exit-line' is a remarkable stage-trick, and very rare in Shakespeare's works (there were long distances to be negotiated on the stages of his time). In default of words, the attention of the audience is intensified on the inward feelings of the character who has just suffered a complete reversal of fortune and has spoken little of it. The least experienced actor would recognize this opportunity, while great ones have used it to powerful and still memorable effect; so Irving's audience knew that Shylock walked 'away to die in silence and alone', and Kean's 'withering sneer, hardly concealing the crushed heart' was the 'crowning glory of his acting' in this role.[10] Such concentration of attention may well be permitted here, for Shylock is leaving the play as well as the stage; but even so, Shakespeare rapidly followed it with new business, widening the focus

[10] *Blackwood's Magazine* (Dec. 1879) and J. Doran, *Their Majesties Servants* (ed. 1897), pp. 430–1; see also my 'The Realization of Shylock', *Early Shakespeare* (Stratford-upon-Avon Studies, 3), ed. J. R. Brown and B. Harris (London, 1961).

by a sudden transition to general talk about having dinner, and to game of disguised identities, initiated in the most sprightly and mocking manner by Portia and Nerissa.

These moments of intense focus can continue to affect the play long after they have passed. The memory of Shylock, kept alive by Jessica's presence in the final act and by direct reference to him, is liable to influence the reception of all the succeeding action, causing the audience—or some of them—to question the fullness or security of the various joys-in-matrimony which are presented.

Not all members of the audience will experience this double view: the relaxation of a predominantly wide focus gives scope for it, but it also precludes its enforcement. And this seems to have suited Shakespeare's purposes, for in later comedies a permissive, double view of the stage became one of his most useful and distinctive means of counteracting superficiality and giving definition within the wide frame.

We have already noticed that the disguises involved in the plots of the comedies were used to provide two or more centres of interest within a single scene, and so help to maintain the general width of focus. In some scenes, however, they give rise to a further mode of double vision or double focus, for two 'persons' are then seen in a single 'figure'. Occasionally the view of the person within the disguise sharpens into a momentarily intense and precise focus on innermost thoughts and feelings. This cannot last too long or be too overwhelming in effect, because the disguise must soon be re-established in accordance with the exigencies of the plot. In *As You Like It*, the device is used freely, especially in the long, central scene (IV. i) between Rosalind, disguised as Ganymede, and Orlando who believes that the seeming youth is only impersonating the Rosalind he loves. Drawing Orlando out to confess and re-confess his love, Rosalind easily assumes the role of a witty, outspoken, disinterested Ganymede pretending to be a Rosalind: but the performance is not perfect. The true Rosalind as well as the supposed Ganymede takes part in the dialogue: 'Then love me, Rosalind', says Orlando and 'Yes, faith, will I' answers Rosalind, and 'Fridays and Saturdays and all' adds 'Ganymede', turning it to laughter. 'Ganymede' draws Celia in to act as the priest at a make-believe wedding, so that the true Rosalind within him may hear Orlando's vows and make hers in return with her double voice. The interchange is like quicksilver, for 'Ganymede' has continually to redirect the conversation so that it veers away from tenderness to scorn or laughter, or to an abrupt demand that Orlando shall again affirm his love. In a later scene (V. ii), Silvius, Phebe and Orlando vow faithfulness and service to their respective loves:

> *Phebe.* Good shepherd, tell this youth what 'tis to love. . . .
> *Silvius.* It is to be all made of faith and service;
>   And so am I for Phebe.
> *Phebe.* And I for Ganymede.
> *Orlando.* And I for Rosalind. . . .
>
> (V. ii. 76–85)

and 'Ganymede' then dares to add his voice, knowing that the true Rosalind speaking within him will not sound out of key, without ardour, even though he speaks a riddle:

> And I for no woman.

The others do not question these words; indeed Orlando finally addresses Rosalind as if she were truly present, and 'Ganymede'—or is it Rosalind?—has to change the tune abruptly, calling:

> Pray you, no more of this; 'tis like the howling of Irish wolves
> against the moon.   (V. ii. 102)

In hesitation, in simply spoken words, and in the quick veering away to a new line of attack, the audience may sense the deepest thoughts and feelings of Rosalind. Within the predominantly wide focus of the comedy, a double vision gives a kind of flickering intensity, and during a few moments of avowal, for some of the audience, the dramatic focus may be still, deep and intimate.

The revelation of a different consciousness existing beneath the main comic or romantic world is used in a more settled and controlled way in the later comedies, without resort to disguise. At the height of the absurd trial-scene in *Much Ado*, the practical Sexton quietens the stage with his own sober view that Hero has 'suddenly died'. He is not answered, so there is probably a moment's silence before he resolves to tell Leonato, and then comic momentum reasserts itself and the audience is back in the world of Dogberry's ambitions. In *As You Like It* Jaques often establishes his own dispirited, experienced view of the world, to be laughed at or ignored, the next instant as other realities are asserted. He sees the absurdities of passionate conviction, and has himself lost all obvious interest; if he had licence he would rail at others, but he has not and so he sometimes finds peace by being 'sad and saying nothing'. Rosalind suggests that he has gained nothing by travelling: 'Yes, I have gained my experience', he replies, but to no effect, for Rosalind, full of the immediate sensations of love, answers brightly:

> And your experience makes you sad. I had rather have a fool to make me merry than experience to make me sad.   (IV. i. 24ff.)

This is the reality of confident youth, and as Orlando, also free of that world, enters immediately, Jaques' isolated private world is lost to view and he leaves the stage. Such moments are summed up at the end of the play, when Jaques leaves the stage again, saying he is for 'other than for dancing measures'. Once more the audience will momentarily see his reality, lonely and barren; and they will know that impassive, unexcitable experience walks out of the conclusion of the play. This moment is elaborated by Jaques' summing up of the hopes of the Duke and the lovers, and it is prolonged by the others watching him go, forgetting to dance. The Duke has to recall them to the world of hope:

> Proceed, proceed. We will begin these rites,
> As we do trust they'll end, in true delights.
>
> (V. iv. 191–2)

The stage is filled with dancing, and then the comedy can conclude. By introducing another view of the stage—a different tempo, different speech and standards of judgement—Shakespeare has reminded us of its precariousness, of how the lovers give themselves to happiness because of feelings and convictions they can justify to no-one but themselves. And Shakespeare has thereby sharpened the wide dramatic focus.

One of the strangest qualities of Shakespeare's comedies is their unassertiveness. An audience will follow easily and comprehensively the interweaving threads of narrative, and so will enjoy moments of lyricism, humour, fantasy and conflict, and respond to lively speech and varying spectacle; and finally, it will rest assured in a general resolution. Beyond this the comedies make few demands, but offer many opportunities. The life-like details of characterization are not underscored, and are not necessary to an understanding of the development of the action. The ideas, or themes, which shape each of the comedies are never stated explicitly, so that an audience may appreciate the dance-like sequences and the contrasts and reflections between the characters without being made aware of the precise words or movements which give this unity, without having to understand, in general terms, the 'meaning' of the play. The moments which tend to induce an intense focus are not followed by incidents which depend on the knowledge or sympathy given by the closer contact. The moments of double view and unsettled focus may pass unnoticed and yet the audience feel quite at ease, as if in possession of all they need to know. The action, dialogue, narrative and characterization of the comedies are understandable and of lively interest without these elements. To further their comic and dream-like qualities, Shakespeare has used a predominantly wide focus which permits the audience to observe all in relaxed mood and with a wide and comprehensive view; and only unassertively, almost as if by stealth, are there further invitations which sharpen the definitions and reveal more depth and more variety of colour. To many of these invitations an audience can respond unknowingly, so that after a performance its members will find it hard to account for the complexity, depth and subtlety of their involvement.

V

Some twentieth-century productions of *Twelfth Night* illustrate the freedom that the comedies offer to their interpreters as to their audiences. When Beerbohm Tree produced it in 1901, he wrote in the Souvenir Programme of Shakespeare's 'serene utterance of his joyous music', and of 'this delightfully irresponsible comedy', and in performance his own Malvolio dominated the play as an elegant, self-satisfied 'superior person'.[11] In 1907 Viola, played by Julia Marlowe, was easily the central character, and the whole was so 'characterized by deep sincerity' that there was some complaint of 'unnecessary solemnity in the auditorium'.[12] When Granville-Barker produced it at the Savoy, in 1912, the *Morning Post* now pronounced it to be 'alive and alert', with occasional wistfulness in Viola and fantasy in Malvolio.[13] Nearer the present day, in 1941, this unassertive play was performed by the Chekhov Players in New York as 'a highly improvized gambol in which Sir Toby Belch emerges as hero,'[14] and in 1957 at Stratford, Ontario, Mr. Tyrone Guthrie

[11] *Daily Telegraph*, 6th Feb. 1901.

[12] *Yorkshire Daily Post*, 27th April 1907; see also *Evening Standard* 27th April 1907.

[13] *Morning Post*, 16th Nov. 1912.

[14] *New York Times*, 3rd Dec. 1941; see also *New York Herald Tribune*, 3rd Dec. 1941, and S. Young, *Immortal Shadows* (New York, 1948), pp. 200-4.

determined to avoid a 'pretty picture' and instructed his actors to 'be as true to life as possible'. He expected his production to be informed by the notion that 'those who think they are sane are nearest to madness and those who think they are mad come closest to sanity'.[15]

The liberty which has permitted these seemingly contradictory interpretations is clear enough in the last five or ten minutes of *Twelfth Night*. The overall, wide focus is maintained by a crowded stage, decorous verse, and the many entrances and exits which smoothly conclude the various strands of the plot. Shakespeare has prevented the audience from following only the union of the lovers, or only Malvolio's confrontation of the truth, by presenting the first in four separate, incomplete passages and the latter in two. Yet within this wide view of the stage there are many insights, moments which can centre the attention on a single dilemma or character, and these are the opportunities for a theatre director and his actors to exaggerate romantic sentiment, liveliness, boisterous humour or melancholy, according to his own taste. When Orsino's 'savage jealousy' is more 'ripe in mischief' towards Cesario than towards Olivia (as he had earlier listened to his page's story, rather than prosecuted his courtship of his mistress), the sudden release of feeling may cause the audience to follow his words and movements with more questioning intentness than before. And the next moment it may be drawn towards Viola, who almost disregards her disguise as Cesario in a passionate avowal of love to Orsino; and then towards Olivia, who dares at length to call Cesario husband before the world and the scornful eyes of Orsino. Hidden motives, dramatic opposition, helplessness, abrupt interchanges can alert the audience until Viola's uncomprehending but emphatic denial that she is married to Olivia—'No, my lord, not I', spoken to Orsino and not the lady—relaxes the intent focus in a recognition of the absurdity of the impasse.

When the priest enters he testifies to the marriage in such long paced verse that the audience may receive a view of another reality, calm and accepting:

> A contract of eternal bond of love,
> Confirm'd by mutual joinder of your hands,
> Attested by the holy close of lips,

[15] Report of a lecture by Guthrie at the University of Western Ontario; see Birmingham Reference Library, Shakespeare Collection, *Twelfth Night* Clippings Book, 1957.

Strength'ned by interchangement of your rings; . . .
Since when, my watch hath told me, toward my grave,
I have travell'd but two hours.

(V. i. 150–57)

Yet another world is evoked by the entrance of Sir Andrew and Sir Toby: the latter scarcely speaks to those already on the stage and hitherto engaging the audience's whole attention, but rather he relishes his own irascibility and leaves directly with his dependent, Sir Andrew. This time the audience has been shown a restless acceptance of the conclusion, and its attention will settle wholly on the lovers again with a new sense—which has never been formulated in words—of their isolation and simplicity.

A theatre director can, of course, emphasize one or other of these secondary views, or gloss them over, according to his own 'interpretation' of the play. Or again, he can make much or little of two silences: Olivia's when she realizes that she has been infatuated with a girl, and Malvolio's when he realizes that he has lived in the excitement of his own fantasy.

And still the unassertive opportunities of the comedy are not finished. The sustained unison as Viola and Sebastian exchange tokens of identity can provide an awed and intimate moment emphasizing the miraculous conclusion of their story. Feste's remembrance of Malvolio's earlier words can give a disengaged view of the whole comedy rather than a concern for the momentary event, and Malvolio's long-delayed final speech—'I'll be revenged on the whole pack of you'—so concentrates attention on him that an actor can use it either as a release for relaxed laughter or as a helpless plea evoking an intense sympathy.

Those who care for the play itself, as opposed to those who have to present a new and individual production of it, will want all these invitations presented, for it is by their means that the audience is fully involved in the world of Shakespeare's imagination operating in the deepest levels of human consciousness. They are also the moments when most is left to the actor's art to give individual realization to the brief words or silences.

So within the conclusion of this comedy, as the characters walk off the stage, leaving it without lights and without movement, the audience which has 'let the world slip' can 'take it all in'. As Feste is left alone to sing of his own folly, and of the wind and the rain and the several ages of man, they find that their view has been wide enough to comprehend this knowledge, subtle enough to feel it acutely, and free enough to catch echoes of follies and wisdoms of their own.

VI

If directors and audiences are left free to respond with whatever intensity or double consciousness that is suggested to them by the play in performance, actors have a more inescapable responsibility. Their roles start with an abundance of defining words and actions, but these lead towards later moments when textually there is little to rely upon, when the audience may view them more deeply than before and when credibility and effectiveness have to come from the very centre of their impersonations. Once Viola has recognized Sebastian, she has very few words: four lines of a love-confession and four of explanation; yet the audience will watch closely. After Malvolio has been freed, Viola has only a silent approach to Orsino and this must serve to sum up all her performance. On one level this approach to Orsino completes a pattern and ends a narrative; on another, it must speak of a happiness and denote a kind of peace. How much laughter, relief, forgetfulness or understanding is expressed will depend upon the person who acts the part, and upon the entire performance up until that moment.

Again and again Shakespeare ends a role with this kind of opportunity for the actor, where the audience will accept him according to his performance as a whole. In *Twelfth Night* Malvolio and Sir Toby have notably limited final appearances, as far as words go; yet both draw from Olivia an expression of concern, as if Shakespeare felt the need to define a sympathy for their different defeats that might have been awakened in the audience. When Rosalind reappears in women's dress at the end of *As You Like It*, she has only five punning lines to speak before words tumble out again in her Epilogue, when the play is done. The audience follows Bottom through fear and happiness in the wood and is drawn towards him by soliloquies of lively immediacy, but in the last scene he speaks only in the words of his 'tedious brief' play and a few lines of prose to help his stage-audience and offer Epilogue or dance. Nevertheless, the audience will continue to follow his progress intently, imagining no worse of him than he does of himself (as Theseus has hinted). The actor's opportunities in this scene are manifold and can set the crown upon his performance. Bottom will be accepted at last, for what he is, beneath the foolish words he speaks.

Sometimes the end is a kind of riddle, capable of many interpretations; such are Malvolio's last words, or Antonio's in *The Merchant of Venice*. In *The Taming of the Shrew*, the conclusion of the main tale of wooing is accompanied by Petruchio's simple words: 'Why, there's a wench! Come on, and kiss me, Kate' (V. ii. 180). But this is not a simple dramatic moment: has Kate already knelt in submission, or has Petruchio prevented her? does Petruchio kneel with her? does Petruchio embrace Kate before he speaks, or afterwards? how soon does he smile, or laugh? how quickly or slowly does Kate respond? Every pair of actors will make their own decision, and should try to find whatever is appropriate to the way they have played their entire roles; this riddle, this intently perceived moment, demands their most considered, their most truly felt and carefully created response. Even this tempestuous comedy, with a stage full of lively characters at the close, will be accepted partly through the audience's appreciation of what can be revealed only riddlingly in words. In *Much Ado About Nothing*, Benedick and Beatrice are given a run of such speeches before finishing with the explicit but brief and factual: 'Peace; I will stop your mouth' (V. iv. 97).

Shakespeare wrote his comedies with prodigal invention, creating 'worlds' in which members of an audience may 'lose' themselves and view each episode for what the actors' performances and their own imaginations can make of it. Intense focus upon a single character is always momentary, and never sustained for an unbroken sequence. Yet at last the 'dream' grows 'to something of great constancy' (*A Midsummer Night's Dream*, V. i. 26) which is grounded in the deepest, most silent element of human personality, and which is also reflected and sustained by the widest view of the stage, action, words and story.

The achievement is extremely subtle, and the degrees of intensity and double vision vary with each of the comedies. Shakespeare is never a writer at ease with a formula that works to his own and his audience's satisfaction, and it is not surprising that after *Twelfth Night* there came a radical change in his approach to comedy. Thereafter a new analysis is required in order to speak of his presentation of comedy.

For *All's Well That Ends Well*, there is an element of debate or trial throughout the play, and a sustained immediacy in the presentation of Helena in the first three Acts; moreover the older characters and bystanders habitually pass judgements on the younger characters. Together these departures from earlier practice give an unambiguous air of challenge or deliberation to the comedy. *Measure for Measure* has many intense scenes, and a sustained concern with judgement and death; in the Duke there is a character who attempts a control over the lives of others. In *Troilus and Cressida* scenes of wooing, lovemaking and comedy are present alongside political debate, bloody and disastrous battle, and calculated murder; and the last focus is upon the angry unappeased Troilus, not on weddings, celebrations and forgiveness. Then, at the end of his writing career, Shakespeare returned to comedy in plays of fantastic narrative, where theophanies and miraculous elements change the basic focus and reference of the drama; now individual motivation and achievement seem smaller and less significant than the wider issues of the action. From comedies to 'problem' or 'dark' comedies, and then to 'romances', Shakespeare's later development is clear enough. That these plays, with far more obvious seriousness, should follow the early comedies will seem less remarkable in view of the ambitious and precarious dramatic presentation that may be discerned even in the earliest plays.

'Were man but constant, he were perfect': Constancy and Consistency in 'The Two Gentlemen of Verona'

INGA-STINA EWBANK

I

In the early spring of 1855 George Eliot (still Marian Evans) read *The Two Gentlemen of Verona* and found that the play

> disgusted me more than ever in the final scene where Valentine, on Proteus's mere begging pardon when he has no longer any hope of gaining his ends, says: 'All that was mine in Silvia I give thee'!— Silvia standing by.[1]

In itself there is nothing unusual about George Eliot's reaction. Most critics of the play have felt that in this, his first, dramatization of romance narrative Shakespeare was tied and partly defeated by the conventions he was attempting to use. Such 'disgust' as has been expressed has often focused on the last scene as typifying the play's problems: in the unbelievable magnanimity of Valentine (at two girls' expense), thematic considerations appear to override any thought of character development or psychological motivation. As an affirmation of male constancy it may have satisfied an Elizabethan audience; for, insofar as they believed with Geron, in Lyly's *Endimion*, that friendship is 'the image of eternitie, in which there is nothing moveable, nothing mischeevous' and that there is as much difference between love and friendship as between 'Beautie and Vertue, bodies and shadowes, colours and life', they would have seen Valentine's lines as a noble and universally valid climax to the action of the play.[2] But this moment in the play has troubled audiences and readers ever since.

[1] Gordon S. Haight, *George Eliot: A Biography* (Oxford, 1968), p. 178.
[2] *Endimion*, III. iv. 124–7. Cf. M. C. Bradbrook, *Shakespeare and Elizabethan Poetry* (London, 1951), p. 150.

It may have been particularly troubling to George Eliot, who, like Julia, had defied the notions of 'modesty' held by her society, and who may have given special assent to Julia's couplet against a double standard:

> It is the lesser blot, modesty finds,
> Women to change their shapes than men their minds.
>
> (V. iv. 108–9)

If so, her objection would again have been part of a more general one, for Valentine's grand gesture is all the more inconsistent in that, up to the final scene where Sylvia is mutely handed around from one man to another and Julia's chief contribution is a swoon, the women in the play have been the active ones, going forth to seek their lovers, making decisions on a basis of profound love *and* commonsense, while the men talk or write letters and poems about their love. Like Shakespeare's more mature comedies but unlike the traditional friendship story, where the woman tends to be merely an object or a touchstone in the testing of friends,[3] the play has shown us some of the most important parts of the action from a woman's viewpoint. Though it is in Valentine's idealistic words that Proteus' betrayal is forgiven, it is through Julia's eyes and mind that we have seen what that betrayal really means. Valentine's attitude resolves a theme, but it is Julia's heartbreak which, if anything, has proved the human content of that theme on our pulses. Valentine's constancy appears to be built on a dramatic inconsistency; and one wonders how far Proteus' reply to Julia,

> Than men their minds! 'tis true. O heaven, were man
> But constant, he were perfect!
>
> (V. iv. 110–11)

is, wittingly or unwittingly, a self-reproach on the part of the dramatist.

But there is also a background to George Eliot's reaction to *The Two Gentlemen of Verona* which makes it more remarkable and more interesting as a departure point for an exploration of the play's inconsistencies—which indeed makes those inconsistencies more worth

---

[3] As for example in the Titus and Gisippus story in Sir Thomas Elyot's *The Governour*, Book II, Chapter XII, which Geoffrey Bullough prints as a 'possible source' of *The Two Gentlemen* (*Narrative and Dramatic Sources of Shakespeare*, vol. I (London, 1957), pp. 212–17).

exploring—than other similar reactions.[4] She was reading, or rather re-reading, the play during some lonely weeks at Dover, while George Henry Lewes was in London arranging his affairs and hers, as well as those of his legal wife and children. The two of them had just returned to England, after eight months in voluntary exile, to face the music of outraged Victorian morality and to try to build a life together. She trusted the man in whom she had 'garner'd up her heart', but she must also have known how precarious their liaison looked to outsiders, and how even her best friends were praying 'against hope' that the protean Lewes would prove constant. So when, in the evenings, she turned from translating Spinoza's *Ethics* to reading *The Two Gentlemen of Verona*—and it may speak more of her emotional state than of a scholarly desire to be chronologically thorough that she was also reading *Venus and Adonis*, *The Passionate Pilgrim* and some of the sonnets—it was with a peculiar personal involvement. Between the lines of her journal entry we may sense that the play, in provoking disgust, had activated a deep fear at the centre of her life. 'Could men really bandy a noble woman's love about like that?' is how her biographer puts into words what she dared not express, even to herself.[5] Out of the allegedly 'romantic and dehumanized atmosphere' of this play, something must have spoken to her about what it feels like to be alive and loving—and therefore vulnerable.

Now, *The Two Gentlemen of Verona* is not a play usually discussed in those terms. Shakespeare seems not yet to have developed the uncanny way he later has of engaging with our own lives so that our own experiences modify our reactions to his lines, and *vice versa*: so that we read *King Lear* differently once we have an aged parent in the household, or reject Lady Macbeth each time we nurse our babies, or even feel able to 'identify' with the anguish and confusion of the puppet-like movements of the lovers in *A Midsummer Night's Dream*. The sphere of human experience in *The Two Gentlemen of Verona* is not only narrow—excluding alike birth, copulation and death—but it is so restricted by remote codes and patterned by an artificial language that we tend to feel it represents a world to which Shakespeare was not much committed. Perhaps we feel that, if our feelings go out to anyone

---

[4] I am not concerned here with the obvious but superficial inconsistencies of geography, timing, etc., which Clifford Leech discusses in the introduction to the new Arden edition (London, 1969), pp. xv–xxi.

[5] Haight, *loc. cit.*

B

in the play, it is to Launce with his dog Crab. A great deal has recently been written on the dramatic technique of the play, and in particular on the way in which Shakespeare has managed to make the parodic scenes of Speed and Launce (and Crab) into organic parts of the structure;[6] but no one has felt like saying, borrowing T. S. Eliot's words about Tennyson, that the poet's technical accomplishments were intimate with his depths. Most discussions conclude either that Shakespeare was preoccupied with form at the expense of truth to human feeling, or that he was laughing at the feelings embodied in courtly convention, or both—that is, that he criticized the convention most of the time but, with an inconsistency worthy of Proteus, found it dramatically expedient to embrace it at the end. Either way—whether we nod an Elizabethan assent to the friendship code or laugh at 'Shakespeare wringing the last drop of silliness out of Valentine's conventions'[7]—we have an explanation for Valentine's gesture and words which does not involve us, or Shakespeare, very deeply. But George Eliot's reaction, from a disturbed and divided consciousness, prompts one to consider the possibility that Shakespeare is here at least trying, if with very partial success, to be as truthful to troubled, complex human relationships as he was in the sonnet celebrating an apparently similar plot situation, 'Take all my loves' (40). Possibly he is saying about the moment of Valentine's magnanimity *not* 'this is what life should ideally be', nor 'this is not life', but 'this is, and is not, life'.

II

Clearly it will not do to pretend that *The Two Gentlemen of Verona* is really a *Troilus and Cressida*. Clearly this very early play[8] is in many ways a piece of apprenticeship (so that one natural reason for anyone's 'disgust' with it is that it is not as good as the rest of Shakespeare) and

[6] In particular, G. K. Hunter, *John Lyly* (London, 1962), chapter VI; Stanley Wells, 'The Failure of *The Two Gentlemen of Verona*', *Shakespeare Jahrbuch* 99 (1963), pp. 161–73; Harold F. Brooks, 'Two Clowns in a Comedy (To Say Nothing of the Dog)', *Essays and Studies*, 1963, pp. 91–100.

[7] Hereward T. Price, 'Shakespeare as a Critic', *Philological Quarterly* XX (1941), p. 398.

[8] In the absence of external evidence, scholars have varied in their opinions as to where, exactly, to place *The Two Gentlemen* among the early comedies. It could have been Shakespeare's first comedy of all.

a seed-bed for themes, characters and situations which are to be developed in later plays. But it can be unhelpful to pre-judge the play according to notions of development: to assume that the reason why *The Two Gentlemen of Verona* troubles us is that Julia is not as 'rounded' as Viola, that the Proteus–Valentine relationship is not as fully realized as the friendship of Bassanio and Antonio, or that the outlaw scenes do not have the thematic importance of their counterparts in *As You Like It*. What is more helpful, if we want to see what impulses produce the particular inconsistencies of *The Two Gentlemen of Verona*, is to relate the play to the sonnets. Whatever the exact chronology of either play or sonnets, a kinship between them has long been a recognized fact. It consists both of verbal echoes—similar, often Petrarchan, topics and conceits being developed through similar vocabulary—and of a kind of plot similarity.[9] Whatever the true story behind either play or sonnets, in both cases Shakespeare is creating a fiction to explore the joys and agonies, the betrayals and fulfilments, of interconnecting love relationships. Proteus, the betrayer of both love and friendship, is most like the Youth of the sonnets, with an element of the Dark Lady; Valentine and the two girls all share features of the sonnets' 'I': adoration of the beloved, faithfulness, constancy; and Valentine in the end takes up the all-forgiving and renouncing position of, for example, Sonnet 40. Obviously I am not concerned here with 'plot' similarities as indicating any autobiographical truths behind these works: the 'truth' of the sonnets lies in Shakespeare's dramatic ability—unique among Elizabethan sonneteers[10]—to create a sense of 'what it feels like' in a given human situation. Paradoxically, that dramatic ability is less evident in the combinations and permutations of love and friendship (with, it should be noted, the friendship theme being given much less scope than the love theme) which make up the pattern of the play. Nor am I suggesting that a single sonnet, like 40, *justifies* the final scene of the play, but that it may help to illuminate its dramatic inconsistencies.

For, in the end, the really important relationship between *The Two Gentlemen of Verona* and the sonnets seems to me to have to do with Shakespeare's attitude to his own poetry and to the traditions of love poetry in which he finds himself writing. More important than any

[9] Cf. Leech, *op. cit.*, pp. lxix–lxx, and Bullough, *op. cit.*, pp. 210–11.

[10] Cf. G. K. Hunter, 'The Dramatic Technique of Shakespeare's Sonnets' *Essays in Criticism* 3 (1953), pp. 152–64.

local similarities is the fact that the sonnets, like the play, show us Shakespeare working within a well-established convention, both using it and criticizing it—writing, as it were, through and around it. Apart from a handful of simply conventional Petrarchan exercises, his aim (explicit and implicit) in the sonnets is to subordinate his style to his subject matter, to use the convention only insofar as it helps him to render the true image of the person he is writing to and of.[11] Thus, to take an extreme example, what he wants to say about the Dark Lady in Sonnet 130 only makes sense through an evaluation of the Petrarchan convention; yet the real point of the poem remains the 'rareness' of the Lady, not the dig at the convention. Related to this feature of the sonnets is Shakespeare's attitude to language: an apparently paradoxical combination of a tremendous belief in the powers of his own poetry (again both implicit in the writing itself and explicitly stated) with an equally insistent sense that language is inadequate to express the beloved's identity—the quintessential statement being 'that you alone are you' (84). It is in the sonnets that Shakespeare most clearly faces the problem which, of course, he shares with any love poet: that he needs language to define the uniqueness of the beloved and his feelings about him or her, but that, at the same time, language itself is conventional and conventionalizes experience.

When love poetry is transferred to the stage, when the inner drama of a sonnet's 'I' and 'thou' has to be translated into the flesh-and-blood interaction of two lovers and probably also their conflicts with several other 'I's and 'thou's, then the problem is further confounded. In *Romeo and Juliet* Shakespeare partly solved it by contrasting the empty attitudinizing of Romeo's love for Rosaline with the beauty of the formality which surrounds and expresses his love for Juliet, from their first meeting on a shared sonnet.[12] Present-day playwrights, handling a tired and cliché-ridden language, have to face the problem in one extreme form—as Arnold Wesker discovered when he wanted a lover to tell his lady that she had 'autumn soft skin' and found that this would put audiences in mind of TV advertisements for Camay soap[13]

[11] See the helpful discussion of this point in Joan Grundy, 'Shakespeare's Sonnets and the Elizabethan Sonneteers', *Shakespeare Survey* 15 (1962), pp. 41–9.

[12] Cf. the chapter on *Romeo and Juliet* in Nicholas Brooke, *Shakespeare's Early Tragedies* (London, 1968).

[13] See the Epilogue to *The Four Seasons* (*Penguin New English Dramatists* 9, p. 189).

—and generally find it easier to let their characters make love in the flesh than in words. The playwrights of the 1590s were not afraid of verbal cliché in the same way; and the lovers in *The Two Gentlemen of Verona* can liken each other to the sun, or the moon, or the stars, can be blinded by love or weep floods of tears, or generally draw on the stock-in-trade of Petrarchan love poetry. But, as in the sonnets, Shakespeare in this play also shows an awareness that conventionalized language, like conventionalized behaviour, may be false. In this self-consciousness about conventional language and situations lie many of the play's inconsistencies, but also much of its sense of life.

We do not have to read or listen to *The Two Gentlemen of Verona* for very long before we discover a tendency in its main characters to be self-conscious about the language they use, to veer between exuberance and deflation, indulgence in Lyly-like wit games and sudden dismissals of them. In I. i Valentine deflates Proteus' love rhetoric even before he has had time to utter any of it; in II. iv the positions are reversed, as Valentine takes up exactly the role he ascribed to Proteus in the first scene and, in his turn, has his hyperboles punctured:

> *Pro.* Why, Valentine, what braggardism is this?
> *Val.* Pardon me, Proteus; all I can is nothing
>   To her, whose worth makes other worthies nothing;
>   She is alone.
> *Pro.*   Then let her alone.
>   (II. iv. 160–63)

Proteus shifts the sense of Valentine's 'alone'—reminiscent of the sonnets' 'that you alone are you'—with a brusqueness which anticipates Timon's dismissal of the Poet:

> *Poet.*   I am rapt, and cannot cover
>   The monstrous bulk of this ingratitude
>   With any size of words.
> *Tim.* Let it go naked: men may see't the better.
>   (*Timon of Athens*, V. i. 62–5)

This effect of contrast and deflation does not seem to be tied to character as much as to the needs of the situation or scene. In II. iv Silvia initially has something of the same function of commonsense critic as, at other times, is given to Speed or Launce. She undercuts the sparring between Valentine and Thurio, and she exposes the absurdity of Valentine's conceits to the cold light of reason:

> *Val.* This is the gentleman I told your ladyship
> Had come along with me but that his mistress
> Did hold his eyes lock'd in her crystal looks. . . .
> *Sil.* Nay, then, he should be blind; and, being blind,
> How could he see his way to seek out you?
>
> (II. iv. 82–9)

Not that this stops Valentine's flow of images; on the contrary, Silvia has supplied him with the perfect cue for a further conceit,

> Why, lady, Love hath twenty pair of eyes,

and this gives Thurio, too, a chance to have a go after his feeble fashion, so that we have one of the rare occasions in the play where the dialogue, in an anticipation of *Much Ado About Nothing*, arrives at a kind of differentiated group wit. But only a few lines later, as Proteus has arrived and entered upon a courtesy duologue with Silvia, the function of commentator has also passed from her to Valentine:

> Leave off discourse of disability.
>
> (II. iv. 105)

Related to this tendency in the play, and also tied to scene rather than to character, is a reminder, which tends to crop up at key moments, of the impotency of words. Proteus' motivation of the brevity of the parting scene between him and Julia—'For truth hath better deeds than words to grace it' (II. ii. 18)—may in itself be merely conventional, but Julia on her next appearance makes an ironically genuine-sounding statement of the reality of love being beyond the power of words. 'Didst thou but know', she says to Lucetta, 'the inly touch of love',

> Thou wouldst as soon go kindle fire with snow
> As seek to quench the fire of love with words.
>
> (II. vii. 18–20)

The irony is double here, for not only does Julia's paean to her and Proteus' love come just after we have witnessed his decision to abandon her, but the very questioning of the power of words is put in such an exuberant form as to question the question. Ironically, too, Julia's argument is inverted and perverted by Proteus as he threatens to rape Silvia:

> Nay, if the gentle spirit of moving words
> Can no way change you to a milder form,
> I'll woo you like a soldier, at arms' end,
> And love you 'gainst the nature of love—force ye.
>
> (V. iv. 55-8)

And significantly it is, at this point, visual and not verbal evidence that brings about Valentine's recognition: 'nought but mine eye / Could have persuaded me' (V. iv. 64-5). The questioning of language does not loom as large, nor occupy as thematically central a place, in *The Two Gentlemen of Verona* as it does in *Love's Labour's Lost*, but it is in some ways still more disturbing. In *Love's Labour's Lost* reliance on fine words and clever patterns indicates an empty idealism, an ivory tower knowledge of life, which collapses before real experience—be it of love or death. The collapse can be funny, but it can also be poignant, as when the Princess holds up the irrelevancy of the King's diction in the final scene: 'I understand you not; my griefs are double' (V. ii. 740). Berowne—for it takes the wittiest mind to see the limits of wit—is the one to take the point: 'Honest plain words best pierce the ear of grief' (l. 741). And so we are prepared for the play's final resting point, on good deeds versus words. In *The Two Gentlemen of Verona*, 'honest plain words' play little part, and the alternatives to wit are, on the one hand, silence and, on the other, force and brutality.

III

It would be tempting to suggest that in Valentine's passage of *peripeteia* and *anagnorisis* Shakespeare anticipated those moments in his later plays where the reliance on eyes rather than ears is an essential part of his technique as a theatre poet. But it is probably closer to the truth to say that it is one of the moments in a play heavily dependent on its language where we are yet reminded that experience may outrun language. For the technique of this play is almost entirely verbal. Ingenious producers have to add to *The Two Gentlemen of Verona* those scenes of 'pure theatre' which are so important in the structure of other Shakespearian comedies. The social ritual, with the exception of Proteus' serenade, consists (even for the clowns) exclusively of talk;

the text provides for no banquet, no masked ball, no concluding dance
but just a verbal promise of social harmony—

One feast, one house, one mutual happiness—

and, though the Duke promises to 'include all jars / With triumphs,
mirth, and rare solemnity', we are allowed to see none of this take
place. The outlaws do not slay deer or sing; the romance wanderings
include no shipwrecks nor anything more spectacular than an attempted rape, and that a pretty verbal one, too. The spectrum of
lovers, if we include the chaste Sir Eglamour and the 'foolish rival'
Thurio, do not add to the physical life of the play in the fashion of Sir
Andrew Aguecheek or Malvolio, or even the spectacularly unlucky
suitors in *The Merchant of Venice*. So love as courtship, and love and
friendship as social forces, are handled through language alone—to the
point where we feel that characters are used as an excuse for speeches
and the plot as a device to bring about situations where characters can
make speeches or engage in duologues. In this respect the play is still
close to the descriptive-contemplative mode of non-dramatic poetry.
Shakespeare's technique is still limited almost exclusively to three
devices: soliloquy, duologue and the asides as comment.[14] Clearly
the debate structure of Lyly's plays underlies the pattern. And yet,
as I have already suggested, there is also an action *in* the language
itself which makes it uniquely Shakespearian (and relates it to the
sonnets)—a sort of dialectic between a sense that 'much is the force
of heaven-bred poesy' (III. ii. 71), on the one hand, and a doubt
and undercutting of that force (even as that *credo* by the Duke is
undercut by the ironical situation in which it is uttered). Delight in
wit, in verbal conceits and Petrarchan diction, co-exists not only
with the conventional regret that love, in Berowne's words, 'sings
heaven's praise with such an earthly tongue', but also with a critical
awareness that words may substitute for or falsify experience.

Because of this dialectic there is more to the real form—by which
I mean that which relates the parts of the play to each other—of *The
Two Gentlemen of Verona* than a 'structure-ridden' narrative,[15] opening
on a parting in which the themes of love and friendship are
introduced and closing on a double reunion and an exaltation of love-

---

[14] See Wells, *op. cit.*, p. 163.

[15] T. W. Baldwin, *William Shakespeare's Five-Act Structure* (Urbana, 1947),
p. 719.

through-friendship. That structure is obviously there, but it is questioned and explored so that only rarely may we take it at its face value. Longitudinally, the exploration seems to move through three stages. In the first of these—I. i through to the beginnings of Proteus' defection at II. iv. 188—a perspective is established for us in which the play's world of witty artifice, in action as in language, is both celebrated and criticized. The opening scene between Valentine and Proteus moves rapidly through a duologue which, in Lyly's manner, sets up two antithetical attitudes, leaving Proteus alone on stage to clinch the antithesis in a soliloquy:

> He after honour hunts, I after love;
> He leaves his friends to dignify them more:
> I leave myself, my friends, and all for love.
>
> (I. i. 63–5)

At this stage there is no reason to doubt that these lines are a straightforward enunciation of theme, but subsequent action and speeches will question all the key-words: 'honour', 'love', 'friends'—even 'self'. Indeed the last line ominously looks forward to having its meaning revalued when Proteus, in II. vi, discovers that 'I to myself am dearer than a friend' and so leaves his true self for the selfish gratification of pursuing a new love. The Speed–Proteus duologue which completes I. i casts the light of burlesque on courtly wit, but, with its puns on ship/sheep/shepherd/mutton, it also keeps us in a dramatic world where life is dealt with as a kind of linguistic game. In the next scene this perspective is delightfully maintained by Julia's coquetry over Proteus' letter, both in the duologue with Lucetta and in her one-woman show with the letter as the only prop. In a scene like this we obviously do not regard language and action from Launce's unsophisticated point of view: 'to be slow in words is a woman's only virtue'; but, on the other hand, a sense is developing that sophistication may be mere padding. As one of my students recently said, when Julia rips up her letter from Proteus and then changes her mind and from the torn pieces picks out simple phrases like 'kind Julia', or 'passionate Proteus', or just 'Proteus', then we feel that she probably has the essence of the letter and has not lost much by losing the conventional decorations. It is notable—and in the context not just an inherited plot-trick—that so much of the intercourse between characters in this play is carried out by way of letters, a medium even further conventionalized than formal speech. Typically Proteus comes on reading a letter from Julia:

> Sweet love! sweet lines! sweet life!
> Here is her hand, the agent of her heart;
>
> (I. iii. 45–6)

and this, apart from their brief parting scene, is the only dramatic statement of their mutual love—just as later Launce's lady-love exists only through her 'conditions' set down in writing. 'Lines' are made the vehicle, indeed the essence, of 'love' and 'life' in this world, even as the 'hand' that writes is the chief agent and evidence of the 'heart' that feels.

The first scene between Valentine and Silvia (and the only one in which they have any kind of privacy, though even here Speed is present) develops this perspective further: in their relationship at this instance, love is the stuff for words; and the words are delightful and wittily patterned, but at the same time curiously depersonalized. It is absurdly apt that Valentine should have been asked to, *and* been able to, write a letter on behalf of somebody else to an unknown recipient. The separation of word and feeling could not go much further than this, and, unlike the love-blinded Valentine, we do not really need Speed to see how deliberate the absurdity is:

> 'Herself hath taught her love himself to write unto
> her lover.'
> All this I speak in print, for in print I found it.
>
> (II. i. 156–7)

The deliberateness goes outside even Speed's superior awareness (it is significant that the letter-carriers are basically so much wittier than the letter-writers and receivers in the play), to a comment from the dramatist on how in this kind of courtship one situation is interchange-able for another, how relationships are as formalized and as dependent on verbal elaboration as conceits. Indeed, in this part of the play Shake-speare delights in constructing scenes which are, as it were, verbal conceits (and often standard Petrarchan conceits) turned into stage-tableaux—such as Julia's game with names in I. ii and the two parting scenes in II. ii–iii.

The clown scenes are obviously used to puncture by parody this tendency to formalization—without, therefore, demolishing the inherent truth in a conceit. Launce's one-man show with Crab has,

by now, probably received more critical attention than all the other
scenes of the play put together, and deservedly so. It draws together
several other scenes: in technique it echoes Julia's speaking tableau in
I. ii; in his delicious confusion over which prop represents which
member of his grieving family, Launce recalls the gay confusion over
the identities of letter-writers and receivers in II. i but also anticipates
the serious confounding of identities involved in Proteus' betrayal; in
theme, of course, the scene parodies the excessive emotion of the parting between Proteus and Julia which has just taken place. But it is
interesting that, in his rebuking of the silent Crab (hard-hearted as
Proteus is soon going to be), Launce is so much wordier than the
lovers themselves, and also that, within the comic frame of the scene,
the diction and patterning of courtly love poetry came so easily to
Launce. He uses them both seriously and facetiously and in a mixture
of both. His sister is 'as white as a lily, and as small as a wand'. The
'tide', which echoes Proteus' conceit—

> The tide is now—nay, not thy tide of tears:
> That tide will stay me longer than I should—
>
> (II. ii. 14–15)

is wilfully confused with the 'tied' Crab. And there is a mixture of
genuine feeling and mockery in his elaboration on Proteus' image:

> Why, man, if the river were dry, I am able to fill it with my tears;
> if the wind were down, I could drive the boat with my sighs.
>
> (II. iii. 47–9)

So Launce makes comically explicit a critical perspective on the
absorption in the conventional attitudes and language of love—a perspective which the 'serious' scenes have implicity demonstrated—
without in any way denying, as might happen in a satire, the holiness
of the heart's affections or the need to put them into words.

IV

In the second stage of its dialectic—from the end of II. iv through
the rest of Act II and the whole of Acts III and IV—the play seems to
take us in two new directions, on the one hand putting the patterned
and apparently conventional language to serious uses and, on the other,

establishing scenes which are, as it were, counter-conceits and in which
the language and attitudes of courtly convention are found altogether
invalid.

Under the pressure of the serious complications in the plot, those
involving tension of mind and suffering and heartbreak, verbal
ingenuity itself becomes a vehicle for a sense of life. The first sign of
this is Proteus' soliloquy in II. vi:

> To leave my Julia, shall I be forsworn;
> To love fair Silvia, shall I be forsworn;
> To wrong my friend, I shall be much forsworn.
> And ev'n that power which gave me first my oath
> Provokes me to this threefold perjury:
> Love bade me swear, and Love bids me forswear. . . .
> I cannot leave to love, and yet I do;
> But there I leave to love where I should love.
> Julia I lose, and Valentine I lose;
> If I keep them, I needs must lose myself;
> If I lose them, thus find I by their loss:
> For Valentine, myself; for Julia, Silvia.
> I to myself am dearer than a friend;
> For love is still most precious in itself.

(1–24)

In this speech many of the stylistic features of the play are concentrated: the end-stopped lines: the antitheses or paradoxes pivoted on
the caesura or brought out by the perfect symmetry of two consecutive
lines; the patterning of repetitions towards a climax; the argument
through conceits (mainly in such lines as the following pair: 'At
first I did adore a twinkling star,/But now I worship a celestial sun').
But here, instead of drawing attention to itself as it would have
done earlier in the play, and unlike the careful patterning in the apparently similar weighing of love against friendship in *Endimion*,[16] the
verbal scheme truly suggests the staccato movements, the to-and-
froing, the see-saw of impulses within a mind which, while it believes
itself divided, is already set on its course. Compared to Euphues in a
similar conflict situation,[17] Proteus is much less self-conscious or con-

---

[16] Eumenides speaking; *Endimion*, III. iv. 105–20.

[17] Euphues, *The Anatomy of Wit*: see Bullough's reprint of the relevant
passage in *Narrative and Dramatic Sources of Shakespeare*, vol. I (London, 1957),
p. 222.

cerned with looking before and after, much less aware of the appearance of the situation from every viewpoint; indeed the most impressive
feature of this speech is its enactment of gradual self-absorption, until
Proteus gives us the first hint of the Iago figure whose limited self—
''tis in ourselves that we are thus and thus'—is the centre of any argument. The casuistical argument against vows (common, as Clifford
Leech points out, in early Shakespeare) is not merely, or mainly, an
exhibition of clever wit; it produces a dizzy sense of the precariousness
of language. When Lyly's debaters weigh up 'love', in a much more
intellectualized fashion than Proteus, the word remains an entity with
a permanent reference; here it means what Proteus' heedless emotion
wants it to mean: 'I cannot leave to love, and yet I do'. In the mouth of
the unscrupulous, language changes its meaning, and—like Iago—
Proteus can pretend to change actuality through words:

> I will forget that Julia is alive,
> Rememb'ring that my love to her is dead.
>> (II. vi. 27-8)

On the other hand, of course, a metamorphosed actuality can give
a new human content and poignancy to an old game of words, as when
Julia speaks of her heavy task of wooing Silvia on Proteus' behalf:

> I am my master's true confirmed love,
> But cannot be true servant to my master,
> Unless I prove false traitor to myself.
>> (IV. iv. 99-101)

The same is true for Valentine's banishment speech which, one might
almost say, bears the same relation to the partial sonnet which the
Duke discovers on him as Romeo's love for Rosaline does to that for
Juliet. Valentine's discovery that he has so 'garner'd up his heart' in
another person that his own identity can only be defined through her,

> To die is to be banish'd from myself,
> And Silvia is myself; banish'd from her
> Is self from self, a deadly banishment.
> What light is light, if Silvia be not seen?
> What joy is joy, if Silvia be not by?
>> (III. i. 171-5)

passes beyond conventional attitudinizing to an attitude in which verbal patterning is functional and central. It is the sort of recognition which even in naturalistic drama calls for patterned speech:

> George who is good to me, and whom I revile; who understands me, and whom I push off; . . . who can make me happy, and I do not wish to be happy, and yes I do wish to be happy. George and Martha: sad, sad, sad.[18]

There is a genuine ring of agony as the metaphors in Valentine's speech stop being conceits and become live reality—as we can feel if we compare the opening and key line of his poem to Silvia,

> My thoughts do harbour with my Silvia nightly,

with his outcry in the banishment speech,

> Except I be by Silvia in the night,
> There is no music in the nightingale;
> Unless I look on Silvia in the day,
> There is no day for me to look upon.
> She is my essence . . .
>
> (III. i. 140 and 178–82)

The echoes here of themes and images from several sonnets may help us to see that, as in the sonnets, Shakespeare is working *through* the convention. At least one of the finest moments in the play is arrived at—much like Sonnet 130, 'My mistress' eyes are nothing like the sun'—through a kind of anti-sonnet technique. When Silvia questions the supposed Sebastian about Julia, 'Is she not passing fair?', and Julia replies by fictionalizing herself,

> She hath been fairer, madam, than she is.
> When she did think my master lov'd her well,
> She, in my judgment, was as fair as you;
> But since she did neglect her looking-glass,
> And threw her sun-expelling mask away,
> The air hath starv'd the roses in her cheeks,
> And pinch'd the lily-tincture of her face,
> That now she is become as black as I,
>
> (IV. iv. 147–54)

then her nouns—the looking-glass, the sun, the roses, the lily-tincture —are those of the Petrarchan convention; but her verbs—neglect,

[18] Edward Albee, *Who's Afraid of Virginia Woolf?*, Act III (Penguin edition), p. 113.

throw away, starve, pinch—enact the reality behind the convention, the vulnerability of the roses and the lilies. We are, at one and the same time, reminded that 'brightness falls from the air' and made to sense 'what it feels like' in the particular dramatic situation. As fiction and reality in Julia's narrative meet in 'That now she is become as black as I', language has become truly dramatic, indeed hardly more than a stage-direction.[19]

V

If Shakespeare's handling of convention and language at this stage of the play suggests a new seriousness and critical alertness, then we might in this context re-view two scenes which are often criticized for the wrong reasons and which, it seems to me, are in fact carefully controlled counter-conceits. The first is the one where Valentine with unbelievable stupidity gives away to the Duke his love for Silvia and his plan for elopement with her. The Duke's ruse of asking Valentine to 'tutor' him in how to court 'a lady in Verona here / Whom I affect' provides the scaffold for a duologue (especially III. i. 89–105) which is a take-off on conventions of courtship in the rest of the play. The main comic point lies not just in Valentine's stupidity but in the free-wheeling, or in terms of Valentine's consciousness almost mesmeric, effect which the convention has once the duologue is under way, so that the right key-word planted by the Duke will provoke the right (in terms of convention *and* of the Duke's intentions) response from Valentine:

> Duke. That no man hath access by day to her.
> Val. Why, then I would resort to her by night.
> Duke. Ay, but the doors be lock'd and keys kept safe,
> That no man hath recourse to her by night . . .
> Val. Why then a ladder quaintly made of cords,
>
> (III. i. 109ff.)

and so on. Shakespeare is, by the structure of the dialogue and by a slight quaintness of syntax, exaggerating the mechanical effect of

---

[19] In the passage from the *Diana Enamorada* which is the source of this scene, Felismena (Julia) tells Celia (Silvia) about the former love of Felix (Proteus) and the effect of the betrayal upon the scorned lady; but the conversation turns into an abstract discourse on the relationship between 'content of minde' and 'perfect beautie' (see Bullough, *op. cit.*, pp. 243–4), whereas Shakespeare's passage is concretely and dramatically emotive.

patterned speech; for the Duke is putting to use the question–response
technique which Kyd employed to dramatize Balthazar's love-worries:

> Yet might she love me for my valiancy:
> Ay, but that's slander'd by captivity.
> Yet might she love me to content her sire:
> Ay, but her reason masters his desire.
> Yet might she love me . . .
> Ay, but . . . [etc.]
>
> (*The Spanish Tragedy*, II. i. 19ff.)

In the Shakespearian situation, love behaviour and language is seen to
have become a mechanized gesture, the lover a puppet who can be
manipulated at will by a detached outsider. Valentine is not just
stupid[20] but a comic character in the Bergsonian sense. Not only is
the love convention, in attitudes and speech, tested and found absurd
but, in a microcosm of the whole play's pattern, it is seen to explode
in violence. The image with which the Duke starts his dismissal of
Valentine may, in its magnitude, seem to ameliorate the situation by
exalting it:

> Why, Phaethon—for thou art Merops' son—
> Wilt thou aspire to guide the heavenly car,
> And with thy daring folly burn the world?
> Wilt thou reach stars because they shine on thee?

But that, too, explodes in ugly, unvarnished brutality:

> Go, base intruder, over-weening slave,
> Bestow thy fawning smiles on equal mates.
>
> (III. i. 153–8)

If this situation is artificial, there is yet a sense of life in its implicit
comment on artificiality and its effects.

The second scene to be set in this context is that in which Proteus,
the most wickedly clever character in the play, in response to Silvia's
reproaches can only produce two identical, and identically feeble,
excuses:

> I grant, sweet love, that I did love a lady;
> But she is dead. . . .
> I likewise hear that Valentine is dead.
>
> (IV. ii. 101–9)

[20] Nor do I think that the scene can be summed up as 'situation at variance
with character' (Wells, *op. cit.*, p. 167).

To see this as 'so feeble that it reflects from the incompetence of Proteus to that of the dramatist'[21] is to disregard the criticism built into this scene and its relation to the rest of the play. Much like Valentine in the scene just discussed, Proteus is moving as a puppet of the courtly love code, which for a situation like this prescribes, in Valentine's words to the Duke:

> If she do chide, 'tis not to have you gone,
> For why the fools are mad if left alone.
> Take no repulse, whatever she doth say;
> For 'Get you gone' she doth not mean 'Away!'
>
> (III. i. 98–101)

The trouble is that Silvia does not go by the courtesy book but by genuine human reactions. Proteus, who was so voluble a letter-writer to Julia and so articulate in sacrificing an old love to a new, is inventive enough as long as he can play with conceits in the wooing-the-reluctant-mistress game:

> *Sil.* Who is that that spake?
> *Pro.* One, lady, if you knew his pure heart's truth,
> You would quickly learn to know him by his voice. . . .
> *Sil.* What's your will?
> *Pro.* That I may compass yours.
>
> (IV. ii. 83–8)

But he cannot cope with a woman who persists in taking a severely practical view of his wit (ll. 89–90) and in being ruthlessly literal about the conceit of his 'pure heart's truth' (ll. 91–5). So, as she gives him the wrong cues (as against the all-too-right ones in the case of the Duke vis-à-vis Valentine), he has no language to reply with but a cry of 'dead'. Once, indeed, he thinks he has picked up a cue, as Silvia assures him that in Valentine's grave (if he is dead) 'my love is buried':

> Sweet lady, let me rake it from the earth.

---

[21] Leech's note at IV. ii. 109. The corresponding passage in *Diana Enamorada* supplies Felix (Proteus) with an eloquent argument (see Bullough, pp. 241–2), which further suggests that Proteus' 'incompetence' is deliberate on Shakespeare's part.

But Silvia quickly disabuses him of the idea that he has found an idiom
through which he can advance his interests:

> Go to thy lady's grave, and call hers thence;
> Or, at the least, in hers sepulchre thine.
>
> (IV. ii. 111–13)

From this deadlock—'he heard not that', the listening Julia significantly
comments—the only way forward is via a totally new conceit, that of
Silvia's picture, which leads to a sonnet game on 'shadow' and 'substance' (ll. 120–27). The presence of Julia and the sleeping Host
throughout this scene enables Shakespeare not only to puncture
Proteus' conceits and inanities with Julia's sharp asides but also to con-
struct a situation which consists of several layers of non-communica-
tion. And the scene closes on Julia's words, as directly in contact with
human reality as Desdemona's 'Faith, half asleep':

> it hath been the longest night
> That e'er I watch'd, and the most heaviest.
>
> (135–6)

So, in exploring its world of romantic courtship, *The Two Gentlemen of Verona* repeatedly and in various ways reminds us that there is
a world elsewhere. We are made to delight in the beauty and wit of
the romance world, but we are also made to sense that it is fragile and
vulnerable, ready to topple over into absurdity on the one side and
brutality on the other. The sense of life that informs the play is something like a tightrope walk, and the scene which I have just discussed
is an epitome of the tightrope pattern.

But IV. ii (which is generally regarded as the best scene in the play)
is also an indication of where the play's radical dramatic weakness
lies: in the tendency for each scene to form, much as each Shakespearian sonnet does, a kind of 'still' from a play,[22] a virtually self-contained
picture of human relationships. Shakespeare has obviously had difficulties in translating the 'I' and the 'thou' (and occasionally 'she') of
the sonnets into the multiple voices and interactions of a dramatic
structure. The lovers hardly ever meet: apart from the last scene, each
twosome comes together in two scenes,[23] but even then their contacts

---

[22] Cf. G. K. Hunter, 'The Dramatic Technique of Shakespeare's Sonnets', *loc.
cit.*, p. 154.

[23] Proteus and Julia meet to part in II. ii, and with Julia disguised as 'Sebastian'
in IV. iv; Valentine and Silvia meet in the letter-game in II. i, and in the

are often perfunctory. There is nothing like Romeo's and Juliet's minds meshing in a sonnet, nor like the formalized intimacy of the couples and cross-pairings in *Love's Labour's Lost* and *A Midsummer Night's Dream*. Lovers appear apart, talking about their love; and paradoxically Valentine and Silvia 'meet' more in his banishment speech than in any actual co-presence on stage. The same is true for the two friends: their relationship is most alive and meaningful in Proteus' soliloquy in II. vi. All this means that the fulfilments in Act V—which forms what I have here called the third stage in the structure of the play—operate in something of a vacuum. When Valentine, faced with Proteus' perfidy, speaks of his friend as physically and morally part of himself—'one's own right hand / Is perjured to the bosom'—and voices an almost Cleopatra-like sense that the whole world has turned a stranger, then these words do not have tentacles which reach back into the play.

VI

The real inconsistency, then, of this play, and the one which becomes most apparent when he tries to dramatize constancy, is that Shakespeare is trying to use as his raw material what characters say (attitudes) rather than what they are (people). Plot is forever crystallizing into attitudes, and the structural pattern is one of scenes, each demonstrating one or more attitudes to love (or friendship). Some scenes are entirely contained in a single emblematic stance, like the two versions of parting with dear ones in II. ii and II. iii; some, like II. iv, move through a whole gamut of attitudes—more by adding one tableau to another than by causally linking each with the other. The longest scene of all—III. i (374 lines)—is the longest not because more happens (the final scene in which so much happens is less than half as long) but because we move through a particularly wide range of stances: through moments deeply moving, moments which implicitly reveal their own absurdity, and moments which explicitly deflate the love code (Launce's and Speed's duologue on Launce's mistress). And what applies within the longer scenes also holds true for the relationship between scenes in the play as a whole. Their interconnection is determined not by growing and changing personalities but by their evaluation of the word and concept of 'love'. In other words, Shakespeare is trying to handle

---

sparring of II. iv; Proteus and Silvia have a brief encounter of civilities in II. iv, and then meet in the abuse scene of IV. ii.

dramatic structure as if it were the verbal structure of a sonnet. To show what I mean, I should like at this point to return to Sonnet 40, which not only is very close in idea to Valentine's renunciation but also helps us to see why in *The Two Gentlemen of Verona* Shakespeare produced a work which is ultimately less dramatic than many of his sonnets.

It is necessary to quote the sonnet in full:

1 Take all my loves, my love, yea, take them all;
What hast thou then more than thou hadst before?
No love, my love, that thou mayst true love call;
All mine was thine before thou hadst this more.
5 Then if for my love thou my love receivest,
I cannot blame thee, for my love thou usest;
But yet be blam'd, if thou thyself deceivest
By wilful taste of what thyself refusest.
I do forgive thy robb'ry, gentle thief,
10 Although thou steal thee all my poverty;
And yet love knows it is a greater grief
To bear love's wrong than hate's known injury.
    Lascivious grace, in whom all ill well shows,
    Kill me with spites; yet we must not be foes.

Without pressing the analogy, one might suggest that the handling of the word 'love' in the sonnet forms something of a paradigm of the way individual scenes have been structured and related to each other in *The Two Gentlemen of Verona*. The syntax of sonnet line 3 produces a clash between the three different uses of 'love', so that each comments upon and modifies our attitude to the other—much like what happens in the sequence of scenes iv, v and vi in Act II of the play. The shock-effect and cross-evaluation brought about by the apparent paradox of line 5 is similar to the operation of II. vi and vii: Julia's affirmation of her faith in Proteus' love following immediately upon his betrayal. The structure of relationships in the multi-dimensional scene IV. ii, where Julia suffers more from her unrequited love than Proteus from his, is based on much the same combination of paradox and antithesis as lines 11 and 12 in the sonnet. And similarly one can see a parallel mode of composition in the second quatrain of the sonnet and the Launce/Crab—Julia/Proteus—Julia/Silvia scene of IV. iv. Pivoted on the paradoxical self-sacrifices of Launce on behalf of his dog and Julia on behalf of her lover, as the quatrain is on the lines 'Then if for my love thou my love receivest, / I cannot blame thee, for my love thou usest', the scene shows a similar structure of attitudes: overall wit and inter-criticism of parts, overall lightness around a real heartbreak.

But when we come to look at the total achievement of the pattern in the sonnet and the play, respectively, its limitations in the play become apparent. In the sonnet, through the verbal action of devices like pun, paradox, antithesis and oxymoron, the pattern becomes an enactment of the poet's feelings for his friend; and the meaning of this 'love' grows both more specific and more evocative, until it is defined —or, rather, held in suspension—in the contrary pulls of the couplet. Verbal ingenuity is entirely in the service of the dramatic evocation of 'what it feels like'. This is, of course, exactly what happens to the word-patterns and images in Shakespeare's mature plays; to a key-word like 'see' in *King Lear*, which changes and grows in human meaning, from Lear's first to his last 'see' and right through to Edgar's closing 'never see so much'. The sonnet is dramatic, too, in its dynamic form: what may look like a static attitude in the opening line develops through the fourteen lines into a live and complex relationship. The final 'yet we must not be foes' is both a desperate appeal and an affirmation—a far more troubled statement than the apparent non-chalance of the first line. It reveals the quality which perhaps most definitely bespeaks the dramatist in the sonnet: the dual voice (or viewpoint), which asserts and yet also questions, affirms an utter self-effacement in devotion and is yet also aware of the absurdity of such an attitude—the ability, in other words, to be both inside and outside an experience.

The play is less dramatic on all these counts. The character inter-action and development which *should* translate the verbal action of the sonnet is lacking, and so the sense of 'what it feels like' is fitful and there is no overall dynamism. In the structural climax marked by Valentine's couplet,

> And, that my love may appear plain and free,
> All that was mine in Silvia I give thee,

'my love' *should* be a more meaningful dramatic reality than the 'love' bandied about in the opening debate of the play. (The dénouement of *Twelfth Night*, for example, shows how the word 'love' has been through just this dynamic process.) But in fact it is not. Nor is the ending sustained by that complex viewpoint which we find in the sonnet (and again in the final scene of *Twelfth Night*). Involvement and detachment have alternated during the first four Acts, sometimes (as in IV. ii) coalescing; but in the last scene, and particularly in Valentine's lines, the drama seems to fall between the two.

If, with due care, we continue the sonnet analogy, it would appear that Shakespeare conceived this last scene in much the same way as in several of his sonnets he used a surprise couplet—one which, after twelve lines of argument in one direction, leaps to a sudden reversal with an antithetical 'Yet' or 'But' or 'Ah, but'.[24] In the sonnets where this happens, the break in the logic and the frequent introduction of a new simplicity (not to be mistaken for facility) suggests that the couplet records more of a desperate wish-fulfilment than a real conclusion, a willed belief rather than a state of emotional conviction. The same seems to me to be true for the last scene of *The Two Gentlemen of Verona*. The trouble (the ultimate inconsistency) is that there is a theoretical pressure on the scene which is not practically realized. The connections, both thematic and verbal, between Valentine's situation and other instances of inconstancy and betrayed trust in Shakespeare —not least, of course, in the sonnets—indicate that pressure.[25] The sonnets which contain a reversal in the couplet are all in one way or another concerned with what Derek Traversi has called 'the necessary flaw at the heart of passion'[26]—the fear that one's love and trust may be betrayed—and this fear, it seems to me, is what Shakespeare tries and fails to instil as an undertone in the scene. The central episode is dealt with in an extraordinary shorthand fashion.[27] There are 24

[24] Thirteen sonnets use the couplet in this way: 19, 30, 34, 42, 60, 84, 86, 91, 92, 131, 133, 139, 141. For a somewhat negative critique of their technique, see Edward Hubler, *The Sense of Shakespeare's Sonnets* (Princeton, N. J., 1952), pp. 26–7.

[25] R. Warwick Bond, in the 'old' Arden edition of the play, draws attention to similarities between Valentine's language and that of Henry V to the traitor Scroop (*Henry V*, II. ii. 138ff.); and also to Imogen in *Cymbeline*, III. iv. 62. Other betrayals, in the plays and sonnets, though with no reference to *The Two Gentlemen*, are discussed in the fascinating article by M. M. Mahood, 'Love's Confined Doom', *Shakespeare Survey* 15 (1962), pp. 50–61.

[26] *Approach to Shakespeare* (London, 1946), p. 46.

[27] It is of course possible that this is due to textual cuts between early performances and the first appearance of the play in print, in the Folio. But even if the interchange between Valentine and Proteus was originally longer, and was abbreviated for an age no longer interested in a love–friendship debate, this makes only a quantitative difference to my argument.

lines between Proteus' attempted rape and Julia's swoon, and in these we are bounced from one extreme attitude to another: disillusionment and reproach, penitence, forgiveness and demonstration of magnanimity. The shock to Valentine's consciousness is hauntingly expressed:

> Proteus,
> I am sorry I must never trust thee more,
> But count the world a stranger for thy sake.
>
> (68–70)

But thereafter the experience does not seem to pass through either character's mind. We are asked to accept it through general truths and universal statements, like Valentine's motivation of his forgiveness:

> Who by repentance is not satisfied,
> Is nor of heaven, nor earth; for these are pleas'd
> By Penitence th'Eternal's wrath's appeas'd.
>
> (79–81)

In a sonnet like 'Why didst thou promise such a beauteous day' (34), which also turns from reproach to sudden forgiveness, the reversal in the couplet is organically part of the whole, for it embodies the very point of the poem: the irrationality, recognized as such and yet treasured, of a deep commitment. Nor is the couplet a simple reversal, for there is a strong undertone of irony in the way its imagery relates to the rest of the sonnet and contradicts the assurance it is supposed to state:

> Ah! but those tears are pearl which thy love sheds,
> And they are rich, and ransom all ill deeds.

How can the artificiality of pearl be commensurate with, still less compensate for, the unnatural hurts which the friend has inflicted?[28] The irrationality of Valentine's argument is not placed in a saving perspective—Speed and Launce have disappeared at this stage of the play, and the women are mute. Nor is there any room for irony in the interchange between sinner and forgiver: Proteus' plea that 'hearty sorrow / Be a sufficient ransom for offence' is taken with the simplest 'Then I am paid' from Valentine. Nor do Valentine's lines have any

[28] Professor Mahood suggests that the last line 'may well be spoken with deep irony to the man who thinks his patronage can pay for his unkindness' (*Shakespeare Survey* 15, p. 53).

of the interpenetration of grief and the desire to forgive which dominates Sonnet 34.

It is easy enough to say that Shakespeare has here tried to do what
he did not yet have the dramatic language or sense of structure to do.
But before we condemn his failure, we should spare a thought for the
magnitude of what he was trying to do. Perhaps his shorthand technique here is a first approach to the insight that one person's complete
forgiveness of another, who has sinned vastly towards him or her, is
a miracle beyond articulation in words—as the wordlessness of the
reunion between Hermione and Leontes and the near inarticulacy of
Cordelia's 'no cause, no cause' would suggest. In the dénouements of
the other comedies there are either no sins to forgive, only mistakes
to rectify, or else the serious repentance and forgiveness take place off
stage (*As You Like It*) or are structurally played down (*Much Ado
About Nothing*). We have to go to the qualified forgiveness of Isabella's
plea for Angelo, or even as far forward in Shakespeare's career as
Prospero's surprisingly bitter speech of forgiveness (*The Tempest*,
V. i. 130–34), before we find a dramatic language and situation which,
like Sonnet 34, tells us that, short of a miracle, forgiveness does not
obliterate the offence.

The reason why I have paid so much attention to what is *not* there
in *The Two Gentlemen of Verona* is that it is the combination of what *is*
there with what is not that makes it a disturbing play. Certain aspects
of its structure and language, as I hope to have shown, enable us to be
in two minds at once: to accept and criticize the life presented to us.
We are aware of the beauty *and* precariousness of the romance world.
But individual characters' speeches cannot reach to the kind of *felt*
uncertainty which is there in Helena's inability to settle for complete
trust—'And I have found Demetrius like a jewel, / Mine own, and
not mine own' (*A Midsummer Night's Dream*, IV. i. 188–9)—and
which rankles in many of the sonnets:

> Thee have I not lock'd up in any chest,
> Save where thou art not, though I feel thou art,
> Within the gentle closure of my breast.

(48)

It is that uncertainty within the closest relationships ('where thou art
not, though I feel thou art') which I think Shakespeare has wanted to
render in *The Two Gentlemen of Verona*, and which gives a peculiar

poignancy to Proteus' outcry: 'O heaven, were man / But constant, he were perfect.' If the ending is an example of ineptitude in early Shakespeare, then the very ineptitude suggests the troubled vision of a man who cares immensely about love and friendship, what they do to people and make people do to each other. Perhaps in the end the surface of this play is intimate with the depths; but perhaps, also, that intimacy will emerge more readily in the study, in the company of the Folio and the Sonnets, than in the theatre. Perhaps *The Two Gentlemen of Verona* must ultimately be seen as that rare phenomenon in Shakespeare's corpus: a play where the sense of life is greater in reading than in seeing it. If so, there will never be a fitter audience for it than George Eliot at Dover, stirred, perturbed—and disgusted.

III

Shakespeare Without Sources

STANLEY WELLS

I

WE are accustomed to the study of Shakespeare's plays by way of his sources. It is a common, and often rewarding, critical technique. But there are a few plays in which Shakespeare did not adapt existing sources. These are, chronologically, *Love's Labour's Lost*, *A Midsummer Night's Dream*, and *The Tempest*.[1] Other plays might almost be included in this list, and even these three show the influence of his reading, though in them the influence is local rather than pervasive. But in these three plays Shakespeare seems himself to have been responsible for the main story line, however much he may have drawn on his reading for points of detail. In this chapter I want to look at these plays as a group,

[1] These are the only three plays for which the Summary table in Kenneth Muir's *Shakespeare's Sources* (Vol. 1, London, 1957, pp. 255–7) gives 'Not known' under the heading 'Main Source'. In his Appendix of plays 'of which the sources are not precisely known' he adds *Titus Andronicus*, *The Two Gentlemen of Verona*, *The Taming of the Shrew*, *The Merry Wives of Windsor*, and *Timon of Athens*, and does not include *A Midsummer Night's Dream*. But of *A Midsummer Night's Dream* he says 'There was probably no comprehensive source' (p. 31). *Titus Andronicus* may be a revision of an earlier play, or may be based on an earlier version of the eighteenth-century chapbook. *The Two Gentlemen of Verona* has, as Muir says, an 'ultimate source' in Montemayor's *Diana*, which, directly or indirectly, provided the basic narrative material. *The Taming of the Shrew* has undisputed origins in folk-tale and, for its sub-plot, Gascoigne's *Supposes*. *The Merry Wives of Windsor* may be based on a lost play. In any case, it is textually corrupt, and there is internal and external evidence that it stands outside the main stream of Shakespeare's achievement. The basic material of *Timon of Athens* is from Plutarch; Muir believes 'there may have been a dramatic source' (p. 260). Of *The Tempest*, Muir says 'There were a number of minor sources . . . but it is highly probable that there was a main source as yet unidentified' (p. 261). I feel that the resemblances, considered in this chapter, between *The Tempest* and some of Shakespeare's earlier plays encourage the belief that this play, too, is of Shakespeare's invention.

and to explore the ways in which Shakespeare's mind worked when he was inventing plots rather than adapting them.

Though some scholars would assign a very early date to *Love's Labour's Lost*, there is fairly general agreement that it was written only shortly before *A Midsummer Night's Dream*, probably about 1594 or 1595. So it would not be surprising that these two plays should have much in common. *The Tempest* is probably Shakespeare's last non-collaborative play, but it is perhaps a mark of the essential unity of his achievement that structurally the play with which it has most in common is an early one, *The Comedy of Errors*. The irregular spacing of my three plays among the canon may warn us against attaching excessive significance to resemblances among them. If they were more evenly spaced, we might more reasonably look in them for an index to Shakespeare's development. But they are not.

The simplest resemblance is that they are all comedies. We may remember Dr Johnson:

> his disposition, as Rymer has remarked, led him to comedy. In tragedy he often writes, with great appearance of toil and study, what is written at last with little felicity; but, in his comic scenes, he seems to produce, without labour, what no labour can improve . . . in comedy he seems to repose, or to luxuriate, as in a mode of thinking congenial to his nature . . . his comedy often surpasses expectation or desire. His comedy pleases by the thoughts and the language, and his tragedy for the greater part by incident and action. His tragedy seems to be skill, his comedy to be instinct.[2]

This pronouncement might seem to receive support from the observation that Shakespeare's three most original plays are comedies. It would be fair to object that he could hardly have invented the plots of history plays, and that in his time tragedies, too, were generally based on historical events (though of course *Macbeth*, for example, is further from its main source than *Richard II* or *Julius Caesar*, and the events of *Titus Andronicus* seem, happily, to have little basis in recorded fact). But comedies form the bulk of his output, and Johnson is arguing partly on the basis of style, so perhaps the evidence in relation to sources does indeed support the view that Shakespeare's natural instincts led him towards comedy.

[2] From the *Preface* (1765); *Dr Johnson on Shakespeare*, ed. W. K. Wimsatt (Penguin Shakespeare Library, 1969), p. 64.

II

The resemblances among the three plays I am considering seem to hinge on *A Midsummer Night's Dream*. *Love's Labour's Lost*, that is to say, is closer to *A Midsummer Night's Dream* than to *The Tempest*; and *The Tempest* resembles *A Midsummer Night's Dream* more than it resembles *Love's Labour's Lost*. The two earlier plays offer obvious points of comparison. Both have a highly patterned structure. The characters fall neatly into groups. In *Love's Labour's Lost* we have the King of Navarre and his three courtiers, balancing the Princess of France and her three ladies, attended by Boyet; Armado and his foil, Moth; Holofernes and Nathaniel with their foil, Dull; and the clowns, Costard and Jaquenetta. The principle of division is partly social; but it is also, more importantly, conceptual. Armado, Holofernes, and Sir Nathaniel represent a kind of polarization of some instincts of the lords: a pushing to the extreme of their tendency to verbalization and their pedantry. They provide an *exemplum horrendum* of the destination to which the course the lords have adopted is likely to lead. Costard and Jaquenetta delightfully represent a simplification of the lords' (and ladies') baser selves, the all-too-natural instincts that they are over-anxious to quell. The characters are not entirely static. In particular, Armado's fall from his ideals provides an example no less horrendous than the intensity with which he pursues them. But it is clear that in constructing this play Shakespeare has created his characters in order to embody a set of ideas.

In *A Midsummer Night's Dream* the characters are equally obviously grouped. There are the fairies, the two groups of lovers (Theseus and Hippolyta on the one hand, and the four younger lovers on the other), and the mechanicals. It is not as easy to think of the characters of this play in conceptual terms as it is in *Love's Labour's Lost*. But it is clear that Theseus and Hippolyta show greater maturity than the younger lovers, and that this relates to the disjunction of reason and love on which Bottom remarks. If the play had been much simpler than it is, the fairies might have been more idealized than they are, and the mechanicals cruder; but Shakespeare has chosen to give his fairies some all-too-human characteristics. In doing so he perhaps emphasizes the humanity of his play, the fact that human life can be confounded by misfortune, that happiness is dependent partly upon chance, the fortunate conjunction of accidental circumstances (represented by the reconciliation of Oberon and Titania), as well as upon the will of man, that is by his reason swayed. But let me not try to abstract a scheme when Shakespeare has taken obvious pains to conceal it. It is enough to notice that the characters fall clearly into homogeneous groups, and to suggest that the over-ruling characteristics of each group are designed to contribute to the play's intellectual coherence.

The patterned structure of the two plays is further dependent upon the disposition of scenes involving the character groups, and the layout of the incidents. This could be demonstrated by means of a structural analysis of both plays, but it seems unnecessary. The plays have a different overall structure, of course; but they are equally neat. *Love's Labour's Lost* is the more original, with its curious ending that projects a happy resolution into a future which stretches well beyond the time-scheme of the play. Before this it has moved to a climax of complication in the overhearing scene (IV. iii), in which much of our pleasure derives from the gratification of our expectations as each character is succes-sively exposed. The corresponding scene in *A Midsummer Night's Dream* is the night scene in the forest, in which Puck plays his tricks upon the lovers, followed by the separate episode of their awakening (III. ii and IV. i). The patterning of *A Midsummer Night's Dream* is very prominent at this stage of the play, with the awakening in turn of Titania, the lovers, and Bottom.

An obvious structural parallel between the two plays is the giving over of most of the last act of each to a play-within-the-play. Again *Love's Labour's Lost* might be felt to be the more sophisticated, since in it the play-within-the-play is enclosed within the main action, whereas in *A Midsummer Night's Dream* it is rather an appendage to the action, having a celebratory function. If one were presented simply with a structural analysis of the two plays one might be forgiven for deducing that *Love's Labour's Lost* was the later. In both plays the play-within-the-play has the structural function of bringing groups of characters together, though to different effect. In both it has, also, common though not identical thematic functions. In *Love's Labour's Lost* there are in effect two plays-within-the-play, the first, and simpler, being the masque of Muscovites which provides the discomfiture of the lords, and a consequent adjustment of their relations with the ladies, which is a necessary preliminary to their forming together an audience for the entertainment that is to be offered to them by their social inferiors. As in some of Shakespeare's other comedies, notably *All's Well that Ends*

Well, embarrassment is a prime source of comic effect in this play; and, as also in other plays, it is succeeded by an improvement in the relations of the embarrassed and their observers. After the ladies have embarrassed the lords, they settle down together to embarrass those who are performing for them the patently ludicrous pageant of the Nine Worthies. That it is patently ludicrous helps us to preserve sympathy with the mockers as well as the mocked. The same is true of *A Midsummer Night's Dream*, where the noble characters, their own differences resolved, together form a somewhat restive audience for a performance by their social inferiors.

The characters of both plays are obviously concerned with right behaviour. Those of *Love's Labour's Lost* repeatedly fail to achieve it. This is why the happy ending has to be deferred. And one of their areas of failure is in courtesy. The lords' interruptions of the pageant eventually provoke Holofernes' rebuke: 'This is not generous, not gentle, not humble.' The line strikes with more force in its dramatic context than its phrasing might seem to merit, partly perhaps because it is likely to embarrass the theatre audience as well as the one on the stage, causing both to reflect on the quality of their laughter. In *A Midsummer Night's Dream* the aristocratic characters similarly mock the play that is being performed for them, and in that play the interruptions are more fully developed. But they are also less disruptive because, while in *Love's Labour's Lost* the comments are addressed directly to the actors, in *A Midsummer Night's Dream* they are almost always made by one member of the stage audience to the others, even though they are sometimes overheard by the actors. Relations become strained, and Moonshine has his moment of exasperation, but good will triumphs, and the play reaches a conclusion which its actors, at least, can feel to be successful. In *Love's Labour's Lost*, however, the play becomes a fiasco with the climax of Armado's embarrassment, when he is 'infamonized among potentates' by the revelation that Jaquenetta is quick with child by him. The stage is, designedly, a shambles before the moment of total embarrassment; a moment that, in successful performance, embraces the audience as well as everyone on stage, when the wordless, sombre figure of Marcade rebukes our laughter.

Marcade's entrance forces the characters of the play not merely into seriousness, but into a level of seriousness deeper than any they have shown so far. The Princess apologizes on behalf of the ladies if they have been guilty of lack of courtesy. She asks that the lords will

> excuse or hide
> The liberal opposition of our spirits,
> If over-boldly we have borne ourselves
> In the converse of breath.

(V. ii. 720–23)

Berowne makes a similar apology on behalf of the men, and the play draws to an end with the lords' promise to undergo a more serious kind of retreat than that to which they had committed themselves in the play's opening lines, one which involves not merely restraint and moderation but also the active pursuit of good works. Rosaline's reply to Berowne's protest 'Mirth cannot move a soul in agony' is a marvellous expression of an ideal of courtesy that, once it is made, can be seen to have underlain the whole action of the play:

> A jest's prosperity lies in the ear
> Of him that hears it, never in the tongue
> Of him that makes it; then, if sickly ears,
> Deaf'd with the clamours of their own dear groans,
> Will hear your idle scorns, continue then,
> And I will have you and that fault withal.
> But if they will not, throw away that spirit,
> And I shall find you empty of that fault,
> Right joyful of your reformation.

(V. ii. 849–57)

It is a moralistic speech, however lightened by the intelligence of style in which it is expressed. It is paralleled by Armado's vow to 'hold the plough' for Jaquenetta's sake for three years, and it is surely not too much to say that the play ends by recommending the virtues of restraint, moderation, penitence, generosity and courtesy. Unfortunately the text is uninformative about just how the action should end, but I think it is significant that the final dialogue of the cuckoo and the owl is not interrupted by its stage audience. It seems desirable that the noblemen, their ladies, and the yokels should join together to respond to the performance of the songs with generosity, gentleness and humility.

A Midsummer Night's Dream shows a similar concern with courtesy, and with moderation and restraint. The ardour of Theseus and Hippolyta in their opening exchange is a controlled one. Soon afterwards, Hermia is warned of the harsh external restraints that will be imposed upon her if she fails to moderate her desires in obedience to her father. As Hermia and Lysander lie down in the wood, she bids him,

> for love and courtesy
> Lie further off, in human modesty;
> Such separation as may well be said
> Becomes a virtuous bachelor and a maid.
>
> (II. ii. 56–9)

Helena, thinking that her companions are mocking her, says

> If you were civil and knew courtesy,
> You would not do me thus much injury.
> Can you not hate me, as I know you do,
> But you must join in souls to mock me too?
>
> (III. ii. 147–50)

An ideal of courtesy is implied in this play, as in *Love's Labour's Lost*, even though none of the characters finds that he can easily live up to it. Mockery is a denial of the ideal, a failure of the imagination. However bad the play they are watching, says Theseus, 'in courtesy, in all reason, we must stay the time.' And this goes along with an ideal of married chastity without which all is strife and dissension, but which, observed, will earn Oberon's blessing:

> So shall all the couples three
> Ever true in loving be.
>
> (V. i. 396–7)

A Midsummer Night's Dream is not as heavily moralistic as *Love's Labour's Lost*, but I think it shows similar moral concerns.

III

The Tempest, too, has a highly schematic structure which, in its neo-classical concern for the unities, seems a deliberately far cry from the episodic freedom of the other romances. In this play, again, the characters fall into obvious groups. As in *A Midsummer Night's Dream*, though not in *Love's Labour's Lost*, some of the characters are supernatural. They bear, however, some resemblance to the subsidiary character groups in *Love's Labour's Lost* in that, more easily than the fairies in *A Midsummer Night's Dream*, they can be seen as a polarization of characteristics of the main characters. Even Berowne, in the overhearing scene, feels 'like a demi-god'. Oberon, Puck and Titania all have power over the elements, and all influence the lives of the human characters. In *The Tempest* Shakespeare creates a kind of amalgamation of these three figures in one human being—Prospero, who is possessed of limited supernatural power; and one wholly supernatural one—Ariel, who, as the agent of Prospero's power, has affinities with Puck. The supernatural aspects of Caliban have no parallel in the earlier plays, but Bottom seems to be one of his less harmful ancestors, and there are stronger resemblances with another of Shakespeare's invented characters, Barnardine in *Measure for Measure*, in which play the Duke also affords parallels with Prospero.

Obviously, the use of the supernatural in itself amounts to a denial of naturalistic intent, if not a declaration of the symbolic, and this seems to link with the general absence from these plays of detailed psychological characterization.[3] Often the function of the character in the overall design seems of more significance than his individual reality. In making his characters expressive of general attitudes, Shakespeare creates special problems for his interpreters. The actors, and their director, have to decide to what extent they should emphasize the representative aspects of their roles, and to what extent they should attempt to invest them with personal characteristics. Not, of course, that Shakespeare himself cannot when he wishes provide an abundance of individualizing touches, as he does especially among the low-life characters such as Costard and the mechanicals. This faculty is less

[3] Absence of detailed characterization, along with thinness of plot, has encouraged comparisons between some of Shakespeare's comedies and certain types of opera. Northrop Frye says 'when we look for the most striking parallels to *Twelfth Night* or *The Tempest*, we think first of all of *Figaro* and *The Magic Flute*' (*A Natural Perspective* (New York, 1965), p. 25). Opera composers have had similar thoughts. Britten's *A Midsummer Night's Dream* is one of the best of Shakespearian operas. *The Tempest*, though it has produced no acknowledged masterpiece, has tempted opera composers more than any other of Shakespeare's plays—Winton Dean finds over thirty operas based on it ('Shakespeare and Opera', in *Shakespeare in Music*, edited by Phyllis Hartnoll (London, 1964), p. 104). And *Love's Labour's Lost* and *The Tempest* are the two plays that come nearest to providing us with a Shakespearian opera by Mozart. There exists an adaptation of *Love's Labour's Lost* as an alternative libretto to *Così fan tutte*; and one of the saddest aspects of the fact that Mozart died when he did is that he is said to have just agreed to set a text based on *The Tempest* (Dean, pp. 91 and 108). The thought of a post-*Magic Flute* opera by Mozart on this theme is awe-inspiring. Let us hope that it awaits us in heaven.

c

apparent in *The Tempest*, in which Trinculo and Stephano are less fully developed than some of their comic forbears, and in which some of the lords seem to be pushed close towards abstraction—or not to emerge very strongly from it. Miranda and Ferdinand are not perhaps much less real than the lovers of the other plays, but they are certainly no more so, and in the log-carrying episode, for instance, Shakespeare risks incredulity in pursuit of his symbolic purpose—it is not, after all, likely to do Ferdinand much harm to spend an hour or two carrying wood, yet this is imposed on him as a probationary task of almost as much significance as Berowne's year-long sick-visiting.

There is a real parallel between the tasks that Prospero requires Ferdinand to perform in order to make sure that he does not under-estimate his good fortune in winning Miranda and the closing episodes of *Love's Labour's Lost*. One reason for this obviously symbolic action in *The Tempest* is that Shakespeare is here attempting the difficult task of compressing the material of romance—usually highly episodic in form—into the tight structure of a play that, instead of rambling in both space and time as most romances do, is set in a single locality within a very few hours. In such stories it is conventional for the hero and heroine to be separated by misfortune, and to demonstrate their love by remaining true to one another in spite of the perils and tempta-tions set before them in their wanderings. Ferdinand's log-bearing is a rather lightweight substitute for the trials usually experienced by heroes of romance, and Prospero's homilies on chastity, along with Ferdinand's reassuring responses to them, though they seem uncharac-teristically explicit in their moralization, serve their purpose as a sub-stitute for the assurances of virtue that a narrator can convey in a prose or verse romance. Anyhow, it is clear that Shakespeare, for whatever reason, felt a desire to stress this theme, since he does so at the expense of credulity. Chastity finds its highest celebration in the masque, in which Ceres and Juno, the products of Prospero's art, virtually repeat the teaching that he himself has just given.

The masque is *The Tempest*'s play-within-the-play, coming at a much earlier point of the action than in the two previous plays. It is performed by characters of higher social status than its audience—spirits, no less; it is heard with respectful attention until its presenter himself puts an end to it; and it provides not a test of the audience's courtesy, but rather an ideal, and an exhortation. It does not involve all the character groups of the play, and its interruption is the result of

Prospero's memory of one that it does not, 'Caliban and his confeder-ates'. The interruption is reminiscent of that in *Love's Labour's Lost*. In that play, Costard's news about Jaquenetta discomposes the per-formers, while Marcade's news discomposes the audience. The moment of interruption in *The Tempest* is, perhaps, technically less well managed. Prospero's awareness of evil comes from within himself; there is no objective correlative to strike the audience. Though he composes himself enough to speak comfortingly to Ferdinand and Miranda, he then has to turn his thoughts to his preparations to 'meet with Caliban'. Though misfortune and evil were felt in the earlier plays, it is only in this one that a confrontation and resolution are arranged, and this is one of the reasons why *The Tempest* seems a more deeply serious play than the other two.

The blessing that Ceres and Juno invoke on the virtuous lovers recalls Oberon's blessing on the house in *A Midsummer Night's Dream*. It also looks forward to at least two works of art written later than any of these plays—Jonson's masque, *Pleasure Reconciled to Virtue*, and Mil-ton's *Comus*, which seems to have been influenced by both *A Midsummer Night's Dream* and *The Tempest*, and also by the Jonson masque. *Pleasure Reconciled to Virtue* ends with a firm recommendation of virtue addressed to Prince Charles, and *Comus* of course is much concerned with chastity. This resemblance might be held to support the hypo-thesis that has been put forward in relation to all the Shakespeare plays I have been discussing, especially *A Midsummer Night's Dream*, that they are 'occasional' plays written, as masques were generally written, to celebrate—and perhaps to influence—a special occasion. *A Midsummer Night's Dream* is often said to be a play for a wedding as well as about weddings, and it has been suggested that the masque in *The Tempest* was an addition for performance during the wedding celebrations of the Princess Elizabeth in 1613. If this were so, the emphases on virtue might be regarded as tributes to the occasion. The hypotheses lack evidence to support them. If they were true, the plays would be likely to look out to their intended real-life audiences in the way that the masque in *The Tempest* does to Ferdinand and Miranda. It is possible that the moral attitudes discernible in the plays are attributable to dramatic decorum and literary convention; but it is also possible that they reflect Shakespeare's own convictions, and that he believed deeply in the importance of the virtues implied in *Love's Labour's Lost*, demonstrated in *A Midsummer Night's Dream*, and virtually preached in

The Tempest. The plays do not suggest that the virtues are easily attained, or that failure to attain them automatically entails damnation. The moral attitudes the plays seem to endorse are straightforward, traditional ones; but at the same time the plays reveal a sensibility that is aware of the complexity of moral issues, that can allow sympathy with Caliban's sense of injustice even while it approves the values that have created this sense.

IV

One of the most characteristic devices in Shakespearian comedy is the adaptation into dramatic form of the pastoral myth, using what is sometimes called 'the place apart', often a forest, as a symbol of a set of circumstances in which the characters are able to free themselves from their past and achieve a development which seems to release their true, so far repressed, selves. *As You Like It* provides the most obvious example, and *King Lear* shows a tragedy borrowing the same device. So far as my three plays are concerned it is only lightly adumbrated in *Love's Labour's Lost.* Appropriately, the action of this play takes place in a park, not a forest. The formality of a park suggests the artificiality, and essential unnaturalness, of the decision the lords have forced upon themselves. The device is fully present in *A Midsummer Night's Dream,* with its escape of the lovers into the forest at night. *The Tempest* extends the idea still further, for here, except for the preliminary scene of shipwreck, the entire action is set in a place where, Gonzalo will say —perhaps over-optimistically—all the characters found themselves 'when no man was his own'. The other plays, too, are concerned with self-discovery and self-realization. We may remember the climax of Berowne's marvellous speech on love:

> Let us once lose our oaths to find ourselves,
> Or else we lose ourselves to keep our oaths.
> It is religion to be thus forsworn;
> For charity itself fulfils the law;
> And who can sever love from charity?

(IV. iii. 357–61)

With these lines the lords together recognize their folly, and decide to 'lay these glozes by'. The moment was well marked in John Barton's Stratford-upon-Avon production (1965) by a casting aside of their academic gowns (though it suggested an unusual gloss on 'glozes'). But the lords have a long way to go before they will be completely cured.

In *A Midsummer Night's Dream* a parallel moment is the awakening of the lovers, when there comes a 'gentle concord' into the world, and when Helena finds Demetrius,

<blockquote>
like a jewel,
Mine own, and not mine own.
</blockquote>

(IV. i. 188-9)

(Benjamin Britten, in his opera based on the play, seizes on these words and makes of them a complete quartet, each of the lovers using them of his or her partner. It is the emotional climax of the work.)

In the association, then, of the 'place apart' with the theme of self-discovery, Shakespeare in these plays uses and develops a technique that he made peculiarly his own.

V

The resemblances among these plays, in point of technique and also of content, on which I have commented may seem no more revealing than the information that there are salmons in the rivers of both Monmouth and Macedon. But they may, more usefully, suggest characteristic workings of Shakespeare's mind. Obviously these workings might be sought in other plays in which Shakespeare was more dependent on sources. But this is beyond my present scope. More relevant to my purpose is an idea that has been propounded about all these plays: that, to a rather exceptional degree, they betray a preoccupation on the part of the dramatist with his own art. In this way, too, they may be unusually personal documents. Writing about *Love's Labour's Lost*, F. P. Wilson says 'One of his special preoccupations in the play is the function of language in society.'[4] It is surely undeniable that in constructing this play Shakespeare was strongly motivated by his interest in the means of communication, in the fact that words can obscure meaning as well as reveal it, that an excessive concern with the means of communication may inhibit true expression, that feeling can communicate itself in spite of words rather than through them. (The interest is especially strongly felt also in *Much Ado About Nothing*.) It is no accident that the most important communication in *Love's Labour's*

[4] *Elizabethan and Jacobean* (Oxford, 1945), pp. 109-10.

Lost is the ostentatiously wordless one made by Marcade's mere presence.

If *Love's Labour's Lost* is largely about words, it is also noticeably conscious of itself as a play. Perhaps the harshness of the final episode is softened for us by the way the play draws attention to its own mode, helping us to detach ourselves from the action. 'Our wooing doth not end like an old play', says Berowne, acknowledging from within the action that the postponement of the happy ending for a 'twelvemonth and a day' (and thus possibly for ever) is 'too long for a play'.

A Midsummer Night's Dream shows an even broader concern with Shakespeare's own art. On a simple level, this is evident in the fact that all the mechanicals' scenes show the preparation and performance of a play. That it is an amateur performance is rendered the less significant by Theseus' remark 'The best in this kind are but shadows . . .'. But on other levels, too, the play shows concerns which relate to the endeavours of the imaginative artist, to such an extent that David P. Young, in his full-length study of the play, can conclude that this 'is Shakespeare's *ars poetica*, embedded in a perfected example of his art', and that it must therefore 'be regarded as one of his most important plays and a touchstone for the understanding and interpretation of others'.[5] If this is so, it is not surprising that Shakespeare should have felt the need to shape the play from within rather than work through an existing story. Young amply demonstrates Shakespeare's concern with the imagination, made most explicit in Theseus' well-known lines (V. i. 2–22). Hippolyta's reply is even more important, admitting that

> all the story of the night told over,
> And all their minds transfigured so together,
> More witnesseth than fancy's images,
> And grows to something of great constancy;
> But howsoever, strange and admirable.
>
> (V. i. 23–7)

These speeches are strategically placed just before the performance of the mechanicals' play, which is to provide both an illustration of its actors' own imaginative failures and a test of the imaginative capacities of their betters. The play firmly, though with a wise gaiety, asserts the basic importance of the imagination in human life, the fact that a world of dreams can grow 'to something of great constancy', and the con-

[5] *Something of Great Constancy* (New Haven and London, 1966), p. 179.

stant though shifting harmonies of the last act demonstrate the need for imaginative tolerance in successful relationships. On these the forces of nature bestow their blessings.

In *The Tempest*, too, Shakespeare's concern with his own art emerges most clearly from the play-within-the-play, especially in the great speech of Prospero which has become the best-known of all celebrations of the glorious transience of theatrical art. But just as, in that speech, the theatrical imagery serves as a metaphorical expression for an experience which, actually theatrical, is fictionally supernatural, so in the play as a whole Shakespeare's concern with his own art is subordinated to a much broader concern with the opposition between constructive good and destructive evil, whether in the individual human consciousness or on any scale up to the cosmic. That Shakespeare was to an unusual degree working to a conceptual pattern in this play is suggested by its peculiar susceptibility to allegorical interpretations. That none of these interpretations seems satisfactory is a measure of the success with which he has effected the sea-change of the bare bones of his concepts into something richly suggestive and strangely elusive. Whether we see Prospero as animal-tamer, employer, father, probation officer, magistrate, theatre director, colonial administrator, creative artist, Shakespeare, an embodiment of the imagination, a Christ-figure, God, or even (as Wilson Knight does) as 'a matured and fully self-conscious embodiment of those moments of fifth-act transcendental speculation to which earlier tragic heroes, including Macbeth, were unwittingly forced',[6] we see a figure whose power to do good is real, but always limited both by his own imperfections and by circumstances over which he has no control. The splendours of his vision vanish at the remembrance of the need for action against his adversaries. Lacking at last both the spirits that have helped him and the art with which he was able to enchant, he is doomed to despair unless the audience grants him its prayers. It is natural to see in Prospero a reflection of his human creator, and to see in the play a concern with the creations of the artistic imagination, creations which at their strongest have a power of transfiguration, yet which are terrifyingly dependent for their power upon the sympathetic imagination. *The Tempest* at its first performance might have held its audience spellbound: it might have been hooted off the stage. So, Shakespeare seems to say, with all

[6] 'The Shakespearian Superman', in *The Crown of Life* (London, 1947), p. 208.

the works of man; their value has no absolute existence. Nothing is but as 'tis valued. Gonzalo may enthuse, Sebastian and Antonio may mock; Ferdinand may adore, Caliban may try to violate. And the response of the audience, upon which all that Shakespeare has to say depends for its effect, is equally uncertain. In *The Tempest* Shakespeare wrote not only about his own art, but about that of all who work through the mind.

VI

The Tempest is a wonderful, infinitely subtle, if enigmatic play. *A Midsummer Night's Dream* is one of Shakespeare's most popular plays. *Love's Labour's Lost* is handicapped by its topicalities, but with judicious abbreviation is capable of highly successful performance. Still, if we considered these three plays in relation to the remainder of Shakespeare's output, we should not necessarily regard them as the height of his achievement. One or other might happen to be a favourite of ours. We might, like Frank Kermode, 'be prepared to maintain that *A Midsummer Night's Dream* is Shakespeare's best comedy'.[7] We might easily feel that *The Tempest* is a personal utterance of unparalleled intimacy, related to the great tragedies in the same way that a late Beethoven quartet is related to the greatest of his symphonies. But obviously these plays do not have the grandeur of *King Lear*, the elemental passion of *Othello*, the emotional range of *Hamlet* or *The Winter's Tale*. The artist who betrays a preoccupation with his own art may seem a little limited, even if at the same time he relates his art to a wide range of human activity, as Shakespeare does in *The Tempest*. If these plays only had survived, I think we should not rate Shakespeare so highly as if, for example, we had only *King Lear* by which to judge him. And it is possible that Shakespeare realized this. Perhaps it is significant that *Love's Labour's Lost* and *A Midsummer Night's Dream* were, so far as we can tell, written at about the same time. If *A Midsummer Night's Dream* really is 'Shakespeare's *ars poetica*', it would be very natural that, having written it, he should go on to put his art into practice in very different ways. The resemblances among these three plays may suggest that, left to his own inventive powers, Shakespeare was apt to confine himself to a comparatively narrow range of techniques and themes. And I wonder if, aware of this, he made a wholly

[7] 'The Mature Comedies', in *Early Shakespeare*, ed. J. R. Brown and B. Harris (Stratford-upon-Avon Studies 3, London, 1961), p. 214.

conscious effort to extend his range by compelling himself to work through stories not of his own making, set often in civilizations other than that to which he belonged, expressive even of moral attitudes that were not his own. He is highly derivative; perhaps the most literary of great dramatists. Paradoxically, this might help to explain why he is also the most wide-ranging, the most personally elusive, the most original in the fullest sense of the word. Perhaps one of the reasons why we find it so difficult to pin Shakespeare down is that he so often wears other men's clothes and speaks with their accents.

But even when he does so, we can often see him using methods and expressing ideas similar to those I have discerned in his invented works. I have suggested that in them we can often see him working to a pre-determined scheme; and I have pointed to his use in these plays of highly patterned structural devices. On the whole, and particularly in his later plays, we do not think of Shakespeare as a specially tidy-minded dramatist. Sometimes he seems not fully to have subjugated recalcitrant source material to an overriding creative concept, with the result that he produces a structure of more grandeur than regularity. In some of his greatest plays he seems to have started with an idea of character—as in Coriolanus or Cleopatra—rather than based a character on an idea. In the three plays I have been discussing the idea seems often to have come first, as in Holofernes and, more complexly, Caliban. An awareness derived from his sourceless plays of his capacity to body forth a structure of ideas in character and action should lead us to exercise caution before assuming absence of preconceived design in plays in which a superficial neatness of structure is not apparent. Shakespeare may have sometimes accepted an existing narrative and elaborated it in such a way as to produce episodes that have the function of cadenzas rather than elements of a fully integrated design. At one time Launce's soliloquies in *The Two Gentlemen of Verona* might have been felt to belong to this category. Most modern critics would not support this view. Certainly the speeches show Shakespeare's ability to improvise with wonderful inventiveness upon a basic theme. But to over-emphasize his improvisatory powers may take us too far back to the concept of a Shakespeare warbling his woodnotes wild with no thought for where the next tune was coming from. There is ample evidence in the plays of Shakespeare's early maturity that he could, and did, some-times lay out a play with intense consciousness of design in both the larger structural elements and the verbal detail. Apart from the two earlier plays on which I have been concentrating, we may think of *Richard III*, with its highly formalized disposition of historical-based material, or of the patterns created in *Romeo and Juliet* by the counter-pointing of the attitudes of Mercutio and the Nurse alongside those of the hero and heroine. Later in his career, too, Shakespeare writes scenes in which a conceptual basis is evident. The graveyard scene in *Hamlet*, for instance, is probably Shakespeare's addition to his source. In the apparent spontaneity of the gravediggers' prose it might seem a prime illustration of his improvisatory faculty; yet it is not difficult to discern behind the easy movement of the scene a carefully programmed series of confrontations with death, mounting from the gravediggers' unimpassioned handling of anonymous remains through increasingly familiar encounters until Hamlet is in the grave with the dead Ophelia. Our appreciation of Shakespeare's developing capacity to hide his framework, to weave a pattern so complex that it resembles a work of nature rather than one of art, should not lead to scepticism about the presence of his artistry.

Although I have temporarily isolated three of Shakespeare's plays, I do not wish to make exaggerated claims for them either in themselves or as keys to the understanding of Shakespeare. But I suggest that in them Shakespeare does, as Dr. Johnson put it, repose in 'a mode of thinking congenial to his nature'; that they reveal something of his personal concerns, especially in relation to his art; and that, by remembering how his mind worked in them, we may be helped in our approach to plays where he owed more of his narrative material to other writings.

IV

Grace, Art and the Neglect of Time in 'Love's Labour's Lost'

JOHN DIXON HUNT

I

IT is surprising that Alexander Pope, who cut whole pages of *Love's Labour's Lost* from his text, did not appreciate the play: for, like his own satire, it moves from a density of contemporary reference to wider, more permanent explorations of human effort. These larger meanings have often been obscured by too much dedication to the play's (usually elusive) topical references or by too myopic an anxiety about the intricacies of its Elizabethan word-play.[1] Recent productions have rescued the play from the archaeologists and displayed it as a drama of coherent style, which Granville-Barker recognized,[2] of charm and considerable point.

But the literary critics hang back. In recent discussions[3] of the comedies it still seems destined to be considered as prologomenon to later and (such is the implication) more worthwhile work. The modern Arden editor is a particularly notorious case: he finds his greatest satisfaction in recognizing among the characters of this play the prototypes or 'trial runs' for later, more famous creations—Berowne and Rosaline for Benedick and Beatrice, the 'clowns' for Dogberry and Verges, even Armado for Falstaff. While he hails *Love's Labour's Lost* as 'still very much alive' and professes to admire its 'excess of high spirits and invention', he might just as well join Hazlitt in wishing to be rid

---

[1] The most learned inquiries into the play's topical allusions are Frances A. Yates, *A Study of 'Love's Labour's Lost'* (Cambridge, 1936), M. C. Bradbrook, *The School of Night* (Cambridge, 1936) and W. Schrickx, *Shakespeare's Early Comedies* (Antwerp, 1956).

[2] *Prefaces to Shakespeare* (Princeton, 1947), II, p. 423.

[3] For example, John Russell Brown, *Shakespeare and his Comedies* (London, 1962), Peter G. Phialas, *Shakespeare's Romantic Comedies* (Chapel Hill, N. C., 1966) and Richard Cody, *The Landscape of the Mind* (Oxford, 1969).

of the play: for he neglects its *meaning*. Yet the insights and wisdom of
this comedy are separate neither from its fun nor from its contemporary
involvements. What we must learn is to attend not just the school of
Night but the academe of wider Elizabethan concerns and to see how
these can still be in touch with our own. It is possible to open these
perspectives from the play's very first speech. The King of Navarre
argues for a three-year academic course (so it is apt that the eighteenth-
century adaptation of the play was called *The Students*), but his mode of
argument alerts us to rival calls upon his court's time. Ferdinand is aware,
obviously, of the traditional opposition of contemplative and active life:

> Our court shall be a little academe,
> Still and contemplative in living art.

Yet some lines later, in the images of chivalric honour and combat that
come readily to the King's rhetorical aid, we may perhaps find hints
of the simplistic nature of his decision. The wide concerns of courtier
and governor are to be surrendered to a 'little academe'; the proportioned life of the former especially is to be somewhat neglected. For 'all
the houres of the days divided into honourable and pleasant exercises,
as well of the bodie, as of the minde'[4] is the properly balanced regimen
of the courtier—this we learn from Hoby's translation of Castiglione,
an edition of which appeared in 1588, probably a few years prior to
Love's Labour's Lost. For the courtiers of Navarre martial and physical
prowess is to be exercised against their 'own affections / And the huge
army of the world's desires'; only in that 'war' shall they earn a fame to
palliate death's blow. One could argue that the King is wittily aware of
this tendentious conceit as he warms to his peroration. But in the
opening of his speech he seems far less alert to the full significance of his
ambitions:

> Let fame, that all hunt after in their lives,
> Live regist'red upon our brazen tombs,
> And then grace us in the disgrace of death;
> When, spite of cormorant devouring Time,
> Th'endeavour of this present breath may buy
> That honour which shall bate his scythe's keen edge,
> And make us heirs of all eternity.

(I. i. 1–7)

The King's plea is not funny in itself—the humour will arise from the
consequences of his plan—for it rests upon man's constant anxiety to

---

[4] Everyman edition (London, 1956), p. 19.

evade time's claims upon him.[5] Navarre and his lords aim at post-humous and lasting fame, based upon intellectual endeavours now. The 'brazen tombs' nicely announce the hollow audacity of worldly ambitions. Yet the (syntactical) dominance of 'cormorant devouring Time' and the meagreness of 'this present breath' are early clues to what the lords only learn by the play's end, that they must move within and not outside time's demanding rhythms.

But another demand and another, far more elusive, rhythm are announced in the third line. The comedy will play fondly and fre-quently with the idea of 'grace' and its action may partly be seen as the demonstration of the double meaning of that word: 'attractiveness or charm belonging to elegance of proportions', and 'divine influence operating in men to regenerate and sanctify' (OED). The achievement of both these graces within the world of nature and time, together with the recognition of their congruence, is the lesson which the larger academe of the play tries to teach the noble lords.

They begin by acquiescing in the King's scheme. The ambiguity of his third line is precisely whether divine grace will redeem the degradation of their physical death or whether they will be seen to have attained only intellectual favour. Berowne soon argues that books will not in fact yield the former:

> Why, all delights are vain; but that most vain
> Which, with pain purchas'd, doth inherit pain,
> As painfully to pore upon a book
> To seek the light of truth; while truth the while
> Doth falsely blind the eyesight of his look.
> Light, seeking light, doth light of light beguile;
> So, ere you find where light in darkness lies,
> Your light grows dark by losing of your eyes.
> Study me how to please the eye indeed,
> By fixing it upon a fairer eye;
> Who dazzling so, that eye shall be his heed,
> And give him light that it was blinded by.
>
> (I. i. 72–83)

Though his language only plays with theological conceit and his wit is self-delighting, Berowne nevertheless deploys an established

5 See Bobbyann Roesen (Anne Barton), 'Love's Labour's Lost', Shakespeare Quarterly IV (1953), pp. 411–26. A fine essay and a notable exception to my strictures of note 3.

Renaissance truth that sustained many amorous encounters. In *The Book of the Courtier*, Castiglione explains it thus:

> But speaking of the beautie that we meane, which is onely it, that appeareth in bodies, and especially in the face of man, and move this fervent coveting which wee call Love, we will terme it an influence of the heavenly bountifulnesse, the which for it stretcheth over all thinges that be created (like the light of the sunne) yet when it findeth out a face well proportioned, and framed with a certaine lively agreement of several colours, and set forth with lights and shadowes, and with an orderly distance and limits of lines, thereinto it distilleth itselfe and appeareth most welfavoured, and decketh out and lightneth the subject where it shineth with a marvellous grace and glittering . . . (Everyman edition, p. 304)

The grace of woman's beauty is the focus and temporal abode of the 'heavenly bountifulnesse' of divine grace. *Love's Labour's Lost* reminds us of these commonplaces often enough: in the modish rhetoric of Longaville's sonnet—'My vow was earthly, thou a heavenly love; / Thy grace being gain'd cures all disgrace in me' (IV. iii. 62–3)— a pun that aptly reverses the King's initial ambition; in the Princess's playful, but literally accurate, wish that her ladies mask themselves so that 'not a man of them shall have the grace, / Despite of suit, to see a lady's face' (V. ii. 128–9); in the king's growing recognition of the Princess as a 'gracious Moon'; (IV. iii. 226) in the fresh perspectives that Berowne gains—

> We to ourselves prove false,
> By being once false forever to be true
> To those that make us both—fair ladies, you;
> And even that falsehood, in itself a sin,
> Thus purifies itself and turns to grace.
>
> (V. ii. 760–64)

What the noble lords commit themselves to at the start of the play, as Berowne delights in pointing out to them, is a life that denies all access to the 'grace' of a lady's favour. Specifically, it prohibits any encounter with the Princess of France, who is encouraged by Boyet on her first appearance to be 'as prodigal of all dear grace / As Nature was in making graces dear' (II. i. 9–10). She is also, if we need other testimony, 'A maid of grace and complete majesty'. This hint of harmony and complete proportion in the Princess is perhaps Berowne's implied criticism of the King's less than total dedication to all the courtly arts.

But what he implies then is later made quite explicit. The King's vow forces him to neglect hospitality or the 'attractiveness and charm' of elegant courtesy as well as denying him access to a higher grace. The Princess makes this immediately clear to him:

> King: Fair princess, welcome to the court of Navarre.
> Princess: 'Fair' I give you back again; and 'welcome' I have not yet.
> The roof of this court is too high to be yours, and welcome
> to the wide fields too base to be mine.
> King: You shall be welcome, madam, to my court.
> Princess: I will be welcome, then; conduct me thither.
> King: Hear me, dear lady: I have sworn an oath—
> Princess: Our Lady help my lord! He'll be forsworn.
> King: Not for the world, fair madam, by my will.
> Princess: Why, will shall break it; will, and nothing else.
> King: Your ladyship is ignorant what it is.
> Princess: Were my lord so, his ignorance were wise,
> Where now his knowledge must prove ignorance.
> I hear your Grace hath sworn out house-keeping.
>
> (II. i. 90–103)

It is perhaps only a happy accident that her formal mode of address to the King in that final line underlines her recognition of his inadequate courtly graces. The disjunction of those courtesies is usually linked to the nobles' exclusion from the divine influence that they should seek, Berowne argues, in woman. For when the King, ready enough to break his vow and receive the Princess, invokes only social necessities, Berowne obliquely reminds him of larger considerations:

> Necessity will make us all forsworn
> Three thousand times within this three years' space;
> For every man with his affects is born,
> Not by might mast'red, but by special grace.
>
> (I. i. 147–50)

It is almost precisely in those terms that Castiglione's Cardinal Bembo explains the influence of divine love or grace upon youthful passions.

We have seen how the Princess insists upon an outward and visible sign of their withholding grace from the lords when she orders her ladies to mask. There are other visual reminders of the theme. After their abortive and rather ridiculous appearance as Muscovites or

Blackamoors, the King and his nobles return (V. ii. 310) in their proper
habits. It seems to me that this should probably be the first time in the
play when we see them in full and elegant courtly attire. There must,
for example, be some visual token of their renunciation of worldly
ambition upon taking academic vows, some alteration of dress[6] perhaps
to suggest their dedication to study and to being (in Armado's phrase
to Moth) 'well-educated infant(s)'. And their childishness and delightful immaturities continue through the poem-reading sequence, recalling
another *aperçu* of Armado that, for Cupid, 'his disgrace is to be called
boy'. The resumption of adult demeanour is signalled in their dress—
'all in their proper habits' is Rowe's useful editorial stress—as well as in
their resumption of gracefulness and courtesy:

> Teach us, sweet madam, for our rude transgression
> Some fair excuse.

> (V. ii. 431–2)

And by the end they also recover that grace of conduct so lacking in
their initial encounter with the Princess:

> *Princess:* Ay, sweet my lord, and so I take my leave.
> *King:* No, madam; we will bring you on your way.

> (V. ii. 860–61)

Though it wants 'a twelvemonth and a day', the lords have already
begun to abjure that 'loose grace' of which Rosaline accuses Berowne.
They are once again, in the Princess's eyes, 'gracious lords'.

II

It is love that ensures the lords' courtly and spiritual 'redemption'.
So it may not be too inappropriate to recall the connections between
love and grace that Calidore is taught in the sixth Book of *The Faerie
Queene* or that preoccupy the Renaissance humanists. Pico celebrated the
'unity of Venus ... unfolded in the trinity of the Graces'[7] and, as
Edgar Wind has explained in this connection, the three graces symbolize

[6] In Elizabethan terms it might well be the absence of cloaks and swords; a
modern production might make the point with the lords in short Oxford
gowns.

[7] Quoted by E. Wind, *Pagan Mysteries in the Renaissance* (London, 1967),
p. 114). See generally on this topic pp. 26–35 and 113–27. Richard Cody (*op.
cit.*) subjects the play to a more extensive examination of its Platonic antecedents and notes some interesting painterly analogues.

the proper portions of giving, accepting and returning. The King of
Navarre is sent to school during the play precisely to learn the lesson
that such a humanist vision as Botticelli's *Primavera* seeks to impart.

It is worth remarking first how relevant to the dramatization of the
theme of grace is the Princess's embassy. Berowne's first allusion to the
'surrender up of Aquitaine' is brief and noncommittal. But the thirty or
so lines devoted to it later touch more firmly upon the virtues of giving,
accepting and returning:

> You do the King my father too much wrong,
> And wrong the reputation of your name,
> In so unseeming to confess receipt
> Of that which hath so faithfully been paid.

> (II. i. 153–6)

And from here the scene slides imperceptibly into another aspect of the
King's diminished gracefulness:

> Meantime receive such welcome at my hand
> As honour, without breach of honour may
> Make tender of to thy true worthiness.

> (II. i. 168–70)

To which the Princess, with what a performance could colour with a
gentle and courteous irony, responds: 'Sweet health and fair desires
consort your Grace.'

The renewal of grace through their love for the Princess and her
ladies comes to the lords only after a recognition of its place in time.
For them, as it were, the graces only dance when they learn to accept
the contiguity that Botticelli demonstrates between Venus and *primavera*:

> *Berowne:* The spring is near, when green geese are a-breeding.
> *Dumaine:* How follows that?
> *Berowne:* Fit in his place and time.
> *Dumaine:* In reason nothing.
> *Berowne:* Something then in rhyme.
> *King:* Berowne is like an envious sneaping frost
> That bites the first-born infants of the spring.
> *Berowne:* Well, say I am; why should proud summer boast
> Before the birds have any cause to sing?
> Why should I joy in an abortive birth?
> At Christmas I no more desire a rose
> Than wish a snow in May's new-fangled shows.

> (I. i. 97–106)

Berowne's point is not taken. Yet he insists upon the ridiculous activity involved in trying to spite cormorant devouring time (a sense of 'spite' the King did not presumably intend). Only due acknowledgement of seasonal propriety can ensure full rather than vain delights. We are told in *Proverbs* XXVI: 'As snow in summer, and as Rain in Harvest, so is Honour unsuitable for a Fool'. The foolishness of the King's scheme lies in its departure from a due sense of 'fitness' and in the unsuitable 'honour' he aims at with his academy: an honour which 'shall bate his scythe's keen edge' does not serve, as to their chagrin they discover, the needs of hospitality. By the play's end they begin to realize the wisdom that Berowne offered earlier 'in rhyme' and that they *and he* chose to neglect.

The play's concern with time is consolidated in the penance imposed upon the King and his lords at the end. The imagery of the Princess's speech recalls the frosts and roses of Berowne's earlier plea and makes plain the terms of her request and the standards of her emotions:

> There stay until the twelve celestial signs
> Have brought about the annual reckoning.
> If this austere insociable life
> Change not your offer made in heat of blood,
> If frosts and fasts, hard lodging and thin weeds,
> Nip not the gaudy blossoms of your love,
> But that it bear this trial, and last love,
> Then, at the expiration of the year,
> Come, challenge me.
>
> (V. ii. 785–93)

She subjects their professed affections to a cycle of seasonal change: their love will be tested both by its survival in time and by its ability to outlast it.

The lords' 'neglect of time' is confessed by Berowne after Mercade has brought the news of the Princess's father's death. The King is perhaps the first to recognize that time neglected means missed opportunities:

> The extreme parts of time extremely forms
> All causes to the purpose of his speed;
> And often at his very loose decides
> That which long process could not arbitrate.
>
> (V. ii. 728–31)

They have neglected time both in their original vow to live outside it in pursuit of intellectual honour and in the artifice of their courtly dalliance with the ladies. Now, abruptly and sadly recalled to the rhythms of temporal existence, they find decisions have often to be made in the instants of time. Yet the King, for reasons which I shall discuss later, still cannot make the Princess understand. It is Berowne, with 'honest plain words', who tries to communicate with her. But she professes to find their courtship merely 'as lining to the time', only an elegant display of courtly graces, The King, alert too late to the demands of time, grows desperate:

> Now, at the latest minute of the hour,
> Grant us your loves,

but the Princess, always more secure in her assessment of its necessities, can only recognize

> A time, methinks, too short
> To make a world-without-end bargain in.
>
> (V. ii. 775–7)

The King has changed his sense of eternal priorities and still finds the present breath cannot buy the grace he seeks.

III

The frustration of the lords' courtship and their apprenticeship to time after the play's end bring us to other considerations. Berowne, as usual, is quick to announce at least part of the relevant theme:

> *Berowne:* A twelvemonth? Well befall what will befall,
> I'll jest a twelvemonth in an hospital.
> *Princess:* Ay, sweet my lord, and so I take my leave.
> *King:* No, madam, we will bring you on your way.
> *Berowne:* Our wooing doth not end like an old play:
> Jack hath not Jill. These ladies' courtesy
> Might well have made our sport a comedy.
> *King:* Come, sir, it wants a twelvemonth and a day,
> And then 'twill end.
> *Berowne:* That's too long for a play.
>
> (V. ii. 858–66)

This is followed first by Armado's confession of agricultural penance ('I have vowed to Jaquenetta to hold the plough for her sweet love three year') and then by the songs—sung by the country people about seasonal change and nature's own decorums or indecorums and dominated by the 'When . . .' of temporal obligation.

An accepted commonplace about the play is that it compares art and reality; but the terms of that comparison, as usually allowed, are too simple. As some Renaissance aestheticians would show (Sidney is convenient for the discussion of this play), art's best efforts were to be found in the imitation of nature, in the rendering of her brazen world into gold without any loss of reference to that world. Costard stumbles upon the problem thus:

> For mine own part, I am, as they say, but to parfect one man in one poor man . . . It pleased them to think me worthy of Pompey the Great; for mine own part, I know not the degree of the Worthy, but I am to stand for him.   (V. ii. 500–6)

The problems that editors have (and, one suspects Costard has) with *parfect* (Q: i.e. perform) or *perfect* (Ff)[8] centre precisely upon how much Costard's rudimentary dramatic skill can imitate the 'reality' of Pompey and how good an idea his art has of the reality that it imitates. Most of the comedy of the Worthies Pageant comes from our noticing this discrepancy between the 'realities' of worth presented and the inept dramatic art of the performers. But those most eager to laugh are the courtiers themselves—it is that 'merriment' that Mercade interrupts.

Not only does their mirth at the expense of the actors seem unkind, it is also presumptuous. For they are all guilty of that excess of art over reality which we term affectation. The courtiers' own activities have often betrayed similar distortions of reality in their concerted pursuit of courtly arts. The 'living art' that will make Navarre the wonder of the world is apparently the study of 'things hid and barred . . . from common sense'. Their delight in Armado is not altogether ironic, one feels; he is another whose pursuit of art, like their own, though more bizarre, ignores the real:

> 'There did I see that low-spirited swain, that base minnow
> of thy mirth,'
[*Costard:* Me?]
> 'that unlettered small-knowing soul,'
[*Costard:* Me?]
> 'that shallow vassal',
[*Costard:* Still me!]

[8] See Variorum edition by H. H. Furness (Philadelphia, 1904), p. 277.

'which, as I remember, hight Costard,'
[*Costard:* O, me!]
'sorted and consorted, contrary to thy established proclaimed edict and continent canon, which, with, O, with—
but with this I passion to say wherewith—'
[*Costard:* With a wench.] (I. i. 236–48)

It is to this Armado's keeping that the lords commit Costard, the one
intrusion (besides Berowne's seasonal plea) of common sense into their
academe.

Costard is not free himself from affectation's taint, for it is an infection
that touches not only Navarre's court but the inhabitants of his coun-
tryside as well. But though he affects courtly wit, his basic attitudes
('this maid will serve my turn, sir') are closer from the start of the play
to human verities than either the court's or Armado's. If we are to
believe Costard later (V. ii. 668), Armado has served *his* turn too upon
Jaquenetta, which only emphasizes the discrepancy between his
language of love ('a most dainty man') and his sexual appetite. Even his
agricultural penance at the end smacks of yet another affectation, derived
perhaps from Virgil's *Georgics* (Virgil was another Mantuan of whom
it could be said, 'who understands thee not, loves thee not').

It is often argued that the chief judgement of this play lies in its
'comparison between affectations, illusions and simplicity'.[9] I would
prefer to argue that its satire is designed to insist upon the precious and
precarious balance necessary in all arts (those of living as much as of the
court or stage) between what is formal and calculated and what is
spontaneous and partakes of life. We have been told, for example,[10]
that Shakespeare thought of wooing in terms of an ideal order in
Love's Labour's Lost; but, as his sonnets equally insist, that ideal order
of courtship can never cease to be in permanent contact with such
exigencies as lust or time. Ideal orders deliver a golden art *out of*, not at
the expense of, the brazen world.

The characters in *Love's Labour's Lost* who strive most ridiculously
for golden worlds are Armado and Holofernes. The one parodies the
courtly world of the play, the other the intellectual; they also serve
to alert us to absurdities and affectations among the courtiers. The
proper diets, both for mind and body, are concerns that re-echo from
Longaville's protestation of loyalty to the King's academic plans—'the

9 John Russell Brown, *op. cit.*, p. 75.
10 *Ibid.*, pp. 129–30.

mind shall banquet though the body pines'—to Nathaniel's 'He hath not eat paper, as it were, he hath not drunk ink' and to Moth's and Costard's decisive judgement upon the meeting of Armado and Holofernes:

> Moth: They have been at a great feast of languages and stol'n the scraps.
> Costard: O, they have liv'd long on the alms-basket of words.
>
> (V. i. 33–5)

It may be Holofernes and Armado that remind us most directly of Pope's Dunces, but the King and his friends are also, if less obviously, dedicated 'to the study of *Words* only in Schools'.[11] Holofernes delights in the mere profusion and coruscation of words—

> ripe as the pomewater, who now hangeth like a jewel in the ear of *caelo*, the sky, the welkin, the heaven; and anon falleth like a crab on the face of *terra*, the soil, the land, the earth.   (IV. ii. 3–6)

Where the base vulgar have one word, Armado's taste is for several: 'It doth amount to one more than two', or 'the posteriors of this day'. It often seems to me that an almost Dunciadic ingenuity is sometimes expended upon interpreting the verbal wit of *Love's Labour's Lost*, when, as the laughter in most productions testifies, it is the *lack* of intrinsic meaning that is the play's concern. The satire is upon those who 'passion to say wherewith' and whose thread of verbosity is drawn finer than the staple of their argument. The irony of 'O base and obscure vulgar' is that ordinary speech sharpens rather than obscures our understanding. It may lack elegance and decorum, but it points clearly to *things*. Holofernes' poem on the deer robs the deer of any semblance of reality.

The relevance of these 'comic' scenes to the play's concern with art and reality is aptly summarized by Holofernes himself, when he praises Ovidius Naso 'for smelling out the odoriferous flowers of fancy, the jerks of invention . . . *Imitari* is nothing'. But imitation, or that proper regard by the arts for the realities they reveal, is everything. Goodman Dull speaks 'no word all this while', because in his poor simple way he believes that words refer to things: 'Me, an't shall please you: I am Anthony Dull.' His is almost a heroic cry in the face of so much

---

[11] Note by Pope and Warburton to *The Dunciad* IV, 501. See 'Twickenham' edition of Pope's *Works* (London, 1963), V, 391. This theme is alluded to briefly by P. G. Phialas, *op. cit.*

language with little or no referential aim. Dull understands 'none neither' of one hundred and fifty lines in V. ii, because few of them point at all directly to the things he expects language to tell him about. He is surrounded by foolish extravagant spirits, 'Full of strange shapes, of habits, and of forms.' Nothing better than the fuss Costard makes about 'remuneration' and 'guerdon' illuminates the discrepancy between reality and the language that fails to convey it: 'O sweet gardon! Better than remuneration—a 'leven-pence farthing better'.

It is also an illustration of the extent to which the court is also liable to neglect imitation, for Berowne's 'guerdon' is as *précieux* as Armado's latinism. Although the 'comics' and the lords are mostly kept apart till the last, long scene of the play, there are cross-references and connections to remind us of their relative places on the scale of affectation. They are all what Dull calls 'book-men', or Boyet, 'book-mates'. So when the King's party desert their books for courtship, their language seems to bear very little more relation to the contingencies of human life than the schoolmaster's and his friend's. Armado is obviously ridiculous when he 'turns sonnet' (becomes words?) or when in seeking authority for his conduct he consults not reality but the storehouse of learning and mythology. Yet the noblemen do exactly the same:

> *Berowne:* The king he is hunting the deer; I am coursing myself.
> They have pitch'd a toil; I am toiling in a pitch—pitch
> that defiles. Defile! a foul word. Well, 'set thee down,
> sorrow!' for so they say the fool said, and so say I, and I am
> the fool. Well proved, wit! By the Lord, this love is as
> mad as Ajax.   (IV. iii. 1–8)

In their more contrived effusions the language easily and amusingly escapes reality, as the King's sonnet confesses:

> O queen of queens! how far dost thou excel
> No thought can think nor tongue of mortal tell.
>   (IV. iii. 36–7)

To borrow a formulation from a more serious context, words without thoughts cannot go even to the heaven of a lady's face; nor thoughts without words. Dumaine is perplexed by this difficulty of matching the two:

> This will I send; and something else more plain,
> That shall express my true love's fasting pain.
>   (IV. iii. 117–18)

The as yet unexpressed deprivation that causes Dumaine's anguish may be a lover's commonplace or a lover's euphemism. If the latter, then we are even more forcibly recalled to the distance between the lord's language and their real objectives. Berowne's 'rhymes are guards on wanton Cupid's hose; / Disfigure not his slop' is another and sharper reminder of that distance. If rhymes are used to decorate love, they should not be fixed to Cupid's codpiece, for the role of that sartorial fixture is not easily disguised or prettified. Yet rhymes also guard or protect the lover-poet from either perceiving or explaining his real purpose and therefore, it is implied, should not be fastened to the codpiece and give the game away. The language of the nobles' sonnets and poems is ridiculous, at least for Berowne, because it bears no relationship to their sexual urges. So it has always seemed to me an apt irony that Berowne's flowery letter miscarries to that straightforward girl, Jaquenetta, to whom the 'earthly tongue' of his verses could not be earthy enough and for whom 'thy parts' would carry a more explicit and simple meaning than Berowne's 'learned tongue' contrives for the phrase.

One of the more awkward speeches for Berowne in the theatre is that at the end of Act III, because it is usually found difficult to establish his attitude and tone. But if we see Berowne caught in the contrary forces of courtly language on one side and an intelligent appraisal of sexual realities on the other, it is not surprising that he betrays those insecurities.[12] There is an almost unbridgeable gap between

> A whitely wanton with a velvet brow,
> With two pitch balls stuck in her face for eyes;
> Ay, and, by heaven, one that will do the deed,
>
> (III. i. 186–8)

and the language of love-rhymes accompanied by the repertoire of suitable studied gesture ('folded arms . . . signs and groans'). Berowne is the first one and, for a time, the only lord to be delighted by these discrepancies:

> O, what a scene of fool'ry have I seen,
> Of sighs, of groans, of sorrow, and of teen!

[12] Though, as I shall show, I cannot accept Professor Edwards' conclusions about *Love's Labour's Lost* itself, I found his discussion of this theme in the sonnets and the play itself very helpful: see Philip Edwards, *Shakespeare and the Confines of Art* (London, 1968).

O me, with what strict patience have I sat,
To see a king transformed to a gnat!
To see great Hercules whipping a gig,
And profound Solomon to tune a jig,
And Nestor play at push-pin with the boys,
And critic Timon laugh at idle toys!

                                        (IV. iii. 159–66)

His theatrical imagery, to which I shall return, shows his quick awareness of the arts of love-making, the necessary 'feigning' that poetry
promotes.

Once their broken vows are discovered, the lords at least drop the
subterfuge of concealing their affections. But for all their rediscovery
of certain natural obligations, across which their academic pretensions
had cut, they cannot as easily learn a corresponding truth of language.
Berowne celebrates the first:

As true we are as flesh and blood can be.
The sea will ebb and flow, heaven show his face;
Young blood doth not obey an old decree.
We cannot cross the cause why we were born.

                                        (IV. ii. 211–14)

But he quickly finds himself involved in the 'flourish of all gentle
tongues' and in the Babel of love conceit that occupies the lords after
the exit of Costard and Jaquenetta. The 'traitors' stay behind—i.e. those
who have broken vows—but the 'true folk' who leave are also those
whose language readily avoids 'glozes' and deals plainly.

This scene with the lords is the centre of interest for those who seek
topical references in the play to Chapman and 'the School of Night'.
Much of that inquiry seems to ignore the play's larger meanings; but
one particular item of contemporary allusion does perhaps hold clues
to this particular stage in the play's development of its themes. Miss
Frances Yates[13] has examined certain controversies centred around
Bruno's dislike of the Petrarchan idealization of women and the
impact of those controversies in Elizabethan England. What they can
teach us about Love's Labour's Lost is not that Shakespeare intended any
precise allusions to contemporary figures, but that he saw in such
disputes material for his own dramatic exploration of certain encounters
between art and reality. The lords' good-humoured wrangle after the

13 Op. cit., chapter vi.

discovery that Berowne too is in love touches upon the conflict between love as mere body (Dumaine's coarse joke at lines 279–80) and the neo-platonic realization that in a lady's grace resides a divine benediction; upon the relationship of various arts of language to various sorts of truth about love; and upon the presence of art in both rhetoric and cosmetic. It is the King who recalls them from these (at present) only sportive debates to the overriding fact—'Are we not all in love?' Yet Berowne, while he argues them wittily out of their vow, provides them with no more secure rhetoric for their affections. Indeed, despite his earlier cynicism, he praises their 'fiery numbers' and the arts that only love can teach:

> But love, first learned in a lady's eyes,
> Lives not alone immured in the brain,
> But with the motion of all elements,
> Courses as swift as thought in every power,
> And gives to every power a double power,
> Above their functions and their offices.
> It adds a precious seeing to the eye:
> A lover's eyes will gaze an eagle blind.
> A lover's ear will hear the lowest sound,
> When the suspicious head of theft is stopp'd.
> Love's feeling is more soft and sensible
> Than are the tender horns of cockled snails;
> Love's tongue proves dainty Bacchus gross in taste.
>
> (IV. iii. 323–35)

However sharpened the lover's senses become, however love's sighs temper the poet's ink, he has not yet any firmer sense of what language to use or of its relation to human realities. Nor is that surprising, if we remember the sharp differences of attitude that characterize his and the other lords' discussion of women, a range of response paralleled in the 'comic' scenes by Holofernes' 'soul feminine' to Costard's 'the child brags in her belly'.

IV

The marvellous last scene of *Love's Labour's Lost* weaves almost musical patterns with the ideas the rest of the play has canvassed. So far we have been introduced to rival notions of grace and to the arts of academe and court, and we have laughed readily at their absurd affectations. Before the play ends we should have begun to recognize what it may take sometime after the play is over (if not exactly a year and a day) for us to appreciate fully—the new and more compelling variations upon his themes that Shakespeare offers.

In their return to the more obvious courtly pursuit of writing love poetry and entertaining their ladies with a masque, the lords recover more of that outward grace they neglected as scholars. There begins to be some consonance between their art or language of living and the world in which they have to live. They also anticipate a recovery of that heavenly grace that comes with a lady's favour; but, as we have seen, the Princess has to teach them that even the larger grace has its natural rhythms. This lesson in its turn is closely bound up with what the drama chooses to say about art.

When Berowne protests that twelvemonth and a day is too long for a play, he alludes at once to the dramatic act we witness in the theatre and to the games he and his friends have played until then. They have been led easily to indulge in 'play', for the grace that consists in elegance and proportion of manners and that comes so readily to the courtiers may itself be a game. This is surely implied by the Princess—

> We have receiv'd your letters, full of love;
> Your favours, the ambassadors of love;
> And, in our maiden council, rated them
> At courtship, pleasant jest, and courtesy,
> As bombast and as lining to the time.
>
> (V. ii. 765-9)

Berowne has already admitted playing 'foul play' with their oaths, and he continues by using the language of children's games:

> All wanton as a child, skipping and vain,
> Form'd by the eye and therefore, like the eye,
> Full of strange shapes, of habits, and of forms,
> Varying in subjects as the eye doth roll
> To every varied object in his glance;
> Which parti-coated presence of loose love
> Put on by us . . .
>
> (V. ii. 749-55)

From his concealment in the poem-reading scene he saw it all as an infants' game of Hoodman-blind. As Boyet's account (V. ii. 89ff.) of their Muscovite rehearsal suggests, the lords undeniably enjoy their

charades and play them with considerable grace and skill. As Moth says
about the presentation of Hercules in the pageant, so we feel about the
nobles' breaking of their academic vows—

> That is the way to make an offence gracious, though few have the
> grace to do it.
>   (V. i. 120–21)

Yet the noble arts of courtship themselves may become absurd: 'A lady
walled about with diamonds' and the huge translations of hypocrisy
with their comparisons to 'twenty thousand fairs' have nothing of
proportion and so little of grace in them. The Princess is shrewd enough
to see this excess and manages to suggest how the king's early dedication to academic life has fed this graceless attempt at courtly courtship:

> Folly, in wisdom hatch'd,
> Hath wisdom's warrant and the help of school,
> And wit's own grace to grace a learned fool.
>   (V. ii. 70–72)

Rosaline is also quick to recognize what Berowne needs and she
determines to play him at his own game, namely to

> wait the season, and observe the times,
> And spend his prodigal wits in bootless rhymes.
>   (V. ii. 63–4)

Their 'waiting the season' requires more than Rosaline intends at
this stage. The grace which, according to the Princess's intentions, they
deny the men by covering their faces also seems to deprive them of
outward elegance in their Muscovite masque. The disruption of the
harmony of the dance is perhaps some visual indication of the failure
of the Muscovite game. The lords recover their poise only when they
resume their proper habits, when they renounce a game in which
imitari was nothing. But Boyet reminds us, as the dance stumbles over
the lovers' verbal exchanges, that the ladies are themselves as predis-
posed to mere verbal ingenuity as the men and even, not too remotely,
as the pedants:

> The tongues of mocking wenches are as keen
> As is the razor's edge invisible,
> Cutting a smaller hair than may be seen,
> Above the sense of sense.
>   (V. ii. 256–9)

The return of the lords in 'their own shape' is echoed in the re-appearance of the ladies unmasked. The 'shapeless gear' of Russian disguise provided no recognizable form for the lovers' encounter and no real language of exchange. Berowne realizes afterwards that their wits had not 'the grace to grace it with such show'. But when the ladies mock them with tales of a 'mess of Russians' they make a charming show of recovering their gracefulness, and yet their sense of how to 'play' the scene is still precarious.

Berowne continues the customary hyperbole of an Elizabethan lover, because it is an act he knows and can play with facility:

> Your capacity
> Is of that nature that to your huge store
> Wise things seem foolish and rich things but poor.
> (V. ii. 374-5)

But Rosaline proves an awkward audience and his capitulation to her some lines later pretends to renounce all arts and all play:

> O, never will I trust to speeches penn'd,
> Nor to the motion of a school-boy's tongue,
> Nor never come in vizard to my friend,
> Nor woo in rhyme, like a blind harper's song.
> Taffeta phrases, silken terms precise,
> Three-pil'd hyperboles, spruce affectation,
> Figures pedantical—these summer-flies
> Have blown me full of maggot ostentation.
> I do forswear them; and I here protest,
> By this white glove—how white the hand, God
> knows!—
> Henceforth my wooing mind shall be express'd
> In russet yeas, and honest kersey noes.
> (V. ii. 402-13)

There is a momentary lapse ('a trick / Of the old rage'), because it is not a part he can yet sustain. But he feels his new role deserves some recompense:

> Write 'Lord have mercy on us' on those three;
> They are infected, in their hearts it lies;
> They have the plague, and caught it of your eyes.
> These lords are visited; you are not free,
> For the Lord's tokens on you do I see.
> (V. ii. 419-23)

Yet this expectation of grace is thwarted by the ladies in yet another delightful modulation of this scene. They can demonstrate that the new-found 'sincerity' was also only a game—'Following the signs, woo'd but the sign of she'. Again the scene bubbles into an exchange of mockery, and in its turn this 'fair fray' is transformed into a combined mockery of the Worthies (signalled by Berowne joining forces in wit with Boyet). The gentles are always, in Holofernes' phrase, 'at their game'.

The Worthies Pageant is mocked with an increasing failure of generosity and self-perception and on the lords' part at least with much lack of grace. For the pedants may affect courtly pastimes in proposing some 'delightful ostentation or show' and their acting may too quickly betray the distance between what the Princess calls their 'zeal' and their 'form'; but it is ultimately all of a piece with the games or 'set(s) of wit well played' that have until now preoccupied the nobles. It is not their *forte*, for their world has its own kinds of excellence and games—'He is a marvellous good neighbour, faith, and a very good bowler.' Yet if Nathaniel is 'o'erparted' as Alexander the Great, what are we to make of Berowne's new role of sincere lover? Does it announce, like Holofernes' thespian ambitions, that '*Imitari* is nothing'?

V

Love's Labour's Lost deliberately postpones any answers, for they are possible, if at all, only after twelve months and a day. I do not share the view that sees 'the characters and conventions of comedy . . . being rather brutally treated . . . Canvas scenery is taken outside the theatre and asked to be real mountain and forest.'[14] Nor is it so simply moralistic as Bacon's 'it is not good to stay too long in the theatre'. Those involved onstage in the action certainly seem to think they are reproved for their games and pastimes; even the Princess feels herself as much reprimanded as any in face of Mercade's 'tale'. They all have quick recourse to 'some forlorn and naked hermitage', to 'honest plain words' or to visitations of the sick. But surely we in the audience should place Mercade's 'tale' and theirs in a different light and regard it with a wider vision: not as an injunction to escape from games and play, but a reminder that so much of our daily conduct consists in games, a living art with rules and

14 Edwards, pp. 46–7. Cf. Roesen (*op. cit.*, p. 414) on the 'ultimate victory of reality over artifice and illusion'.

decorums of its own.[15] If any characters in the play recognize this, it is perhaps the Princess and her ladies; for their gaiety and easy conduct come in part from their knowing that life requires from each of them a fluent performance.

The play ends, after all, not with the dedication to 'mourning houses' and hospitals, as some critics seem to suggest, but with another game— with the dialogue in song that should have ended the play of the Worthies. Here, perhaps for the first time in the play, imitation is everything. The debates of the play are held in the unresolved exchange between the extremes of Winter and Spring; realities of adultery and running noses are not neglected by an art where words and music move harmoniously and in time; the actors, too, maintain their roles without even a 'little fault'. It is all a game when men dressed as owls and cuckoos represent winter and spring; but for once it is a game that, recognized as such, nevertheless delights and instructs us in its attention to real things.

These songs obviously reaffirm the seasonal emphases of Berowne in the first scene and the Princess in the last. Yet their dialogue is unresolved not only as the traditional debate between winter and spring but as a conflict of art and life. For they are pastoral eclogues, holding in marvellous equilibrium the idealism of meadow flowers, shepherds piping and picturesque prospects with the ruder actualities of country life. The play continues to beg the question of what language, what rules the 'real' life requires. Armado's solution is obviously a shade ridiculous—'holding the plough' for Jaquenetta's sweet love. Although he acts as prologue and epilogue for the pastoral songs, this fantastical Spaniard is still a 'child of fancy' and there is perhaps a clue to his continuing affectation or taste for art at the expense of life in his commendation of Apollo, the god of poetry. This 'phantasime' still lacks grace in his antics and proportion in his vows and in choosing to dismiss Mercury he neglects the god who traditionally was the 'leader of the graces'[16] and who is seen to conduct them across the pageant of Botticelli's *Primavera*.

[15] C. L. Barber has explored how the play is 'a set exhibition of pastimes and games' in *Shakespeare's Festive Comedy* (Princeton, 1959). But his emphasis is still that these are judged within 'a larger rhythm' (p. 91) of the 'everyday situation' (p. 108), whereas I would prefer to think that even everyday situations demand their own rules for play, as modern psychologists have insisted— see Eric Berne, *The Games People Play* (London, 1966).

[16] Wind, *op. cit.*, pp. 121–2. One of the difficulties for the actor playing

So we are ultimately left guessing whether the actors in these delightful games properly understand the connections between grace, art and time. Berowne's 'Russet yeas and honest kersey noes' is a witty identification of the new language of sincere love with the 'simplicities' of pastoralism. We shall never know whether his extra-mural year will teach him the rules of the new game and allow him as delightful a language as the others he has used, and whether he will find grace in Rosaline's eyes.

Armado is whether he should subdue the personality of 'phantasime' for the neutrality of his final role. My feeling would be, on the contrary, that he needs to be a child of fancy till the very end.

V

'The Merchant of Venice', or the Importance of Being Earnest

D. J. PALMER

I

'*The Merchant of Venice* is the simplest of plays,' wrote Harley Gran-ville-Barker, 'so long as we do not bedevil it with sophistries.'[1] And so it is, provided also that we do not take its moralizing too seriously, for the sophistries are already there. In the two climactic scenes of the play, for instance, Bassanio wins Portia by turning sententious rhetoric against itself,

> So may the outward shows be least themselves;
> The world is still deceiv'd with ornament.
> In law, what plea so tainted and corrupt
> But, being season'd with a gracious voice,
> Obscures the show of evil? In religion,
> What damned error but some sober brow
> Will bless it, and approve it with a text,
> Hiding the grossness with fair ornament?

(III. ii. 73–80)

while Portia succeeds in the trial scene by proving herself a better equivocator than Shylock.

This is the most sententious of all the comedies before the problem plays. Moral issues stare us in the face, so that, as Frank Kermode has observed, 'only by a determined effort to avoid the obvious can one mistake the theme of *The Merchant of Venice*'.[2] However the theme or moral argument of the play is formulated, as the conflict between justice and mercy, or the antithesis of prodigality and usury, or the

---

[1] Harley Granville-Barker, *Prefaces to Shakespeare* (Second Series, London, 1930), p. 68.

[2] Frank Kermode, 'The Mature Comedies', *Early Shakespeare*, ed. J. R. Brown and B. Harris (Stratford-upon-Avon Studies 3, London, 1961), p. 224.

use of riches spiritual and material, it is based on the opposing values of Belmont and Venice. Yet Shakespeare's treatment of the theme is not 'obvious' in the sense that led Stephen Gosson to exempt the old play called *The Jew* from his general censure of the stage in 1579, for its edifying representation of 'the greedinesse of worldly chusers and the bloody mindes of Usurers'.[3] The themes are very similar, but whether or not Shakespeare was indebted to *The Jew* for the double plot of the caskets and the bond, *The Merchant of Venice* resists the simple categories of a morality play. Those critics who have felt, for instance, that the powerful characterization of Shylock upsets the balance of the dramatic structure are right at least in their perception of forces that complicate and cut across the moral alignments of the theme. Our sympathies are too often divided, and action too often contradicts avowed principle, to allow us to feel secure in those symmetrical antinomies of value set up between Belmont and Venice. If Shylock were merely a conventional stage-Jew, if Jessica did not 'steal' from her father in every sense of the word, if the quality of Christian mercy towards Shylock were less strained, Bassanio's 'worth' more in evidence and Antonio's self-righteousness less so, then the moral issues would be more clear-cut but the play correspondingly less interesting.

The play's overt sententiousness serves a dramatic purpose similar to that which T. S. Eliot found for 'meaning' in poetry: 'to satisfy one habit of the reader, to keep his mind diverted and quiet, while the poem does its work upon him: much as the imaginary burglar is always provided with a bit of nice meat for the house-dog'.[4] Our attention is often held by moral arguments of one kind or another, while a different order of awareness and response is being solicited by other dramatic means. Thus in I. iii there is a contention between Shylock and Antonio on the rights and wrongs of usury, in which Shylock grounds his justification for lending money at interest on scriptural authority, citing as precedent the account in Genesis 30 of how Jacob earned his hire as shepherd to his uncle Laban:

> Mark what Jacob did:
> When Laban and himself were compromis'd
> That all the eanlings which were streak'd and pied
> Should fall as Jacob's hire, the ewes, being rank,

---

[3] Stephen Gosson, *The School of Abuse* (ed. E. Arber, English Reprints, London, 1869), p. 40.

[4] T. S. Eliot, *The Use of Poetry and the Use of Criticism* (London, 1933), p. 151.

In end of autumn turned to the rams;
And when the work of generation was
Between these woolly breeders in the act,
The skilful shepherd pill'd me certain wands,
And, in the doing of the deed of kind,
He stuck them up before the fulsome ewes,
Who, then conceiving, did in eaning time
Fall parti-colour'd lambs, and those were Jacob's.
This was a way to thrive, and he was blest;
And thrift is blessing, if men steal it not.

(I. iii. 72–85)

But the issue of usury is only a pretext for insinuating other analogies between the story of Jacob and the dramatic situation. Like Jacob, Shylock is a worm that eventually turns, and his identification with Jacob's cunning in getting the better of this bargain prefigures his own use of the 'merry bond' for revenge upon Antonio. Antonio, on the other hand, exonerates Jacob from deception while convicting Shylock of casuistry: 'The devil can cite Scripture for his purpose.' It is indeed a scene bedevilled with sophistry, for as Antonio shifts the moral issue from usury to an *ad hominem* attack on Shylock's false-seeming, it is clear that the antagonism between them runs far deeper than a business rivalry or a theological dispute. The story of Jacob's manipulation of animal passions is itself a mirror of the equivocal way in which both Antonio and Shylock try to gain the moral advantage from an antipathy that is seated in the blood. Shakespeare is not concerned to present the case for or against usury itself.

In this 'simplest of plays', the true simplicity resides in the primacy of natural feeling. Like Jacob's 'fulsome ewes', the characters behave according to the laws of 'kind', not according to the precepts and doctrines of the moralist. As Shylock says,

affection,
Mistress of passion, sways it to the mood
Of what it likes or loathes,

(IV. i. 50–52)

and opposing extremes of excess and deficiency in temperament, in the 'senses, affections, passions' of the blood, create the possibilities for tragic or comic resolution which are kept open until the climactic passions of the trial scene. If Jacob is a figure of the power to control and direct natural feeling, that power is conspicuously denied to the moralist in an action which bears ample witness to Portia's observation that 'the brain may devise laws for the blood, but a hot temper leaps o'er a cold decree' (I. ii. 15). The eloquence of moral deliberation and exhortation, 'good sentences, and well pronounc'd' (I. ii. 9), finally gives way to the ultimate simplicity of silence in which 'the touches of sweet harmony' (V. i. 57) are heard.

While Stephen Gosson approved *The Jew* for its morality, the spirit of Shakespeare's play is closer to Sir Philip Sidney's reply to Gosson in *An Apology for Poetry*:

> Wherein, if we can, show we the poet's nobleness, by setting him before his other competitors, among whom as principal challengers step forth the moral philosophers whom, me thinketh, I see coming towards me with a sullen gravity, as though they could not abide vice by daylight, rudely clothed for to witness outwardly their contempt of outward things, with books in their hands against glory, whereto they set their names, sophistically speaking against subtlety, and angry with any man in whom they see the foul fault of anger.

'Dost thou think, because thou art virtuous, there shall be no more cakes and ale?' The moralist, traditional enemy of the comic spirit, not only bedevils us with sophistries, but fails where the poet succeeds in moving the affections:

> For suppose it be granted (that which I suppose with great reason may be denied) that the philosopher, in respect of his methodical proceeding, doth teach more perfectly than the poet, yet do I think that no man is so much *philophilosophos* as to compare the philosopher in moving with the poet.
>
> And that moving is of a higher degree than teaching, it may by this appear, that it is well nigh the cause and the effect of teaching. For who will be taught, if he be not moved with desire to be taught? and what so much good doth that teaching bring forth (I speak still of moral doctrine) as that it moveth one to do that which it doth teach?[5]

In the play as a whole, the story of Jacob, 'the skilful shepherd', has another significance: like T. S. Eliot's 'imaginary burglar', it is a figurative analogy to Shakespeare's own art, which deceives with 'outward shows' to move us through feeling to imaginative conception.

Jacob is not the only magician-figure in *The Merchant of Venice*.

[5] Sir Philip Sidney, *An Apology for Poetry*, ed. Geoffrey Shepherd (London, 1965), pp. 104–5, 112.

When Bassanio describes Portia in terms of the myth of the Golden Fleece at the end of the play's first scene,

> For the four winds blow in from every coast
> Renowned suitors, and her sunny locks
> Hang on her temples like a golden fleece,
> Which makes her seat of Belmont Colchos' strond,
> And many Jasons come in quest of her,
>
> (I. i. 168–72)

the allusion associates her with Medea, who fell in love with Jason and used her necromantic arts to help him win the Golden Fleece. Medea is the central figure in Ovid's version of the myth (*Metamorphoses*, Book VII), which Shakespeare must have had in mind, for Ovid pursues her subsequent career as the play does in its later reference to the legend:

> In such a night
> Medea gathered the enchanted herbs
> That did renew old Aeson.
>
> (V. i. 12–14)

Aeson was Jason's father, and after Medea has betrayed her own father by marrying Jason and returning with him to Greece, she employs her skills to restore Aeson to youthful vigour by opening his veins with a knife and replacing his aged blood with the juice of 'the enchanted herbs'. The rest of Medea's story takes a more sinister turn, as she uses her magic in treachery and murder. Thus 'with hir suttle guile / Of counterfetted gravitie' (as Arthur Golding translated it, Book VII, lines 398–9), she persuades the daughters of King Pelias that his life can be renewed as Aeson's had been, and so lures them into cutting their father's throat. Her wickedness reaches its peak in the murder of her own children (again with a knife) and in the attempt to deceive her second husband Aegeus into poisoning his son Theseus.

What begins as a romantic love story therefore turns into tragedy, but there is a logic in this progression, for each of Medea's crimes, directed against the ties of kinship, is a repetition of her original betrayal of her father in helping Jason win the fleece. Significantly for Shakespeare's purposes, Ovid begins his tale with Medea's struggle between moral restraint and unbridled passion:

> Aeetas daughter in hir heart doth mightie flames conceyve.
> And after struging verie long, when reason could not win

The upper hand of rage: she thus did in hir selfe begin:
In vaine, Medea, dost thou strive: some God what ere he is
Against thee bendes his force. For what a wondrous thing is
    this?
Is any thing like this which men doe terme by name of Love?
For why should I my fathers hestes esteeme so hard above
All measure? sure in very deede they are too hard and sore.
Why feare I lest yon straunger whome I never saw before
Should perish? what should be the cause of this my feare so
    great?
Unhappie wench (and if thou canst) suppresse this uncouth
    heat
That burneth in thy tender brest: and if so be I coulde,
A happie turne it were, and more at ease then be I shoulde.
But now an uncouth maladie perforce against my will
Doth hale me. Love persuades me one, another thing my skill.
The best I see and like: the worst I follow headlong still.
                                        (Book VII, ll. 10–25)

A few moments after Bassanio has linked her with the legend of the
Golden Fleece, we find Portia at the beginning of the second scene in
Medea-like conflict between loyalty to her father and the natural desire
to choose her own husband, echoing the last of the lines quoted above:

It is a good divine that follows his own instructions; I can easier
teach twenty what were good to be done than to be one of the
twenty to follow mine own teaching. The brain may devise laws
for the blood, but a hot temper leaps o'er a cold decree; such a hare
is madness the youth, to skip o'er the meshes of good counsel the
cripple. But this reasoning is not in the fashion to choose me a
husband. O me, the word 'choose'! I may neither choose who I
would nor refuse who I dislike; so is the will of a living daughter
curb'd by the will of a dead father.   (I. ii. 12–22)

Yet here the differences between Portia and Medea begin. Portia is not
in love with any of the 'strangers' who have come Jason-like to
Belmont, as she makes clear by mocking at their eccentric dispositions.
And since they refuse to accept the conditions of her father's will, she
can unlike Medea gladly vow loyalty to her father: 'If I live to be as old
as Sibylla, I will die as chaste as Diana, unless I be obtained by the
manner of my father's will' (I. ii. 95). Portia is contrasted rather than
identified with Medea, but the parallels are there in the play to intensify
the sense of possible disaster. From Ovid's tale Shakespeare has appro-

priated the related and recurrent significance of 'blood' as the physical basis of passion and of kinship. As Medea rejuvenated her husband's father, Portia will restore the life of her husband's friend, by means of deceptive arts; but Portia's lawful magic prevents the knife from shedding a single drop of blood. It is Jessica instead who betrays her father by marrying a stranger,

> Alack, what heinous sin it is in me
> To be asham'd to be my father's child!
> But though I am a daughter to his blood,
> I am not to his manners,
>
> (II. iii. 16–19)

Like Ovid, Shakespeare opens the action with an 'uncouth [i.e. strange, unknown] maladie'. Antonio's sadness reflects the wayward motions of 'affection, / Mistress of passion', for critics who try like Salerio and Solanio to discover the cause of this sadness are wilfully ignoring its dramatic point: 'In sooth, I *know not* why I am so sad'. Antonio has of late, but wherefore he knows not, lost all his mirth, and this sadness, which gives him 'much ado to *know* myself', sets him apart from those who know him best, his friends. Later in the play, Portia describes friendship as a communion of similar spirits:

> for in companions
> That do converse and waste the time together,
> Whose souls do bear an equal yoke of love,
> There must be needs a like proportion
> Of lineaments, of manners, and of spirit.
>
> (III. iv. 11–15)

The virtually interchangeable names and speeches of Salerio and Solanio suggest just such a shared identity, in contrast with Solanio's reaction to Antonio's distemper:

> Now, by two-headed Janus
> Nature hath fram'd *strange fellows* in her time:
> Some that will evermore peep through their eyes,
> And laugh like parrots at a bagpiper;
> And other of such vinegar aspect
> That they'll not show their teeth in way of smile
> Though Nestor swear the jest be laughable.
>
> (I. i. 50–6)

Antonio's sadness divides the 'equal yoke' of friendship; as Bassanio,

Lorenzo and Gratiano approach, Salerio and Solanio take their leave so abruptly that Bassanio feels there is something wrong:

> Good signiors both, when shall we laugh? Say when.
> You grow *exceeding strange*; must it be so?
>
> (I. i. 66–7)

Friends become strangers, and the encounter between Antonio and Gratiano is just such a contrast of opposing temperaments as that between the 'strange fellows' Solanio described. If Shakespeare confused 'two-headed Janus' with the masks of tragedy and comedy, the image is also picked up in Antonio's assertion that he holds the world as 'A stage, where every man must play a part, / And mine a sad one', to which Gratiano replies, 'Let me play the fool' (I. i. 78–9).

Antonio's sadness sets in motion the forces of division and disharmony which will take the play to the brink of tragedy before it is retrieved as a comedy. His loss of inner equilibrium produces that sense of things drawing apart into opposite extremes which this first scene develops through the talk of contrasting excess and deficiency, though the emphasis upon differences of temperament between friends who should be united by sympathies of feeling, and through the sequence of departures as in turn each of Antonio's friends leaves him.

Shakespeare has adapted to his own purposes Medea's 'uncouth maladie' that turns her affections to a 'straunger'. After the estranging effects of Antonia's sadness upon himself and his friends, in the second scene we hear from Portia about her suitors, who are 'strange fellows' both in Solanio's sense and as foreigners. This prepares us for Shylock's entry in the following scene, since Shylock is essentially the stranger, by temperament and race. Indeed, since it is 'blood' that determines both, Shylock's Jewishness and his disposition are related. The antipathy between himself and Antonio is not only absolute and unqualified, it has its roots in a repugnance that is physical before it finds moral or religious grounding. Shylock's refusal to eat with Antonio, the intensity of his desire instead to 'feed fat the ancient grudge I bear him', matches the extraordinary violence of Antonio's behaviour to him:

> You that did void your rheum upon my beard
> And foot me as you spurn a *stranger* cur.
>
> (I. iii. 112–13)

This is not merely ideological bigotry: they respond to each other through their bodies, in a savage, primitive way, and the essence of such a response is that neither regards the other as a fellow man. With this strong physical feeling between them, it is not surprising that Shylock should propose as forfeit for his bond 'an equal pound / Of your fair flesh'.

'Mislike me not for my complexion': the Prince of Morocco's enjoinder to Portia at the opening of the next scene (II. i) is a fitting comment on the mutual antipathy between Antonio and Shylock. Morocco refers to his black skin, but the Elizabethan word 'complexion' also meant the disposition of the humours in the blood which were believed to determine temperament. Melancholy, choleric, sanguine and phlegmatic humours, mixed in different proportions, make up Nature's 'strange fellows'. Differences of race, by which Morocco and Shylock are identified as 'strangers', are also in the blood, while in yet another sense this blood signifies our common humanity, as Morocco implies when he compares himself to 'the fairest creature northward born':

> And let us make incision for your love
> To prove whose blood is reddest, his or mine.
>
> (II. i. 6–7)

'So may the outward shows be least themselves'. Morocco's challenge, by anticipating Shylock's attempt to 'make incision', also reminds us that the affections of liking or loathing are rooted in the blood. 'Mislike me not for my complexion' is thus an appeal which extends in the play far beyond its immediate context.

Shylock's most powerful appeal for our sympathies also gathers its force from physical imagery, paradoxically arguing from 'kind' to the justification of most unkind cruelty:

> Hath not a Jew eyes? Hath not a Jew hands, organs, dimensions, senses, affections, passions, fed with the same food, hurt with the same weapons, subject to the same diseases, healed by the same means, warmed and cooled by the same winter and summer, as a Christian is? If you prick us, do we not bleed? If you tickle us, do we not laugh? If you poison us, do we not die? And if you wrong us, shall we not revenge? If we are like you in the rest, we will resemble you in that.
>
> (III. i. 50–57)

In its reduction of moral argument to the terrible logic of the blood,

Shylock's passionate eloquence illustrates the sense in which this is 'the simplest of plays'.

III

In Elizabethan usage 'sad' could mean 'serious' as well as 'melancholy'. Thus the merry Gratiano finds Antonio's sadness akin to the grave disposition of the moralist:

> There are a sort of men whose visages
> Do cream and mantle like a standing pond,
> And do a wilful stillness entertain,
> With purpose to be dress'd in an opinion
> Of wisdom, gravity, profound conceit;
> As who should say, 'I am Sir Oracle,
> And when I ope my lips let no dog bark'.
> O my Antonio, I do know of those
> That therefore only are reputed wise
> For saying nothing.
>
> (I. i. 88–97)

Gratiano 'speaks an infinite deal of nothing', as Bassanio observes behind his back, and between these two extremes of excess and deficiency differences of natural disposition are reflected in the use of language. In the unfolding action characters are given ample opportunity to play the moralist: the choice between the caskets is performed by each of Portia's suitors as an exercise in high-minded eloquence, while Shylock and his enemies exchange speeches of self-righteous recrimination. But 'wisdom, gravity, profound conceit' are, as Gratiano suggests, the 'outward shows' of attitudes determined by temperament and the inner motions of the blood; conversely, the rhetoric of sententious deliberation and exhortation, the appeals to precept and doctrine, fail to move the affections to their purpose. Moral argument gives way to equivocation, as 'good sentences and well pronounc'd' are wasted upon the currents of natural feeling.

After Portia's reflections in the second scene on the opposition of a 'hot temper' and a 'cold decree', the clown Gobbo takes up this conflict between moral restraint and natural inclination in a parody of the 'serious' action:

> My conscience says 'Launcelot, budge not'. 'Budge' says the fiend. 'Budge not' says my conscience. 'Conscience' say I 'you counsel well.' 'Fiend' say I 'you counsel well.' To be rul'd by my conscience,

I should stay with the Jew my master, who—God bless the mark!—
is a kind of devil; and, to run away from the Jew, I should be rul'd
by the fiend, who—saving your reverence—is the devil himself.
Certainly the Jew is the very devil incarnation; and, in my conscience, my conscience is but a kind of hard conscience to offer to
counsel me to stay with the Jew. The fiend gives the more friendly
counsel. I will run, fiend; my heels are at your commandment; I
will run.   (II. ii. 20–28)

The sententious arguments of Portia's suitors as they deliberate before
the caskets are hardly to be taken more seriously than this. The means
which Portia's father has devised for selecting a husband show him to
have been both a moralist and an equivocator, the author of riddling
inscriptions on the caskets and sententious little rhymes on the scrolls
within. This is a kind of guessing game which each of the suitors tries
to solve by the processes of reason, but which really works by testing
their temperament and affection to Portia rather than their judgement.
Morocco chooses gold for the perfectly good reason that only the
most precious metal is worthy to contain 'so rich a gem' as Portia, but
the hyperbolic imagery rather than the logic of his speech shows that
it is the spirit of emulation which sways his choice:

> 'Who chooseth me shall gain what many men desire'.
> Why, that's the lady! All the world desires her;
> From the four corners of the earth they come
> To kiss this shrine, this mortal-breathing saint.
> The Hyrcanian deserts and the vasty wilds
> Of wide Arabia are as thoroughfares now
> For princes to come view fair Portia.
> The watery kingdom, whose ambitious head
> Spits in the face of heaven, is no bar
> To stop the foreign spirits, but they come
> As o'er a brook to see fair Portia.
>
> (II. vii. 37–47)

Morocco's own 'ambitious head' attracts him to the golden casket,
because to win her would be to triumph like another Tamburlaine
over 'all the world'. Arragon, on the other hand, disdains 'the fool
multitude that choose by show', a sentiment of admirable integrity,
were it not for his motives:

> Because I will not jump with common spirits
> And rank me with the barbarous multitudes.
>
> (II. ix. 32–3)

Thus as he turns to the silver casket his otherwise unexceptionable moralizing is discounted by his vanity (his very name suggests 'arrogance'):

> 'Who chooseth me shall get as much as he deserves'.
> And well said too; for who shall go about
> To cozen fortune, and be honourable
> Without the stamp of merit? Let none presume
> To wear an undeserved dignity.
> O that estates, degree, and offices
> Were not deriv'd corruptly, and that clear honour
> Were purchased by the merit of the wearer!
>
> (II. ix. 36–43)

'I will assume desert': with this claim Arragon's affection is shown to be more toward himself than to Portia.

Interspersed with these scenes in Belmont is the parallel action by which Lorenzo successfully steals Jessica from her father's house. 'It is a wise father that knows his own child': Gobbo's line serves to point the contrast between Portia's father and Shylock. Jessica's elopement is to take place during the revelry of the masques, and Shylock's attitude to the 'prodigal' and merry-making Christians is that of a strict puritanical sobriety:

> But stop my house's ears—I mean my casements;
> Let not the sound of shallow fopp'ry enter
> My sober house.
>
> (II. v. 33–5)

Yet here, too, the moralist's stance is determined by a bias of temperament, for Shylock betrays an intense physical repugnance to 'the vile squealing of the wry-neck'd fife', while his reiterated instructions to lock up the house suggest that his wise precept ('Fast bind, fast find— A proverb never stale in thrifty mind') is really an emblem of the heart that is closed to human sympathies.

It is more surprising to find Gratiano turning moralist. Bassanio has granted his 'suit' to go to Belmont, on condition that Gratiano will 'allay with some cold drops of modesty / Thy skipping spirit', and Gratiano has promised to

> put on a sober habit,
> Talk with respect, and swear but now and then,
> Wear prayer-books in my pocket, look demurely.
>
> (II. ii. 175–7)

But for the night of masquing Bassanio has specifically entreated him 'rather to put on / Your boldest suit of mirth'. The clothing imagery of these exchanges relates to the 'outward shows' of masquing and to the disguise in which Jessica will deceive her father, but while this elopement is played as romantic comedy between Jessica, Lorenzo and their friends, the scene begins with a curiously solemn exchange between Salerio and Gratiano:

> All things that are
> Are with more spirit chased than enjoy'd.
> How like a younker or a prodigal
> The scarfed bark puts from her native bay,
> Hugg'd and embraced by the strumpet wind;
> How like the prodigal doth she return,
> With over-weather'd ribs and ragged sails.
> Lean, rent, and beggar'd by the strumpet wind.
>
> (II. vi. 12–19)

Such moralizing seems out of keeping not only with Gratiano's character but with the revelling spirit which has been anticipated. Moreover it predicts a turn of events which does not come about, as far as the 'prodigal' lovers are concerned. Lorenzo and Jessica are never to return, while Bassanio and Gratiano will return having won 'the golden fleece'. So comedy will avert the moralist's forebodings, but meanwhile, if Gratiano's sententiousness is out of place, so too is the light-heartedness with which Lorenzo and Jessica steal from Shylock. Lorenzo jests about playing the thief for a wife, and Jessica is coyly 'much asham'd' of her boy's disguise, though not abashed to take her father's ducats: 'Here, catch this casket; it is worth the pains.' The contrast with the casket scenes in Belmont provides the perspective in which we see these 'pretty follies'. Lorenzo's praise of Jessica,

> For she is wise, if I can judge of her,
> And fair she is, if that mine eyes be true,
> And true she is, as she hath prov'd herself,
>
> (II. vi. 53–5)

is in ironic juxtaposition with Portia's description of her suitors as 'deliberate fools' who 'have the wisdom by their wit to lose'. Wisdom and judgement are subject to the affections, for as Portia declared in the second scene of the play, 'this reasoning is not in the fashion to choose me a husband'.

IV

When Bassanio arrives at Belmont, we expect him to win Portia because they love each other. In this 'simplest of plays', the movement of their affections to each other is as primary and absolute as the antipathy that divides Antonio and Shylock. We now also know which of the three caskets Bassanio must choose, having seen the other two opened by Morocco and Arragon. The great mystery, or rather the magic secret, is the process by which Bassanio makes his choice.

Like the previous suitors, he treats his task as an exercise in moral judgement, and he makes a long speech of sententious deliberation. Yet this is neither a debating competition nor a lottery of 'hazard'. Portia tells Bassanio 'If you love me, you will find me out'. In the requirements of a good husband, love would seem to come before eloquence or wisdom. Bassanio's choice will vindicate the 'good inspiration' of Portia's father for posthumously disposing of his daughter in marriage, but what has love to do with an excellent if somewhat platitudinous and lengthy speech on the dangers of false appearance? Portia's love, as Bassanio told Antonio in the opening scene of the play, has already declared itself in 'fair *speechless* messages' from her eyes.

Unlike his unsuccessful predecessors, Bassanio has music while he works, and the song that is played at first seems to have little to do with the situation:

> Tell me where is fancy bred,
> Or in the heart or in the head,
> How begot, how nourished?
>> Reply, reply.
> It is engend'red in the eyes,
> With gazing fed; and fancy dies
> In the cradle where it lies.

(III. ii. 63–9)

We can dismiss the suggestion that Portia is cheating in arranging for a song with enough '-ed' rhymes to give even Bassanio a clue to 'lead'. Not only has Portia renewed her pledge of loyalty to her father's will at the beginning of the scene, but Bassanio would have no reason to pretend for nearly forty lines that he hadn't grasped such a clue; in any case, astuteness is not a prominent feature of our hero's charm. However, the song does provide him with the theme of his speech; if 'fancy' is 'engend'red in the eyes', 'So may the outward shows be least themselves'. Fancy and judgement are opposed, like the heart and the head, and so Bassanio launches into his moral deliberation.

But the speech is shot through with ironies and contradictions that Bassanio seems unaware of. He begins, for instance, by denouncing the very rhetorical arts he uses so well, the 'gracious voice' and 'sober brow' that conceal truth beneath eloquence. This penniless prodigal then rejects gold and silver, and finally, after a most ornamental and highly-wrought argument decrying ornament and artifice, he chooses the leaden casket because its plainness moves him 'more than eloquence'! Bassanio warns us, 'in a word', against

> The seeming truth which cunning times put on
> To entrap the wisest.
>
> (III. ii. 100–101)

Bassanio's reasoning cannot be taken at face value any more than the 'outward shows' he inveighs against. The irony is increased as he now opens the casket, finds 'fair Portia's counterfeit', and in his extravagant admiration of the painter's art contradicts all he has previously spoken against 'seeming truth':

> Here in her hairs
> The painter plays the spider, and hath woven
> A golden mesh t'entrap the hearts of men.
>
> (III. ii. 120–22)

The moralist's condemnation has become the artist's praise.

Bassanio is 'entrapped' by the song in a process that has more to do with 'fancy' than with judgement. Portia creates the mood in which his affections will respond, not to the words of the song, but to the power of the music. It is a solemn mood, not only of dramatic suspense, but of lyrical beauty, in which words themselves melt into the music of pure feeling:

> Let music sound while he doth make his choice;
> Then, if he lose, he makes a swan-like end,
> Fading in music. That the comparison may stand
> More proper, my eye shall be the stream
> And wat'ry death-bed for him. He may win;
> And what is music then? Then music is
> Even as the flourish when true subjects bow
> To a new-crowned monarch; such it is
> As are those dulcet sounds in break of day

That creep into the dreaming bridegroom's ear
And summon him to marriage.

(III. ii. 43-53)

We shall be told more later in the play about 'the sweet power of music', but as this scene is performed in the theatre we can feel its spell directly. Unlike the other suitors, Bassanio does not ponder each casket in turn, but his speech suggests that he is drawn without foreseeing it to his conclusion at the leaden casket. His gravity and intentness of spirit are conditioned by the music, by a continuous swell of harmony moving beneath and blending with his speech. In this way Bassanio's judgement is subject to the movement of his affections, and he utters not wisdom but poetry.

The tone of the scene is one of high seriousness, in keeping with the prevailing spirit of the play, but unlike the sadness of Antonio or the grim humour of Shylock, this graceful solemnity is not inimical to the comic spirit. From the tension of nervous excitement in the dialogue at the beginning of the scene, suspense grows into a sense of wonder and mystery as the ceremony begins, and after Bassanio's unhurried deliberation the climactic moment of the opening of the casket also releases pent-up feelings in the high tide of Portia's outburst,

O love, be moderate, allay thy ecstasy,
In measure rein thy joy, scant this excess!
I feel too much thy blessing. Make it less,
For fear I surfeit.

(III. ii. 111-14)

The language of the moralist becomes an expression of passionate joy, and this overwhelming intensity of emotion is sustained through Bassanio's hyperbolic praise of Portia's picture and its artist, through the contrasting simplicity with which the flesh-and-blood Portia offers herself,

You see me, Lord Bassanio, where I stand,
Such as I am,

until feeling, always primary to eloquence, eventually outstrips the power of words altogether:

Madam, you have bereft me of all words;
Only my blood speaks to you in my veins;
And there is such confusion in my powers

As, after some oration fairly spoke
By a beloved prince, there doth appear
Among the buzzing pleased multitude,
Where every something being blent together,
Turns to a wild of nothing, save of joy,
Express'd and not express'd.

(III. ii. 176–84)

To gain such an admission from the eloquent Bassanio is no mean achievement, though to put into words the inexpressible language of the blood is an even greater triumph of art. Only the ultimate simplicity of silence can follow this, but the moment passes as Gratiano and Nerissa intrude to share the joy, which turns, or descends, into brief merriment before this mood in turn is suddenly dashed with the news of Antonio's mortal danger.

V

'How every fool can play upon the word! I think the best grace of wit will shortly turn into silence, and discourse grow commendable in none but only parrots' (III. v. 38–40): Lorenzo's reflection upon the clown's quibbles comes between Portia's departure from Belmont and the trial scene itself, in which words are strained to their limit. Shylock's obduracy ('I'll have no speaking; I will have my bond') as Antonio is led to prison (III. iii. 17) also ominously anticipates the failure of 'good sentences' to move 'the blood' in the play's climactic scene.

Like Bassanio's choice between the caskets, the trial scene is in outward show an appeal to judgement. Shylock has the letter of the law on his side: if the devil can cite Scripture, it seems he is equally well versed in judicial procedure. The Duke, the court's presiding officer, and Antonio's friends take their stand on the moral law, according to which Shylock is

an inhuman wretch,
Uncapable of pity, void and empty
From any dram of mercy.

(IV. i. 4–6)

Shylock's cruelty is condemned as unnatural, against the law of 'kind' but Shylock grounds his case on a different conception of what is natural, on the arbitrary but fundamental compulsions of our physical being:

> Some men there are love not a gaping pig;
> Some that are mad if they behold a cat;
> And others, when the bagpipe sings i' th' nose,
> Cannot contain their urine; for affection,
> Mistress of passion, sways it to the mood
> Of what it likes or loathes. Now, for your answer:
> As there is no firm reason to be rend'red
> Why he cannot abide a gaping pig;
> Why he, a harmless necessary cat;
> Why he, a woollen bagpipe, but of force
> Must yield to such inevitable shame
> As to offend, himself being offended;
> So I can give no reason, nor will I not,
> More than a lodg'd hate and a certain loathing
> I bear Antonio.

(IV. i. 47–61)

The legal, moral and temperamental attitudes are therefore in conflict with each other, or rather they are three different ways of regarding the situation in court, each at cross-purposes with the other two.

To this state of affairs comes Portia, in her disguise as Balthazar. Her eloquent appeal for mercy is probably the best known speech in the play, a set oration of great legal, moral and passionate force. But the dramatic point of this speech seems to be its virtual irrelevance; it is a piece of superfluous rhetoric, since it achieves no effect whatsoever:

> There is no power in the tongue of man
> To alter me.

(IV. i. 236–7)

Shylock's deafness to such eloquence reflects on the powerlessness of words, however just and reasoned, to move his affections; and later in the scene we have cause to wonder whether the speech has had much effect on its other hearers either.

Portia's disguise is unlike that of Shakespeare's other comic heroines. It is not a means of extending or displaying her true nature, but rather the assumption of a completely different identity. The 'unlesson'd girl, unschool'd, unpractis'd', as she described herself in the caskets scene, is simply not the learned and magisterial figure of the trial scene; even her visit to the aged lawyer Bellario, brief as that must have been, can scarcely be supposed to have produced this transformation. Her acquisition of the arts that she practises in this scene is as magical as Bassanio's choice of the right casket. This disguise contrasts with Jessica's: it is an outward show without moral deception, since Portia is not acting out of self-interest. Balthazar's part in the trial is performed with immaculate professional disinterestedness; 'he' is not tainted by those passions which make a mockery of legal procedure not only in Shylock's behaviour but in that of the prisoner's friends and in the presiding Duke's lack of impartiality. Portia's disguise is an expression of that *selfless* love and shared identity which she described when she first resolved to assist her husband's friend:

> this Antonio,
> Being the bosom lover of my lord,
> Must needs be like my lord. If it be so,
> How little is the cost I have bestowed
> In purchasing the semblance of my soul
> From out the state of hellish cruelty!
>
> (III. iv. 16–21)

As Antonio stands surety for Bassanio, hazarding his own body for his friend, Portia assumes a surrogate body to save him. There is therefore a particular resonance in her command to Antonio: 'Lay bare your bosom.' Antonio's nakedness and Portia's disguise complement each other in giving theatrical expression to the nature of love.

The Shylock who remains unmoved by all the rhetoric of persuasion and vituperation, thus rendering words powerless, is also ironically the Shylock who insists upon the words of his bond: 'nearest his heart, those are the very words', and no surgeon to stop Antonio's wound, because it is not 'so nominated in the bond'. With supreme poetic justice, therefore, he is undone by his own faith in the word:

> Tarry a little; there is something else.
> This bond doth give thee here no jot of blood:
> The words expressly are 'a pound of flesh'.
>
> (IV. i. 300–302)

And how fitting it is that the vital but missing word, and so the hinge upon which the play turns from tragedy into comedy, is 'blood'.

The judgements that are then delivered upon Shylock, sequestering half his estate and forcibly converting him to Christianity, give a new twist to this play of 'good sentences, and well pronounc'd'. Gratiano's vindictive triumph ('A halter gratis; nothing else, *for God's sake!*'), gross as it is, sounds less appallingly self-righteous than the calculated humiliation which is Shylock's 'pardon'. Shylock ends his part in the play not merely thwarted but utterly crushed in spirit:

> *Portia:* Art thou contented, Jew? What dost thou say?
> *Shylock:* I am content.
> *Portia:* 　　　　　　　　Clerk, draw a deed of gift.
> *Shylock:* I pray you, give me leave to go from hence;
> 　　　　　I am not well; send the deed after me
> 　　　　　And I will sign it.
>
> 　　　　　　　　　　　　　　　　　　(IV. i. 388–92)

With the simplicity of these understatements, Shylock's part is over: the rest is silence, as far as he is concerned. The effect of this exit needs no underscoring by such melodramatic business as Irving added, having the broken man falter and collapse on his way out. The unemphatic tone which Shakespeare has secured at this point is precisely the secret of its dramatic impact, and as the play immediately shifts into the light, almost casual, comedy of the rings, Shylock is never mentioned again—a silence that reverberates through the remaining scenes.

VI

The main action of the play is now over, and what remains is like an epilogue, in which there is no more to do but 'converse and waste the time together'. Set in Belmont, the final scene opens with what is surely the play's most striking, and most daring, transition of feeling:

> The moon shines bright. In such a night as this,
> When the sweet wind did gently kiss the trees,
> And they did make no noise—in such a night,
> Troilus methinks mounted the Troyan walls,
> And sigh'd his soul toward the Grecian tents,
> Where Cressida lay that night.
>
> 　　　　　　　　　　　　　　　　　　(V. i. 1–6)

This opening duet performed by Lorenzo and Jessica turns the bitter conflict and equivocations of the trial scene into sweet harmony and tranquillity. We have entered a world of poetic beauty, in which, although the mythological lovers invoked are all tragic (Troilus and

Cressida, Pyramus and Thisbe, Dido and Aeneas, Medea and Jason),
their griefs are distanced by being framed in art and overlaid by lyric
charm. The 'silence of the night' and the recollection of past tragedies
in present happiness establishes a mood of serenity which is deepened
by the playing of music:

> How sweet the moonlight sleeps upon this bank!
> Here will we sit and let the sounds of music
> Creep in our ears; soft stillness and the night
> Become the touches of sweet harmony.
>
> (V. i. 54–7)

Like Bassanio in the caskets scene, Lorenzo is moved by the music
to philosophical gravity. 'Is it not strange,' as Benedick remarks in
Much Ado About Nothing, 'that sheeps' guts should hale souls out of
men's bodies?' And indeed the music that transports the soul through
the senses is the counterpart of that unheard music of the heavenly
spheres and of the harmony in 'immortal souls' of which Lorenzo
now speaks:

> But whilst this muddy vesture of decay
> Doth grossly close it in, we cannot hear it.
>
> (V. i. 64–5)

This silent music is the highest plane of harmony, on which, according
to the Platonic doctrine Lorenzo cites, the souls of the lovers are united.
On this plane, the body is no more than a 'muddy vesture of decay',
but, as in Donne's poem, 'The Extasie',

> So must pure lovers soules descend
> T'affections and to faculties
> Which sense may reach and apprehend,
> Else a great Prince in prison lies.

and from what Donne calls the 'soul's language' of silent harmony, the
lovers now descend to the plane of their affections.

Jessica finds that the music induces a kind of sadness in her disposition: 'I am never merry when I hear sweet music.' 'The reason is
your spirits are attentive,' replies Lorenzo, and he then describes 'the
sweet power of music' over the passions and 'the hot condition of the
blood':

> Therefore the poet
> Did feign that Orpheus drew trees, stones, and floods;

> Since nought so stockish, hard, and full of rage,
> But music for the time doth change his nature.
>
> (V. i. 79–82)

The music of Orpheus stands for Shakespeare's own art, both as a fiction feigned by 'the poet', and as an archetype of the poet's skill in moving the passions. To the Elizabethans the Orpheus myth signified the moral function of poetry, and Shakespeare makes the same use of the myth as Sidney had done, or as Puttenham in *The Arte of English Poesie*:

> And *Orpheus* assembled the wilde beasts to come in heards to harken to his musicke, and by that meanes made them tame, implying thereby, how by his discreete and wholsome lesons uttered in harmonie and with melodious instruments he brought the rude and savage people to a more civill and orderly life, nothing, as it seemeth, more prevailing or fit to redresse and edifie the cruell and sturdie courage of man than it.[6]

Castiglione, too, writes in *The Book of the Courtier* that music

> doth not onely make sweete the mindes of men, but also many times wild beastes tame: and who so savoureth it not, a man may assuredly thinke him not to be well in his wits.[7]

So Lorenzo concludes his speech with a reference to

> The man that hath no music in himself,
> Nor is not mov'd with concord of sweet sounds.
>
> (V. i. 83–4)

As Shylock is remembered here, the whole speech is retrospective in its bearing upon the play's concern with hot tempers and cold decrees. The failure of the moralist to persuade with his 'good sentences', appealing to reason and judgement, is now set in contrast with the poet's claim to be a teacher and law-giver by virtue of his power over the unruly passions. The art of Orpheus with wild beasts recalls that of Jacob, the 'skilful shepherd', who exercised quasi-magical control over the primal passions of the blood. Only the memory of Shylock, who does not savour music, strikes a discord in the lyrical harmonies

[6] *Elizabethan Critical Essays* (2 vols., Oxford, 1904), ed. G. Gregory Smith, ii. 6–7.

[7] B. Castiglione, *The Book of the Courtier* (translated by Sir Thomas Hoby, 1561), Everyman's Library (London, 1956), p. 76.

of this scene; but even as Lorenzo speaks of the man whose affections are as 'dark as Erebus', Portia makes her entrance. Portia, who has subdued just such a man through her skill in counterfeiting, therefore extends the analogies with Shakespeare's own art, and she is associated as a benevolent Medea with the magic of Jacob and Orpheus.

The counterfeiting of Portia and Nerissa over their husbands' rings now shifts the tone of the scene from lyrical enchantment to jesting, as we descend from the spiritual harmonies with which the scene began to the mock-quarrelling of the lovers. And as the spirit of mirth finally supplants the solemnity of silence and 'sweet harmony', the play ends with Gratiano's exuberant bawdiness:

> But were the day come, I should wish it dark,
> Till I were couching with the doctor's clerk.
> Well, while I live, I'll fear no other thing
> So sore as keeping safe Nerissa's ring.
>
> (V. i. 304-7)

It is an obvious lowering of the tone, in every sense, for like Donne's 'Extasie' the scene has moved downward from the plane of the soul, through that of the affections, to the ultimate simplicity of the body's appetites and 'the doing of the deed of kind':

> To our bodies turn wee then, that so
>   Weake men on love reveal'd may looke;
> Loves mysteries in soules doe grow,
>   But yet the body is his booke.

VII

The structure of Shakespearian comedy reflects a principle of Elizabethan aesthetics that 'oftentimes a dischorde in Musick maketh a comely concordaunce'.[8] 'How shall we find the concord of this discord?' asks Duke Theseus in A Midsummer Night's Dream, and the answer lies not only in the characteristic action of the comedies, leading through confusion and conflict to clarification and reconciliation, but also in their blending of contrasting tones and moods. Shakespeare's development in comedy could be traced in terms of the increasing

[8] 'E.K.', Epistle Dedicatory to The Shepheardes Calender, by Edmund Spenser (1579); The Poetical Works of Edmund Spenser, ed. J. C. Smith and E. De Selincourt (London, 1912), p. 417.

subtlety with which disparate elements of tone are brought into con-
cordance with each other, from *The Comedy of Errors* with its fusion of
romantic and Plautine motifs, to the complex and precarious harmonies
of *Twelfth Night.*

The *Merchant of Venice* occupies a special place in this progression,
as a play in which the discords are so powerful that it almost becomes
a tragedy. In *Love's Labour's Lost*, the fragile and artificial comedy is
shattered at the end by the sombre entry of Mercade, bringing news of
death; *The Merchant of Venice*, on the other hand, establishes a keynote
in its opening lines which suppresses the comic spirit of mirth and
merriment. There is little playful laughter and not much wit, until they
break out in the conclusion. Instead the prevailing tone is serious, and
this current of feeling is modulated from Antonio's sadness, through
the grim conflict between Shylock and his enemies, and the solemnity
of the casket scenes, to the gravity which attends even the lovers in
their ecstasy: they are never merry when they hear sweet music.

The seriousness of comedy is itself a paradox, a *discors concordia.*
Yet the comic seriousness of *The Merchant of Venice* lies deeper than its
potential for tragedy or its moral themes; the play operates at the
fundamental level of feeling, as its action stresses the primacy of the
affections, and after the tragic and moral conflicts are over, the serious
spirit is transmuted into the effect of music at Belmont. 'Nothing is
good, I see, without respect,' says Portia sententiously as she hears this
music:

> How many things by season season'd are
> To their right praise and true perfection!
> Peace. . .

(V. i. 107–8)

The harmony is sweeter in the silence of the night, and also after the
discords of the preceding action; this comic resolution reduces the
passions to a serene contentment which is still serious in tone, but from
which the play can come to rest in a relaxed good humour. Among the
happy lovers as they leave the stage, Antonio is the odd man out, the
discord that 'maketh a comely concordaunce', for his part remains 'a
sad one'.

VI

The Owl and the Cuckoo: Voices of
Maturity in Shakespeare's Comedies

R. A. FOAKES

I

I WOULD like to begin by considering Jaques in *As You Like It*. Before
we see him he is described, by one of Duke Senior's attendant lords, as a
melancholy humourist, satirizing court and country, so that we know in
advance of his love of moralizing. This lord's entertaining account of
Jaques addressing the hurt deer suggests the possibility that the stance
of Jaques in a pose, and his words and behaviour when we see him
leave this ambiguity about him, so that we do not know how seriously
to take him. He would mock his companions for leaving 'wealth and
ease', but mocks himself too:

> Here shall he see
> Gross fools as he,
> An if he will come to me.
>
> (II. v. 51-3)

He would be a fool, a professional fool, crying 'Motley's the only
wear' (II. vii. 34), for fools may 'wisely hit' people, making them smart
at the recognition of their own folly or vice. Yet his stance as satirist is
at once exposed as baseless by Duke Senior.

> For thou thyself hast been a libertine
> As sensual as the brutish sting itself.
>
> (II. vii. 65-6)

Besides, Jaques' own mockery and moralizing tend to rebound on
himself, as his most memorable speech, on the seven ages of man,
moving from infancy by stages to nothingness in old age, is at once
refuted by the entry of Orlando with Adam, his faithful and ancient
servant, still of use and helpful, and a living rebuttal of the notion of old
age as 'second childishness and mere oblivion' (II. vii. 165).

Jaques comes off second-best in his sets of wit with Orlando and with Rosalind; to Orlando this 'Monsieur Melancholy' is 'a fool or a cipher' (III. ii. 273), and Rosalind too mocks the emptiness of his sadness, wishing rather 'to have a fool to make me merry than experience to make me sad' (IV. i. 24). In spite of all this, Jaques is not really a sad figure, and the simples of which his melancholy is compounded include a kind of gaiety and a delight in encountering others. In particular he seeks out the fool, and rejoices to meet him, and to exhibit Touchstone's adroitness in repartee to Duke Senior in the final scene. Yet again, in this last scene, the Jaques who has moved easily between the polarities of foolery and melancholy, leaving us uncertain quite how to interpret him, goes off in serious mood, rejecting 'pleasures' to study rather with Duke Frederick, who has 'put on a religious life' (V. iv. 175).

All this is familiar. It suggests various ways of describing Jaques. The pun in his name, perhaps emphasized in the accenting of it in such lines as II. i. 43, can be used to stress in him 'the cynicism of the rake reformed'.[1] He can equally be seen as a 'comic pointer' exposing the folly of others,[2] of courtiers living in the woods, and of Touchstone and Audrey as partners in marriage, or as a comic figure in his own right, luxuriating in his poses. He is often sharp and right in what he says, but can also be mistaken and made almost to seem foolish. However, if we say all these things about him, and further, perhaps, agree that no one

---

[1] H. J. Oliver in his Introduction to the New Penguin Shakespeare edition of *As You Like It* (1968), p. 15. The text here requires the pronunciation 'jakes':

> Lord.   . . . the hairy fool
>   Much marked of the melancholy *Jaques*
>   Stood on th' extremest verge of the swift brook
>   Augmenting it with tears.
> Duke Senior.   But what said Jaques?

No doubt the new Freudian or anal-erotic school of criticism could make much of this, though so far their psychoanalytic attention to the comedies has, blessedly, been slight, but see Norman H. Holland, *Psycho-Analysis and Shakespeare* (New York, 1965) and F. C. Crews (editor), *Psychoanalysis and the Literary Process* (Cambridge, Mass., 1970).

[2] A phrase used by Larry S. Champion in the *Evolution of Shakespeare's Comedy* (Harvard, 1970) to indicate the function of characters who 'help to focus and guide the spectator's laughter' (p. 78).

perspective has a special validity, but rather that the varying aspects contribute to a remarkably interesting and complex figure, we still seem to leave something central about him unexplained. All these things together fail to explain why he is in the play; as a figure richly established, a delightful role for an actor to play, and one who has the final summing-up speech in the play, he has more importance, more stature, than can be accounted for in the terms of character and function I have outlined.

It clearly will not do to locate this stature in the capacity of Jaques as 'touchstone'. Like Touchstone himself, Jaques at times, momentarily, provides a necessary critical perspective, and properly mocks the sentimental pastoralism of courtiers who moralize the discomforts of exile into blessings, as well as the sentimental raptures of Orlando in pinning love-songs on the trees of the forest. Touchstone also from time to time acts as necessary critic, whose judgement is correct, as in his parody of Orlando's easy and overblown verses. So, too, does Rosalind, most notably in her controlling supervision of the lovers in IV. ii. None of them is simply a measure or tester of values in the play. Its splendid balance is arrived at in a subtler and more complex way, as none of the characters, neither of the court nor of the forest, comes through untouched by a gentle but radical criticism; at the same time what is beneficial is brought into dominance in the overall movement of the action to harmony at the end.

I think the function of Jaques becomes clearer if he is considered in relation to time. Other characters in the comedy are conscious of time, and play many variations on the theme. Those inhabiting the Forest of Arden may seem to the outsider to 'fleet the time carelessly, as they did in the golden world' (I. i. 109), or, alternatively, to 'lose and neglect the creeping hours of time' (II. vii. 112). Time may proceed with either a lazy or a swift foot, as Rosalind instructs Orlando: 'Time travels in divers paces with divers persons' (III. ii. 290). Time is also the 'old justice' waiting to try all offenders who fail to keep their appointed time (IV. i. 178). Time is winter and spring, the spring of the song the pages sing, a song begun by the 'pretty country folks', the lovers lying in the fields:

> This carol they began that hour,
>   With a hey, and a ho, and a hey nonino,
> How that a life was but a flower.
>   In the springtime, the only pretty ringtime,

When birds do sing, hey ding a ding, ding.
Sweet lovers love the spring.

And therefore take the present time,
  With a hey, and a ho, and a hey nonino,
For love is crowned with the prime
  In the springtime, the only pretty ringtime,
When birds do sing, hey ding a ding, ding.
Sweet lovers love the spring.

(V. iii. 24–35)

Carpe diem, 'take the present time', they sing, although the present time
in another perspective is not worth much in contrast with 'the antique
world' (II. iii. 57). All these perspectives are there, and all in some sense
valid. Yet all these perspectives are somehow contained within a sense
of 'unmeasured time', of a poetic world in which time does not matter;
as Orlando remarks, 'there's no clock in the forest' (III. ii. 284).

The forest of Arden is a timeless world beset by time, framed within
a play that begins and ends with 'the pompous court' (V. iv. 176). It is
also a world pervaded by a sense of time in its many aspects, and
central to all these is the image embodied in Jaques' great speech on the
seven ages of man. For although this is refuted in its immediate application by the arrival of the good old Adam, it nevertheless embodies a
central truth in the play. From the perspective of the young, life is but
a flower, to be plucked and enjoyed before it fades; from the point of
view of Touchstone, the passage of time by the clock merely illustrates
how men ripen and then rot; and time is also the immediate present,
that hurries or passes slowly according to mood and occasion. Only
Jaques in his speech presents an image of the span of life, in which 'one
man in his time plays many parts'; and the part of lover, so central in
the play, recedes to become one of the many. The action of *As You
Like It* is, so to speak, contained within the larger action suggested in
this speech, that play of life in the theatre of the world in which all men
have to act in ways conditioned by life not art.[3]

3 For an interesting account of other aspects of the relation of Jaques to time,
and of the way in which Jaques sees himself as a historian objectively chronicling
the life of man, see the recent study of *Shakespeare and the Nature of Time* by
Frederick Turner (Oxford, 1971), especially pp. 35–44. Duke Senior is clearly
also a 'mature' character in terms of age, but as a character he is little more than a
figurehead monarch, a cypher, as nothing in him is questioned: he is not
'mature' in the fuller sense developed here.

What Jaques represents here is a voice of maturity. It is not that he is 'right'; indeed, he is no more right than others, and all the perspectives on time are authentic. The point is rather that, although he is mocked on all sides as 'Monsieur Melancholy', Jaques carries a curious authority of voice, an authority derived from the sense he conveys of being mature, of being able to look at what is around him with a humorous detachment, of offering the voice of experience. He has been a sensual libertine at some time, if we can believe Duke Senior, and has evidently outgrown this, to act a part not listed in the roles he describes in his speech, that of intelligent, sometimes satirical, and generally compassionate observer, not so clever as to avoid mockery himself, nor so satirical as ever to suggest bitterness, but sane and reasonable.

II

Another voice of 'cool reason' (V. i. 6) is that of Theseus in *A Midsummer Night's Dream*. At the beginning of the play he looks forward to his marriage with Hippolyta, which is due to take place in four days' time; the throes of courtship are over, and his occupation now is to pass the time agreeably until the wedding. As Duke of Athens he has some slight function in the plot, to judge the cause of Egeus, complaining against his daughter Hermia, in the opening scene, and to act as general patron at the end, but this does not explain why he is given the finest and most memorable speech in the play. Indeed, as in Act I he is stirring up 'the Athenian youth to merriments' (I. i. 12), to make the time pass quickly until the wedding, so in Act V, the marriage completed, he is calling for further entertainment:

> What masques, what dances shall we have,
> To wear away this long age of three hours
> Between our after-supper and bed-time?
>
> (V. i. 32–4)

The voice of Theseus is, however, not that of a bored Duke amusing himself, but that of a ruler, magisterial, intelligent, and also compassionate:

> Lovers and madmen have such seething brains,
> Such shaping fantasies, that apprehend
> More than cool reason ever comprehends.
> The lunatic, the lover, and the poet

Are of imagination all compact.
One sees more devils than vast Hell can hold,
That is the madman. The lover, all as frantic,
Sees Helen's beauty in a brow of Egypt.
The poet's eye, in a fine frenzy rolling,
Doth glance from heaven to earth, from earth to
    heaven,
And as imagination bodies forth
The forms of things unknown, the poet's pen
Turns them to shapes, and gives to airy nothing
A local habitation and a name.

(V. i. 4-17)

The speech is palpable poetry, the climax in some ways of Shakespeare's
own 'frenzy' in giving body to 'the forms of things unknown' in this
play; but within the imagined vision, the 'dream' of the play's title, he has
created a spokesman for 'cool reason' who nevertheless speaks the most
magical verse in the play. This paradox is exemplified further in the
presentation of the 'tedious brief scene' of Pyramus and Thisbe by
Bottom and his crew. The newly married lovers, Lysander and Hermia,
Demetrius and Helena, join Theseus and Hippolyta to watch the play.
Only a short time before, we have seen them 'frantic' with love, and
mad in quarrel, so that Puck, looking on, remarked,

Cupid is a knavish lad,
Thus to make poor females mad;

(III. ii. 440-41)

but now they view the antics of the cast in the play-within-the-play
critically. They are restored to reason, and enjoy with a rather superior
and mocking detachment the buffoonery which turns tragedy to farce
before their eyes.

Their comments on the play of Pyramus fill in the gaps in the action,
and their consciousness that they are watching a play extends the
consciousness of the larger audience in the theatre. Hippolyta under-
standably regards the dialogue between Pyramus, Thisbe and Wall as
the 'silliest stuff' she ever heard, but Theseus sees more deeply that 'the
best in this kind are but shadows; and the worst no worse, if imagination amend them' (V. i. 208). Theseus and Hippolyta, the best in this
kind, are but shadows, as Puck reminds us in his Epilogue,

If we shadows have offended,
Think but this, and all is mended,

> That you have but slumbered here
> While these visions did appear.
>
> (V. i. 412–15)

The characters are all shadows, all part of the dream, and by analogy we, the audience, may be shadows too, acting out our parts on the stage of life (as in the image of Jaques). At the same time, the 'strange and admirable' things wrought by the imagination deserve attention. It is not merely that the 'Hard-handed men' labouring to present their playlet are doing their best to compliment Theseus their Duke, so that, as he says, 'in courtesy, in all reason, we must stay the time' (V. i. 247); their play suffices, in another curious phrase he uses, to 'ease the anguish of a torturing hour' (V. i. 37). It is the highest reach of their imaginations, and in kind belongs with the loftier art to which Theseus and we are more accustomed. It is unreal, shadows, silly stuff, yet real, and necessary to ease anguish, to pass the time. The shadows we see are substantial, and these actors in their fumbling way are trying to reach towards what is expressed by the dance and song of the Fairies at the end, blessing the bride-beds, and promising,

> So shall all the couples three
> Ever true in loving be.
>
> (V. i. 396–7)

Here art, the shadows or dreams embodied in the poet's fantasies, becomes a symbol for a possible order, a harmony, a control over our lives, that we can imagine but cannot achieve.

This vision seems to go beyond reason, and to spring from

> Such shaping fantasies, that apprehend
> More than cool reason ever comprehends.

Yet reason is the agent of control and order in life, as imagination is in art; it is Theseus who bridges the two, reminding us of the need for reason, to moderate and order folly in society, to subdue love to the ceremony of marriage, and to criticize firmly if courteously the inadequacies of the play-within-the-play. The paradox embodied in the dream is that the voice of reason is necessary. Although he is presumably young, like the other lovers, Theseus speaks with authority, and, like Jaques, represents a mature stance. Also like Jaques, he is very conscious of time, not in terms of the immediate present, which is the concern of the lovers, or the indefinite and timeless vista open to the fairies, but rather in terms of demarcating his life, four days to the wedding, three hours between supper and bedtime, a fortnight of honeymoon 'revels and new jollity' (V. i. 359), and then—presumably a return to the workaday round of social obligations and responsibilities. Plays may open up a vision or dream that is out of time, but the voice of reason knows they can only last for a brief interval of entertainment, in which 'we must stay the time', that they are sandwiched between supper and bedtime, as a recreation from the real business of life, here marriage and consummation.

III

Theseus, like Jaques, has his limitations. He has no 'shaping fantasies', not even such a vision as is opened to Bottom in his 'dream', and he recognizes that there are things inaccessible to 'cool reason'. Both characters nevertheless speak with a voice of reason and maturity, and offer what seems to be a necessary corrective to the golden world of lovers. They remind us of the exigencies of time, and set the moment of love or courtship in relation to a larger perspective on life. In these two plays, which involve us directly in worlds of fantasy, in which shepherds from classical pastoral are to be found, and fairies from folklore and Ovidian legend roam at night, voices such as those of Jaques and Theseus may seem to be especially needed. However, I think these two figures also represent a development to a high level of artistry of what is elsewhere a complicating and important feature of Shakespeare's mature comedies.

Most of the comedies have threats of discord or death to set off the harmony and joy with which they end; this is a commonplace, but points to a more sophisticated level of imaginative activity, as represented perhaps by the ending of *Love's Labour's Lost*. Here Armado presents what he calls a 'dialogue' in praise of the owl and the cuckoo, dividing his singers so that one side represents winter, the other spring. The song of spring is naturally a song of love, but in this case the refrain celebrates the cuckoo, the cuckold's bird.

> When daisies pied and violets blue
>   And lady-smocks all silver-white
> And cuckoo-buds of yellow hue
>   Do paint the meadows with delight,

> The cuckoo then, on every tree,
> Mocks married men; for thus sings he,
>> Cuckoo;
> Cuckoo, cuckoo: O word of fear,
> Unpleasing to a married ear!

The song of winter recalls chiefly the harshness of the season, at which the owl stares, singing nightly, ' "Tu-Whit, Tu-Who"—A merry note'

> When icicles hang by the wall.
>> And Dick the shepherd blows his nail,
> And Tom bears logs into the hall,
>> And milk comes frozen home in pail,
> When blood is nipp'd, and ways be foul,
> Then nightly sings the staring owl,
>> Tu-whit;
> Tu-who, a merry note,
> While greasy Joan doth keel the pot.

The delights of spring, the season of love, turn into the sound of the cuckoo mocking married men, while the discomforts of winter are offset by the merry sound of the owl. These songs do not, in other words, present a simple contrast;[4] the cuckoo's mocking voice tempers the season of youth and ardour, but he overdoes it, as not all marriages end in cuckoldry; while the owl—emblem of gravity, age, and a suspect, even foolish, wisdom, for he is blind by daylight—enlivens the season of dull chores, frost and coughing. The cuckoo and the owl have, so to speak, seen it all before; their songs within the songs suggest an ironic detachment, and the 'dialogue' of spring and winter contains within itself hints of those paradoxes and conflicting perspectives developed much more fully in Jaques and Theseus. It is not a matter merely of simple oppositions, the owl versus the cuckoo, age versus youth, winter versus spring, wisdom versus folly, but a much more complex vision in which all are necessary, and counterbalance one another, and in which the wisdom of age may be just as vulnerable and as subject to mockery as the folly of youth. In the world of romantic comedy, in

---

[4] These songs are often treated as a delightful but gratuitous addition by Shakespeare to the play, but their importance in the design of Love's Labour's Lost, and the perspectives they suggest, have been explored by Cyrus Hoy in The Hyancinth Room (1964), pp. 35-8; see also Anne Righter's (Bobbyann Roesen's) essay in Shakespeare Quarterly IV (1953), pp. 411-26.

E

which courtship, the sense of flowering and of release involved in love and wooing is central, a necessary counterbalance is provided by figures like Jaques and Theseus, who represent, in a much more sophisticated and complicated way, the combined ironic stances of the cuckoo and the owl.

IV

In relation to this, *Much Ado About Nothing* is especially interesting. In some ways it resembles *Love's Labour's Lost*, which presents a group of witty and intelligent courtiers as lovers, and makes its prominent older characters, like Armado, fools. So in *Much Ado*, Benedick and Beatrice, though nominally contributing the subplot, in fact steal the show, as the early recording of their names as a title for the play suggest they always did.[5] Shakespeare needed no figure here like Jaques or Theseus, for these central characters themselves are mature, in the sense that they embody a stance of wit or intelligence.

Hero and Claudio are regarded commonly as rather shadowy figures. This is understandable, since Claudio talks in commonplaces of love, which in consequence seems not to be deeply felt, and Hero accepts without demur her social role as one of obedience to her father, which is to say that she is wooed by proxy, and accepts Claudio in silence. This is not to say their love is insincere; for convention and artifice may be vehicles for sincere feeling. Sincerity is not an issue. It is rather that social conventions and outward appearances are of primary importance to Claudio, the young protégé of Don Pedro, Prince of Aragon. He woos Hero in public, by means of the Prince as intermediary; when he thinks her false, he denounces her in public, before the company assembled in church for his wedding. There is a deep irony in his speech as her rejects her, for he has only been concerned himself with 'exterior shows':

> There, Leonato, take her back again,
> Give not this rotten orange to your friend,

[5] Shakespeare's company was paid in 1613 for the performance at Court of a play called 'Benedicte and Betteris', and if this cannot certainly be identified as *Much Ado* (see E. K. Chambers, *William Shakespeare. A Study of Facts and Problems*, Oxford, 1930, II. 343), there seems to be no doubt that King Charles I thought of the play in terms of these characters and wrote their names as a subtitle in his copy of the 1632 Folio of Shakespeare's plays (see J. O. Halliwell-Phillipps, *Outlines of the Life of Shakespeare*, London, 1885, p. 262).

She's but the sign and semblance of her honour.
Behold how like a maid she blushes here!
Oh, what authority and show of truth
Can cunning sin cover itself withal!
Comes not that blood as modest evidence
To witness simple virtue? Would you not swear,
All you that see her, that she were a maid,
By these exterior shows? But she is none.

(IV. i. 30–39)

It was her beauty that attracted him in the first place, and he has never, in the action of the play, sought to look beneath the surface to Hero as a person, so that he is as easily persuaded by what he sees, or thinks he sees, to regard her as a whore. It is appropriate that he should perform a public penance at what appears to be the tomb of Hero, when he is made to believe she is dead, and that he should agree without question to marry the niece Leonato promises to produce, 'were she an Ethiope' (V. iv. 38). He is marrying this time out of a sense of duty and honour, to make public restitution to Leonato, but is naturally delighted to have the living Hero restored to him. Once her name is cleared, her image changes to appear as when he first saw her, and saw only beauty:

Sweet Hero, now thy image doth appear
In the rare semblance that I loved it first.

(V. i. 237–8)

Benedick and Beatrice contrast in their love with Hero and Claudio. The merry war of words between them shows them to be deeply engaged with one another. In spite of their apparent scorn of each other, and of the idea of marriage, a kind of electricity flows between them from their first appearance. They each talk about the other when not talking to one another, and their conscious speech signals even while it superficially denies what one can fairly call their unconscious feelings. The plot of Don Pedro to bring them 'into a mountain of affection the one with the other' (II. i. 330) only makes them recognize and acknowledge what is already clear to the audience, that they are in love. The point is that their involvement with one another is private, not public—so private that they attempt to conceal it from themselves beneath a façade of wit. By being brought to admit it publicly, both of these mockers lay themselves open temporarily to the mockery of others; but they recover their poise brilliantly by the end, in their final acceptance of one another:

> *Benedick:* Come, I will have thee, but, by this light, I take thee for pity.
> *Beatrice:* I would not deny you, but, by this good day I yield upon great persuasion, and partly to save your life, for I was told you were in a consumption.
> *Benedick:* Peace! I will stop your mouth.
>
> (V. iv. 92-7)

In writing of their love, their hands witness against their hearts that it is genuine, yet they will go to the altar protesting they do so merely for 'pity'. Their wit controls their passion, whereas the love of Hero and Claudio is controlled by the conventions of society.

Benedick and Beatrice seem to act as free agents, although they are tricked into revealing their love. This freedom, expressed in the lively play of intelligence in their dialogue, makes them, as Benedick says, 'too wise to woo peaceably' (V. ii. 63), but also protects Beatrice from foolish suitors, and enables each of them to find a worthy partner. The depth of their love is guaranteed by their free and intelligent acknowledgement of it, and it is nonetheless sincere for their ability to joke about it; indeed, they provide a perspective in which the ordinary 'romantic' protestations of Claudio seem feeble. Wit has its limitations, as it can be cruel, and it might be seen as disabling Benedick and Beatrice from recognizing their love; they have to be brought into a 'romantic' frame of mind, like that of Claudio and Hero, as expressed in Beatrice's rhymed couplets at the end of III. i, and in Benedick shaving his beard, changing his costume, and rushing to get a picture of Beatrice. The point is that the witty poise they begin from, and only lose in flashes that reveal the strength of their feelings, includes and transcends such a relationship as Claudio and Hero can hope for.

For their wit is a mark not only of their freedom and equality, but of their understanding of their limitations, and a high degree of self-control: they do not take themselves too seriously. This sense of proportion or balance in them makes us recognize in them a voice of reason in this play; they seem mature to the extent that they are in command of themselves. It is instructive to relate them to another witty heroine, Rosalind in *As You Like It*. She too is generally in command of herself: while acknowledging to Celia how many fathoms deep she is in love, she never loses herself in her passion, and though she reflects Touchstone's description of a true lover to the extent that she 'runs into strange capers', in flirting with Orlando for example, she alone avoids the 'folly' of love. This is brought out especially in V. ii, where she joins the band of passionate lovers in their choric complaint:

> *Phebe:* Good shepherd, tell this youth what 'tis to love.
> *Silvius:* It is to be all made of sighs and tears,
>   And so am I for Phebe.
> *Phebe:* And I for Ganymede.
> *Orlando:* And I for Rosalind.
> *Rosalind:* And I for no woman.
>
>   (V. ii. 76–81)

She makes one of the group of foolish lovers, but mocks them from her disguise, 'And I for no woman', and in the end dismisses them: ''tis like the howling of Irish wolves against the moon'.

Yet this position of ascendancy is barely maintained by Rosalind in the action, because she has no worthy foil, no Benedick-figure, but only Orlando, who is so love-sick that he mars the trees of the forests by hanging bad poems on them addressed to

> The fair, the chaste, the unexpressive she.
>
>   (III. ii. 10)

Rosalind is 'unexpressive', or inexpressible, ineffable—she transcends the possiblity of expression, yet he does nothing but seek to express her, in verses justly mocked by Touchstone. Orlando, thus 'love-shak'd' as he says, can only act for much of the time as a kind of fall-guy to Rosalind, who teases him from behind her disguise. It takes a good actress to prevent Rosalind in consequence from seeming sentimental or arch. It is only through her disguise that she can maintain her witty stance, and it is no concealment of her true sex to the audience; otherwise she would appear as she really is, 'love-shak'd' like Orlando, for she admits to Celia

> I cannot be out of the sight of Orlando. I'll go find a shadow, and sigh till he come.   (IV. i. 193)

Rosalind's self-command is precarious, and sustained by her disguise; Beatrice and Benedick are, so to speak, free in themselves, and do not need such support as a disguise to enable them to maintain a stance.[6]

[6] My argument here runs counter to the well-known generalizations about comedy made by Northrop Frye in his essay 'The Argument of Comedy',

They support one another, being alike in their independence, and together provide a sense of proportion and maturity in the play; *As You Like It* needs a Jaques, whereas a Dogberry is sufficient in *Much Ado About Nothing*.

Dogberry and Verges can be seen as functioning in various ways in the play. It may be said, for instance, that Shakespeare uses them as lightning conductors, delaying the entrance of his clowns until the middle of Act III in order to surround with comic action the denunciation of Hero in church in IV. i, and so both set off and mitigate the emotional effect of the savagery of Claudio. The most notable feature of Dogberry and Verges, nevertheless, is their misuse of words. In this they are opposite to Benedick and Beatrice, who are notable for their control of words, their skill in using them. Indeed, they delight in their skill so much that they play with words, concealing their true feelings, and each is tricked into acknowledging love by overhearing praise of the other, by 'noting', in the punning sense of the title.[7] In a similar way, Dogberry and Verges overhear Conrade and Borachio talking, and learn the truth about the plot against Hero. Dogberry and Verges may in this way be seen as parodying in their incompetence with language the wit of Beatrice and Benedick; they also reflect in a distorting mirror the part played by 'noting' in bringing out the truth, for their inability to grasp the significance of what they overhear contrasts with the immediate understanding of Benedick and Beatrice. To this extent Dogberry and Verges reinforce the supremacy of Benedick and Beatrice in the play.

---

published in *English Institute Essays* (1948), and reprinted in L. Lerner, *Shakespeare's Comedies. An Anthology of Modern Criticism* (London, 1967), pp. 315–25. There he says that in the 'essential comic resolution', a 'normal individual is freed from the bonds of a humorous society, and a normal society is freed from the bonds imposed on it by humorous individuals'. This is too simple, in my view; the challenge for Benedick and Beatrice is to retain their essential freedom, while submitting to the restrictions necessary to maintain society, in their case the bonds of love and marriage. For further comment on this general point, see p. 141 below and the Introduction to my Arden edition of *The Comedy of Errors* (London, 1962), pp. xlix–l.

7 The word 'Nothing' in the title carries a quibble on 'noting', meaning 'observing', and refers to a dramatic action in which what is seen or overheard, and often misunderstood, plays a central part. The reverberations of the word have been explored by Paul Jorgensen in *Redeeming Shakespeare's Words* (Berkeley, Calif., 1962), pp. 2–42.

These two acknowledge their love, which is put to a tough test after the supposed death of Hero, when Beatrice demands that Benedick kill Claudio, so forcing him to choose between the demands of friendship and of love. However, the predominant impression they convey is one of wit, an intelligent mastery of language indicating an ability to master themselves; wit in this sense is a mark of freedom and consequently of character, for character is revealed in modes of being or becoming self-aware. Wit is also here a mark of maturity, of a stance more deserving of respect than others in the play. One other figure to be noted in this connection is Don Pedro. The Prince of Aragon appears to be young, presumably of an age with Claudio and Benedick. He woos Hero on behalf of Claudio, and at one point offers himself to Beatrice, as she jests about her lack of a husband:

> Beatrice: Hath your Grace ne'er a brother like you? Your father got
>   excellent husbands, if a maid could come by them.
> Don Pedro: Will you have me, lady?
> Beatrice: No, my lord, unless I might have another for working days.
>   Your Grace is too costly to wear every day.   (II. i. 291–6)

Although Beatrice goes on to beg pardon for speaking all mirth and no matter, it is not clear whether Don Pedro is merely jesting himself. At the very least, it is noteworthy that he readily offers to play the part of lover and woo Hero, so that Claudio is easily persuaded into jealousy, and that he proposes marriage to Beatrice; he may mock Benedick as 'the married man' at the end, but Benedick has the last word, and there is an edge to it: 'Prince, thou art sad; get thee a wife, get thee a wife' (V. iv. 118). Don Pedro seems to have leanings towards marriage, but remains a lonely figure, left 'sad' or serious amid all the merriment of the ending. As a prince he has dignity, and carries authority, though he shares with Claudio the stigma of too easily believing Hero to be a 'common stale'. He remains a background figure, though often on stage, marked chiefly perhaps by his loneliness; he woos and makes intrigues for others, and is left 'sad' at the end. In this he is reminiscent of Antonio in *The Merchant of Venice*, who begins 'sad', and remains alone among the merry couples (Lorenzo and Jessica, Gratiano and Nerissa, Bassanio and Portia) and the end. In this play Portia, improbably transmuted into an expert lawyer, speaks with the voice of maturity, but like Beatrice and Benedick in *Much Ado*, she is paired off among the marrying couples at the end; and Antonio, like Don Pedro, remains a solitary figure, sharing

in the last scene something of this aspect of Jaques. Like him, they are
not for dancing measures, but represent a slightly discordant element,
something unsatisfied, a pattern not fully resolved, a winter note among
springtime delights more than faintly troubling our pleasure in the joy
of satisfied lovers.

V

In *Twelfth Night* the note of discord is sharper and more insistent,
and the voices of reason or maturity are less secure, so that the overall
effect is of a curiously muted gaiety. It may seem odd to propose Sir
Toby as one voice of maturity early in the play, but he is the effective
centre of the group consisting of Maria, Fabian, Feste, and Sir Andrew
Aguecheek. Sir Toby sponges on Sir Andrew, yet at the same time
provides him with an occupation (wooing Olivia), and, so far as it is
possible, may be seen as educating him. Sir Andrew, a natural fool,
thinks he is witty, and sets off the true wit of Sir Toby, for whom he
provides matter. The finest scene of the early part of the play is II. iii,
in which Sir Toby and his companions create a night of misrule in their
drinking and boisterous singing. Feste's song, 'O mistress mine', a
'carpe diem' plea that

Youth's a stuff will not endure,

(II. iii. 51)

is contradicted by Sir Toby, who *makes* it endure. He is often presented
as old, and, as Olivia's uncle, must be rather older than the lovers in the
play, Orsino, Olivia, Viola and Sebastian, who all presumably share
Orsino's 'fresh and stainless youth' (I. v. 243). It is only in contrast to
their youth that Sir Toby seems old, and part of his attractiveness lies
in his ability to make the gaiety of youth last, as he ends, indeed, by
marrying Maria.

In this scene Feste's song and Sir Toby's gaiety also contradict the
stubborn silliness of Olivia's determination to mourn seven years for
the death of her brother. Malvolio's intervention here is thus especially
unsympathetic. For Malvolio, who alone despises folly—the folly that
reveals itself as wit in the 'admirable fooling' of Sir Toby, and in the
wry comments of Feste—emerges as a fool himself in his solemnity.
He has a point in attempting to stop the 'caterwauling' of Sir Toby and
Feste, and enters as a messenger from Olivia and a representative of

rule, order, and civility; but Olivia's sobriety, her mourning, has been shown as rather absurd, and Malvolio we know is 'sick of self-love' (I. v. 85), and hates festivity in itself out of an intolerant sense of his own superiority. He may be right, but he takes himself too seriously, lacks a sense of humour, and is properly put down by Sir Toby's famous rebuke: 'Dost thou think because thou art virtuous, there shall be no more cakes and ale?' (II. iii. 108). 'Virtue' without good humour, generosity of spirit, or tolerance, deserves no better.

Thus far what Malvolio calls Sir Toby's 'disorders' and 'uncivil rule' seem no great matter, but as the action develops they erupt into cruelty and violence. Maria's plot to make Malvolio suppose Olivia is in love with him succeeds brilliantly, and hilariously, for as long as Malvolio preens himself in his own self-importance, or mortifies his flesh by smiling and wearing cross-garters, he is simply exposing his own folly in imagining that his mistress, sworn to seven years' grief, could look affectionately on him, and so punishes himself. Such grotesque behaviour makes him appear to be afflicted with what Olivia calls 'midsummer madness' (III. iv. 53), and she consigns him to Sir Toby's charge. At this point Sir Toby begins to carry the jest too far, by treating Malvolio literally as mad, shutting him in a dark room, and devising new ways to torment him. He and Maria relentlessly pursue the joke, ignoring Fabian's warning:

> *Maria:* Nay, pursue him now, lest the device take air and taint.
> *Fabian:* Why, we shall make him mad indeed.
> *Maria:* The house will be the quieter.
> *Sir Toby:* Come, we'll have him in a dark room and bound. My niece is already in the belief that he's mad. We may carry it thus, for our pleasure and his penance, till our very pastime, tired out of breath, prompt us to have mercy on him.   (III. iv. 125–33)

To make Malvolio mad indeed would go far beyond Sir Toby's intention, but by his refusal to 'rule' and limit the jest, by his desire to go on till their 'pastime, tired out of breath' yields to mercy, he risks that possibility.

Sir Toby also pushes through his device to make Sir Andrew fight a duel with Viola disguised as Cesario. When the two unwilling swordsmen are first brought face to face (in III. iv), Antonio chances to come by, and would have intervened to fight with Sir Toby, but that he is promptly arrested by the Duke's officers. This warning of how easily

the jest might turn sour, and a mock-fight become a real one, goes
unheeded by Sir Toby and Fabian, who press Sir Andrew to encounter
the 'paltry boy' Cesario once more. The result is real violence, as they
meet with Sebastian in error; the appearance of Sir Andrew with a
'bloody coxcomb', and Sir Toby, also wounded, in the final scene has
an element of shock about it. Although no great harm is done, blood
has been shed, and Malvolio's earlier criticisms of Sir Toby's 'misrule'
come home vividly. Sir Toby's pursuit of a jest in defiance of all
restraint leads him (like his unrestrained drinking) into folly, and folly
turns into madness, into anger, violence, the disturbance of order.

It is tempting to see in the play varieties of folly set against the
'wisdom' of the professional fool, Feste. Orsino, prostrated by love for an
idealized Olivia, shows his folly from the opening scene; he is in love
with the idea of being in love, and affects a melancholy that strains
against his youth and vigour. He likes to feed his mood with music,
notably in Feste's song 'Come away, come away, death', which
carries to the extravagant conclusion of a lonely grave the metaphor
'I am slain by a fair cruel maid', and so conveys a sense that Orsino's
passion is a waste of time, an absurdity, a rejection of life. Feste proves
Olivia a fool to mourn for her brother, and Viola too, though in some
ways like Rosalind in her self-command, is foolish in love, idolizing
the Duke who thinks her a boy.

The folly of love can pass also into madness, as is suggested when
Olivia rushes Sebastian into marriage. To him, the doting Olivia seems
at first so extraordinary, the 'accident and flood of fortune' he meets with
in Illyria so odd, that he thinks he must be dreaming, or else mad:

> Yet doth this accident and flood of fortune
> So far exceed all instance, all discourse,
> That I am ready to distrust mine eyes
> And wrangle with my reason, that persuades me
> To any other trust but that I am mad,
> Or else the Lady's mad.
>
> (IV. iii. 11–16)

Olivia does not in fact know whom she is marrying in such haste, and
while welcoming his good fortune readily enough, Sebastian makes the
point for the audience that love too can become a kind of lunacy. This
parallels the other forms of madness; Malvolio appears mad in his folly,
and is shut up in a dark room and bound—and Sir Toby's pursuit of a

joke beyond reasonable limits leads to a madness of anger, to fighting, and to bloodshed.

Order, balance, harmony, are precariously maintained, and in relation to these varieties of folly and madness, Feste is not established simply as a representative of wisdom. For although Shakespeare pulls Feste out of an involvement in the garden-scene, in which Malvolio finds Maria's letter (II. v.), and substitutes, both here and in the plot to make Sir Andrew and Viola fight, the figure of Fabian, Feste neverthe-less joins Sir Toby in baiting Malvolio in II. iii, torments him again in IV. ii, in the guise of the curate Sir Topas, and gloats over his discomfiture at the end. Feste comes near to being vindictive, to persecuting Malvolio, and all because of a petty and typically humourless remark. It is Feste who mocks him to the last, and who draws from Malvolio his bitter exit-line:

> Clown: Why, 'some are born great, some achieve greatness, and some have greatness thrown upon them'. I was one, sir, in this interlude; one Sir Topas, sir. But that's all one. 'By the Lord, fool, I am not mad.' But do you remember? 'Madam, why laugh you at such a barren rascal? An you smile not, he's gagged.' And thus the whirligig of time brings in his revenges.
> Malvolio: I'll be revenged on the whole pack of you.
>
> (V. i. 357–64)

Malvolio can be seen as a scapegoat, embodying bad qualities in his lack of humour, his solemnity, his hostility to festivity and joy, and sym-bolically expelled here from the society of Illyria, so enhancing the joy of the ending. At the same time, he is punished beyond his deserts, to the point of injury, and if the whirligig of time brings its revenges for Feste, so it may for Malvolio. He seems in many ways life-denying, but festivity itself leads to folly, drunkenness, quarrelling and madness; and in tormenting him, his persecutors begin to show the same lack of feeling, of charity, for which they condemn him.

The ending of the play is very complex, as the comic butt becomes pathetic, and makes his tormentors, especially Feste, appear inhuman. This may be one reason why, after Duke Orsino's short and conven-tional final speech, Shakespeare leaves Feste to sing what is a kind of epilogue. The theme of this song is the passage of time; it compresses into five four-line stanzas something analogous to Jaques' speech on the seven ages of man, here reduced to four, the 'little tiny boy', 'man's estate', marriage and old age. The predominant impression it gives is of folly, knavery and drunkenness, in a world that goes on much the same; but the vague melancholy of the words is counteracted by the gaiety of the song as sung to music. The words put the immediate action of the play into a long perspective, 'A great while ago the world begun', and the last stanza goes on to withdraw us into a position of detachment from the play, one of a repertory performed daily:

> A great while ago the world begun,
>   With hey, ho, the wind and the rain,
> But that's all one, our play is done,
>   And we'll strive to please you every day.

Feste makes us aware not only that the action of the play concerns only a brief part of life, wooing and wiving, but also that the play itself has been a brief entertainment in a workaday world.

What the song offers, in other words, is a voice of maturity. It links with other songs and sayings of Feste, with his consciousness of time and death, with his exposure of cant, and with his awareness that 'Foolery, sir, does walk about the orb like the sun—it shines everywhere' (III. i. 36). It is a voice gay in spite of an undercurrent of sadness, resigned and tolerant in acceptance and understanding, mocking and ironical, yet at the same time earnest, rising to moments of wisdom, but not escaping the passion and folly it is aware of in others, and above all, conscious of the swift flow of time. Feste is Shakespeare's final development in the comedies of the compassionate observer; in his persecution of Malvolio, he becomes involved in the very intolerance he derides, so that he does not speak with a simple moral authority, but rather as a sane, mature, if vulnerable figure, providing what I think is a necessary counterbalance in romantic comedies to the spectacle of lovers, rushing together in the 'very wrath of love', as Rosalind describes Celia and Oliver, or overwhelmed in other ways by their passion, bursting forth like Orsino,

> With adorations, fertile tears,
> With groans that thunder love, with sighs of fire.
>
> (I. v. 239–40)

The voice of cool reason disengages us from the sentiment, and makes us aware simultaneously of the sweetness, the transitoriness, the folly, and the importance of love; and, in the comments of Jaques, Touchstone, and Feste especially, there is conveyed too a sharp sense of the pressure of time, and the brevity of life, adding an ironic complexity to comedies that end in the joyful assurance of love harmonized in marriage.

In other words, the voices of maturity remind us of the world of time outside the play, of the necessary return to social responsibilities that lies beyond courtship, and beyond the joyous but temporary freedoms of Illyria or Arden. These voices urge against the notion of release, of festive comedy, and against Northrop Frye's conception of comedy as liberation from moral and social norms,[8] an insistent counterpoint: the argument of Shakespeare's comedies is the richer for their presence.

[8] In *Shakespeare's Festive Comedy* (Princeton, 1959), C. L. Barber emphasizes Shakespeare's dramatization of 'love's intensity as the release of a festive moment', and says, 'His comedies present experience entirely polarized by saturnalia; there is little *within* the play to qualify that perspective' (pp. 238-9, 1966 edn.). For Northrop Frye's argument, see note 6 above.

VII

Shakespeare's Fools: The Shadow and the Substance of Drama

GARETH LLOYD EVANS

I

IN recent years increased attention has been paid by criticism to Shakespeare's Fools. This increase was, doubtless, fired by the excellently detailed and imaginatively presented work of Enid Welsford[1] which showed the vast antecedents of the character both in art forms and in real life, and suggested its importance to a full understanding of the nature of Shakespeare's imagination. Later, Robert Goldsmith[2] dealt shrewdly with the contradictory nature of the Fool—the contrapuntal effects of his drollery and sage comment. One of the most recent books takes the study a stage further. William Willeford[3] discusses, in both philosophical and psychological terms, the nature of folly and the significance of the relationship of the Fool to the actor and his audience.

The scope of the area for research is well indicated by recalling Leslie Hotson's[4] intricately clever work on the meaning of the word 'motley' and what it implies about the dress of real Fools and their status in royal and noble households. Hotson provided valuable pointers to yet another aspect of study—the nature and status of real Fools in history. At the time of writing, no such study, on a comprehensive basis, has yet appeared. If and when it does far greater attention than hitherto will have to be paid to sources other than literary; the evidence capable of being supplied by the social historian and the art historian is likely to prove immensely valuable in attempting to establish the place

---

[1] Enid Welsford, *The Fool: His Social and Literary History* (London, 1935).
[2] Robert Hillis Goldsmith, *Wise Fools in Shakespeare* (Michigan, 1955; Liverpool, 1958).
[3] William Willeford, *The Fool and His Sceptre* (London, 1969).
[4] Leslie Hotson, *Shakespeare's Motley* (London, 1952).

of real Fools in their society and their relationships with the various forms of entertainment in the early and late medieval periods.

For, indeed, with this figure, the student of Shakespeare is faced with the intriguing fact that an apparently fictional type has an accredited reality. Any Shakespeare Fool has (and there is perhaps a touch of wry irony here) a far more clearly definable and recognizable source than, say, Lear, or any other of Shakespeare's great characters whose 'historical' reality is so shadowy. The student also confronts the unique fact that the realization of the Fool figures on the Elizabethan stage was entrusted to a man who had a unique knowledge of real Fools. Robert Armin, who played Touchstone, Feste, Lear's unnamed Fool and Lavache, knew far more about their typical antecedents than Burbage did of the originals of the parts he played—Lear, Macbeth, Othello and Hamlet. It might, in passing, also be timely to record that Armin knew the difference between true Fools and clown figures like Gobbo far more clearly than many modern directors of Shakespeare's plays who, following a passing mode, seem to wish to put every zany into motley.

Armin serves to remind us that the study of the relationship of the actor to his role has been a marked preoccupation of twentieth-century thinking and writing on theatre matters. What happens to Olivier when he is Macbeth, or to Gielgud become King Lear? Most actors (but strangely fewer actresses) of quality have, in the past few decades, questioned deeply into the nature of their own personalities. It should perhaps not be surprising in a century in which psychology has drifted and sprayed its effects into almost every corner of existence, to find actors particularly prone to be magnetized by the kind of anwers that a probing into the unconscious might reveal. After all, not only is psychology a wonderful boost to the ego but it must be very beguiling to consider the nature of a man whose professional function is not to be himself. Has a chameleon a personality?

The implications of this preoccupation are many, and an indication of the extent to which it can exercise not only the minds of actors but also the modes of directors is Peter Brook's much-hailed production of *A Midsummer Night's Dream* (Straftord-upon-Avon 1970, London 1971). As is customary in an age of shifty and shifting values, the production's importance was over-rated. Phrases more applicable to the plastic enormities of technological discovery like 'break-through' and 'new horizons' were used to evaluate what was an extremely competent display of directorial ingenuity. The truly remarkable fact about the production was, however, its adroit use of a Shakespeare play to illustrate the twentieth-century preoccupation with the nature of the relationship between actor and role. For example, all the actors quite deliberately stepped out of character when they were not required to be an integral part of the spoken or visual action and watched (in their own 'real' personalities as it were) what was happening. It was like the chinese box, and the whole affair very germane to the preoccupation under discussion—partly because the audience wondered how much the non-acting postures that were taken up were, indeed, yet another layer of illusion. Brook's procedure (a sort of anglicized version of alienation) would impose far less strain on an audience's credibilities when the play is a comedy than when it is in any other mode. For an actor, on stage, as himself, to laugh at the antics of his colleagues playing parts and then, in turn, to be laughed at himself, seems curiously right. Yet, for an actor, on stage, as himself, to watch, for example, the murder of Lady Macduff which he set in motion in his role of Macbeth, seems curiously wrong.

Comedy invokes less identification from an audience than does tragedy. In fact, comedy depends for its effects upon a certain distancing. It requires a barely realized mental posture of superiority so that there can be a full deployment of that element that causes us to laugh. If tragedy induces the feeling—'there but for the grace of God and art go I'—then comedy involves the response—'catch me doing or saying that'.

II

If a study of his plays did not convince us that Shakespeare was, in a very direct sense, concerned about the relationship between actor and role, then a reminder of the conditions in which he worked should smother any doubts. The very close involvement with actors in the imbroglio of both public and private theatres must have daily brought him face to face with a practical manifestation of the problems facing the playwright who is not just a visitant but a close working colleague of temperamental actors. Drama created while the eventual executants are breathing over the dramatist's shoulder has a complicated grain that differs from the polished results of the writer's solitary immunity from interference.

What may seem definitive, imperishable, even sacrosanct in the quiet of the study may well be the first element to be transmuted, altered, even replaced when subjected to the various expediencies and histrionic expertise of the rehearsal room. To be aware that Shakespeare's plays were deeply and inevitably subjected (given the nature of the acting companies) to the latter environment immediately raises questions which admit of no final answer but whose very fascination invites speculation. How much of Burbage went into Macbeth? How much of Armin informed the creation of Feste or Lear's Fool? Is there, indeed, any common denominator to roles known to have been played by the same actor in Shakespeare's company?

Some common denominators seem to spring out of the group of tragic heroes known to have been played by Burbage, despite the singular differences we can observe in them. Two examples seem obvious enough. First the actor who played the tragic heroes must have had (and still needs to have) an imagination and a mental and emotional sensibility of a very developed order. These roles are beyond the run-of-the-mill matinee idol; they demand more than technical skill. Second, the actor who played these roles needed (and still needs) to have a quite unusual sensitivity to the appreciation and communication of language. Your rodomontade player will pull off Henry V, your skilled technician and cold-voiced villain will conquer Angelo, and Romeo would be adequately served by one with a sense of music, soft lips and a disposition to sentimentality. But Lear, Hamlet and Macbeth, in particular, demand a huge poetic feeling and an ability to apprehend the implications of the intellectual content of the lines. This is not to ask for an actor of immense intellectual stature, but one of limitless mental and emotional intuitiveness. Such men are rare. It is not enough to say that because Shakespeare was a great poet it is natural that his characters should speak great poetry: a bad actor can make sow's ears out of any poet's silk purses.

It is very tempting to assume that Burbage was possessed of these rare qualities and that this gave Shakespeare a kind of confidence which put no restriction whatsoever on his own imaginative immensity and his verbal splendour. The characters were, so to speak, only possible in the terms in which they eventually came to exist because the actor was big enough to meet the terms—indeed, may well have suggested them.

These kinds of relationships, and others less inchoate and theoretical, might well be multiplied. For example, were the evidence firmer, it might with confidence be expected to apply to all of Shakespeare's major characters. At least it can be said that all the tenuous evidence available points unerringly towards the existence of far closer relationships between actor and role than has hitherto been admitted. One might, indeed, find certain quirks of certain actors being exploited (perhaps covertly) by Shakespeare in the creation of certain characters.

If it is objected that there is too much supposition in this, it should be recalled that the use of the idosyncrasies of players (Green Room raw material, as it were) is far from uncommon in theatre today and has distinguished confirmation for its past usage in the work of Congreve who seems, quite relentlessly and presumably undetectedly, to have caused some well-known actors and actresses of his time to reproduce their own habits in fictional characters without being aware of what they were doing. Shakespeare, the most assiduous picker-up of trifles in the history of drama, could hardly give second place to Congreve in the matter of source-hunting. Equally, it should be recalled that the consanguinity of actor and role is at least suggested by the intriguing substitution of the names of actors for their roles, possibly as a result of a prompter, in II. ii of *Much Ado About Nothing*. Cowley (i.e. Richard Cowley, a member of the Lord Chamberlain's Men) appears three times for Verges, but the entire contribution of Dogberry, which is a major one, appears under the name of Kemp (i.e. Will Kemp) twelve times.

Two points are worth stressing here. First, the scene is, in an obvious sense, a throwaway, barely necessary to forward the action, and its dialogue is almost entirely designed to promote comic business. Second, the comedy of the scene seems arranged to 'feed' Dogberry/Kemp and, moreover, seems deliberately to be leading up to giving him the opportunity for the last solo speech of the scene—ending with 'O that I had been writ down an ass'. In truth, we get very much the same impression from those pantomime and music-hall sketches where a stooge or stooges build up the verbal atmosphere to enable the star comic to explode into his big solo which often ends with a well-known catchphrase.

When the substitution of Kemp for Dogberry for the entirety of the scene is considered, when the nature of the scene is recalled, when its dramatic irrelevance is recorded, is it unreasonable to lean towards a belief either that Kemp wrote it or that Shakespeare did, but in absolute and well-judged servility to the known values of Kemp's comic genius?

Discussion of Burbage and Kemp in these contexts admittedly runs the risk of bogging down in speculation. Where, however, the Fools and Robert Armin are concerned, there is much firmer ground.

We know, with a certainty equal to that applicable to Burbage and his roles, that Armin played Feste, Touchstone, Lear's Fool and probably Lavache. It has been suggested that he also played Dogberry. The evidence for this derives from a line in the dedication to Armin's play *The Italian Taylor and his Boy* (1609) which goes—'I pray you the boldness of a beggar who hath been writ down an Asse in his time'.[5] Faced with the Kemp/Dogberry substitution already referred to, the strong possibility that the Ass phrase was, or became, a popular catchphrase either deriving from, or popularized by, Kemp and, as it is hoped to show, the quite un-Armin qualities required to play Dogberry, the difficulty of accepting the suggestion is very great.

III

It is well known, and it is thoroughly documented by Enid Welsford, that the Court Fools of Shakespeare derive, in essentials, from the real Fools of history. These essentials were transmuted by Shakespeare for his own dramatic puposes but he capitalized very much on his sources. The most obvious of them are:

1) The Fools are conspicuously classless or, at very least, difficult to place with confidence in the social hierarchies. Although, like Feste, they may haunt the houses, mansions, palaces of the high and mighty, they are obviously neither of the upper class nor distinctly of any other. Jaques' reference to Touchstone that he is 'One who hath been a courtier' seems calculatedly vague. Touchstone gives no particular indication of being more than on jester/master terms with the high-born of the play. If he cannot be truly seen as a member of the upper class, neither does he seem to fit well with the lower orders. His marriage to Audrey seems, in every way, a monumental aberration—like is certainly not marrying like in any sense, least of all a social one. Lear's Fool is classless to the point where even to consider his place in the social hierarchy seems ridiculous. Lavache, though listened to, is presented as a confidant whose words are countenanced, not because of equality of social status, but for some other reason.

5 *Works*, edited by A. B. Grosart (London, 1880).

2) This other reason has much to do with the fact that the Fools are conspicuously a law unto themselves. They utilize (as, for example, in Feste's catechizing of Olivia or Lear's Fool's wisdom-shafted jibes) an accepted right to speak their minds. A marked and important feature of this acceptance of a right is, of course, the irony that is embedded in it. They do speak what they think, they are often expected even incited to do so, and yet they can, incontinently, at the whim of the piper's payer, be punished for doing so—'Sirrah, the whip'.

This ironic 'right' to speak is often referred to as a Fool's licence and it is usually assumed that it is a tradition and not a palpable reality—a wry ghost of something that itself has no substance. An example of the way in which the art and social historian may well guide future research into the history of Fools may be indicated by the fact that, in the many depictions of these creatures carved on the underside of choir-stall seats in so many of our cathedrals and medieval churches, there are some who are holding quite conspicuoulsy in one hand what seems like a rolled-up parchment. Whether or not the artist's licence has created a Fool's 'licence'—depicting something that did not exist but was well-known as a tradition—or whether some Fools actually did possess a written licence, is not known, but the matter is amenable to much detailed research.

3) At certain times—and, in the case of Feste, Lear's Fool and Lavache, at most times—their 'comic' utterances, whether in dialogue or mono-logue, are embarrassingly unsimple. It is an area of theatre-experience worth commenting on that the status of Fools in an audience's experi-ence is quite dissimilar to that of the plain comic folk who are some-times found in the presence of the Fools. Martext and Audrey provide uncomplicated laughter; Touchstone does not; Aguecheek by the side of Feste is a funny simple droll. When Feste is being 'funny' in the dialogue with Olivia, Viola and as Sir Topas, we are well aware that 'this is not altogether Fool'. There is little in Lear's Fool that inclines us from a strong feeling that he is less a comic than a prophetic or even tragic figure; and Lavache is more cynic than jester.

It may be added that another element in the audience's experience of these creatures re-emphasizes the complexity of their status. How often, as members of an audience, do we watch and listen to the actor playing the Fool and react a little nervously as he seems to beg for our laughter at his quips about the Vapians and impeticosing gratillity. Our response is so often nervous not only because we recognize the difficulty the actor has in inducing comic responses from what seems intractable material but also because we are reluctant for our neighbours to know that we do not understand the joke. On the contrary, to laugh alone in these circumstances can either be a conceit or a form of desperate insincerity!

It is true, of course, that some of the quips which leave us darkling would have had an immediate response from an Elizabethan audience because of their contemporary allusiveness. It is equally true, however, that there remains an area of their verbal communications which seems opaque for other, mysterious reasons.

4) The Fools have (to use a modern catch-phrase that any good Fool would reduce to mincemeat) a conspicuous withdrawal syndrome. Their involvement in the action, incidents, tensions of the plays is peripheral. This posture is implicitly comprehended on a reading of the plays but becomes explicit when the plays are experienced in the theatre. Feste's withholding of any comment whatsoever and his withdrawal from the action at the sudden intervention of Malvolio in the drunken below-stairs scene is sudden in its impact. In the production at the then Shakespeare Memorial Theatre in 1959, Feste couched beneath a table quietly strumming on a musical instrument—he seemed light years away from Illyria. Even Touchstone, the most socially integrated (to use modern parlance again) of them all, is not at the heart of the play. Comments about him hint at a kind of alienation in his make-up. 'He uses his folly like a stalking-horse and under the presentation of that he shoots his wit' (*As You Like It*, V. iv. 100).

Lear's Fool is the most removed of all. He darts in and out of the play with his wry comments, his unremarked wisdom and warnings, his saws and jingles which seem to come from a time before clock-time began. When he is no longer dramatically needed he disappears from the action with utter finality.

These four characteristics alone entitle us to look closely at these Fools, for a mystery seems to hand here. No other Elizabethan dramatist exploits the real Fools of history in this way. The kind of character that has been described is unique to Shakespeare.

IV

It is suggested that this is partly due to the fact that Robert Armin was unique in Shakespeare's company and that Shakespeare and he had a certain affinity in the sense that each kindled the other's imagination. Armin sensed what Shakespeare wanted, Shakespeare sensed what Armin could give him. Moreover they came together in a working relationship at a time (1599) when the timbre of Shakespeare's dramatic imagination was changing, becoming more complicated. For the kind of comedy he was about to begin writing at this particular time he needed the kind of conception which, it is claimed, Armin instinctively and sensitively understood. Together, they created a figure unique in drama and, through that figure, revealed an attitude towards comedy, acting and drama which is as strange as it is singular.

We know practically nothing about Robert Armin except that he was probably a pot-boy in a tavern, that he was probably anti-puritan and that he wrote plays, tracts and a curious work, *Foole upon Foole*,[6] which is a remarkable if uneven commentary on real Fools and some speculation upon the nature of folly. Armin probably belonged for a time to the Lord Chandos' men but in 1599 or thereabouts he joined the Lord Chamberlain's, replacing the great custard-pie, physical comedian, Will Kemp. The entry of Armin into the company coincided with the appearance and development of the Fool in Shakespeare's plays and with the consequent diminishing in importance of broad physical comedy.

It is reasonable, surely, to believe that Armin brought with him an excited respect for Shakespeare's work. There are a considerable number of both close and possible echoes of Shakespeare's plays in Armin's work—perhaps more in number than in any other Elizabethan writer. Surely only close acquaintance and an attendant admiration could recognize the beauty of the image in *Romeo and Juliet* which goes—'Earth-treading stars that make dark heaven light' and reproduce it as 'Earth's bright-treading stars' in his own play *The Two Maids of Moorclacke*?[7] Again, surely only an intimate acquaintance with a popular play by his colleague could lie behind a remark in the same play—'there are, as Hamlet says, things called whips in store'. The fact that he has misquoted is no argument against intimacy. The modern scholar is only too well aware that familiarity often breeds this kind of carelessness.

Apart from such respect and admiration, it is further suggested that Armin delivered into Shakespeare's mind and greedy imagination a notion of comedy far different from any he had perpended before and,

[6]*Works*, edited by A. B. Grosart (London, 1880).   [7]*Ibid.*

through it, a more complicated notion of the place and function of character in drama.

Some idea of the strength that may lie in the suppositious connections thus made between Armin and Shakespeare may be strikingly indicated by a passage in an epistle signed 'R.A.' but prefixed 'R. Armin' printed in 1590 with a tract entitled *A brief Resolution of the right Religion*. The probability that the actor Armin is one and the same man as R. Armin is strong, and although nine more years were to elapse between the publication of the tract and Armin's joining the Lord Chamberlain's men this is no argument against Shakespeare's having read the tract either before 1599 or indeed having been introduced to it by a new colleague eager to impress the well-known dramatist. The passage in question refers to Puritans and it reads:

> The other vicious and detestable sect are Martinets, who see so far into matters that they oversee themselves, wresting things from the right sense to the wrong, making show of zeal when it is mere folly.[8]

A more evocative general description of Malvolio's colouring it would be difficult to find. The start of recognition which such a passage invokes is frequently repeated in a close examination of *Foole upon Foole* and its companion publication *A Nest of Ninnies* which amplifies some of the comments Armin makes in the former study of Fools. Not only are there occasional sharp reminders of the unusual ambience which Shakespeare's Fools have about them (as in Armin's description of Will Sommers, Henry VIII's Fool: 'His melody was of a higher strain, and he looked as the noon broad waking'), but occasionally it is possible to catch something of the rhythms, the anticlimaxes, guile and shrewdness, and descent into quipping bathos so characteristic particularly of Feste and Touchstone:

> By the first merry emblem I reach at stars, how they fire themselves at the firmament; whether it be with sitting too near the sun in the day, or couching too near the moon in the night I know not, but the hair of their happiness often falls off, and shoots from a blazing comet to a fallen star, and carries no more light than is to be seen in the bottom of Plato's ink-horn, and when they should study in private with Diogenes, in his cell, they are with Cornelius in his tub.[9]

[8] *Works*, edited by A. B. Grosart (London, 1880).　　[9] *Ibid.*

We recall, for example,

> bid the dishonest man mend himself: if he mend, he is no longer
> dishonest; if he cannot, let the butcher mend him. Anything that's
> mended is but patch'd; virtue that transgresses is but patch'd with
> sin, and sin that amends is but patch'd with virtue.
>
> (*Twelfth Night*, I. v. 40–44)

Armin's conception of the subtlety of true folly and his sensitivity
to the language of fooling—one moment a broad quip, then a nerve-
jolting pun, then a mordant comment, all interwoven with strands of
strange verbiage and occasionally decorated with a sad lyricism—is of
the same order as Shakespeare's. What is more, his sense of the wisdom
in folly is absolutely in line with Shakespeare's, not merely in conception (for the idea of wise folly was not original, as both men would
have known from a reading of Erasmus's *Moriae Encomium* (translated as
The Praise of Folie, 1549), but in its form of expression. It is in this that
the uniqueness of the two writers lies.

> Fools questions reach to mirth, leading wisdom by the hand as age
> leads children by one finger, and though it holds not fast in wisdom,
> yet it points at it.[10]

To read Armin's books and to recall Shakespeare's Fools is to be
immediately aware that both men had come to inhabit a country of the
imagination in which the notion of comedy as a mere laughter-maker
had been put aside. To hear Feste mocking Malvolio about whirligig
Time, and Touchstone gravely turning to Rosalind and saying, 'but
as all is mortal in nature, so is all nature in love mortal in folly', to
overhear Viola say, 'This fellow is wise enough to play the Fool', is to
be made aware that we are in a different realm from that inhabited by
Gobbo, Costard, Bottom and their like.

The Fool's comic function in contradistinction to theirs is well
expressed by William Willeford:

> The Fool is a fact, and he is the only fact that cannot be governed
> by the comic dream. . . . He is the reminder that the moment of
> perfection realized by the comic dream is only pretending.[11]

This comment not only suggests something of a clue to the nature of
the Fool's effect in deepening and maturing Shakespeare's conception
of comedy, but also the figure's status as a new kind of *dramatis persona*.

[10] *Works*, edited by A. B. Grosart (London, 1880).   [11] Willeford, *op. cit.*, p. 74.

V

Before the coming of Armin and the Fool, Shakespeare, we may say, had exulted in the comic dream. *Love's Labour's Lost*, *The Two Gentlemen of Verona*, *The Taming of the Shrew*, *The Comedy of Errors*, *A Midsummer Night's Dream* are territories of delight which Shakespeare, no doubt, inhabited with wise joy. The adjective is important because, admittedly, even the earliest comedies are not without dark hues. In them the young playwright's comic spirit occasionally stirs a little restlessly in perturbation about mutability, aware that the sunlight on the garden must harden and grow cold. More than this, even the gayest, most effervescent, most witty moods and modes in these early comedies are rarely self-indulgent. This early comedy looks outward from itself, is purposeful in the sense that it is never allowed to cheapen or minimize, for the sake of mindless laughter, Shakespeare's deep sense of values in the matter of love, fidelity, friendship.

The arrival of the Fool immediately heightened Shakespeare's awareness of the contrast between created dream and ever-incipient reality. In his green days comedy and high exciting romance was able always to hold back the shadows of reality, but now Shakespeare fully realized that the darkness cannot be banished. *Twelfth Night* and *As You Like It* are indeed more poignantly comic, and their sunlight the more welcome and subtle, simply because the Fools are so often reminding us that comic perfection is, in a way, only pretending:

> But that's all one, our play is done.
>   (*Twelfth Night*, V. i. 393)

But the Fool does much more than to remind Shakespeare and ourselves about the pretence of the comic dream. Inside the Fool there lies a mystery about which all we can instinctively say, either in reading or seeing the plays, is that it has something to do with a knowledge and sometimes a purpose which is exclusive to the Fool. This knowledge is connected not with the comic dream per se, but seems, we feel, to lie outside it, and the purpose is curiously stern. It is brilliantly expressed in the speech of Jaques to the Duke and his assembled followers:

> O worthy fool! One that hath been a courtier,
> And says if ladies be but young and fair,
> They have the gift to know it; and in his brain,
> Which is as dry as the remainder biscuit

After a voyage, he hath strange places cramm'd
With observation, the which he vents
In mangled forms. O that I were a fool!
I am ambitious for a motley coat . . .
                    . . . It is my only suit,
Provided that you weed your better judgments
Of all opinion that grows rank in them
That I am wise. I must have liberty
Withal, as large a charter as the wind,
To blow on whom I please, for so fools have;
And they that are most galled with my folly,
They most must laugh. And why, sir, must they so?
The why is plain as way to parish church:
He that a fool doth very wisely hit
Doth very foolishly, although he smart,
Not to seem senseless of the bob; if not,
The wiseman's folly is anatomiz'd
Even by the squand'ring glances of the fool.
Invest me in my motley; give me leave
To speak my mind, and I will through and through
Cleanse the foul body of th' infected world,
If they will patiently receive my medicine.

                    (*As You Like It*, II. vii. 36–61)

The knowledge and the purpose are implicit here. The Fool's knowledge is of the folly of mankind, the fool's ability is to exorcize that
folly. It is as if Jaques is saying that the exercise of the kind of wise
folly possessed by the true Fool can purge mankind's so-called wise
men of their own kind of folly. It is Jaques' ambition to ascend to this
status of high therapy.

Why should Jaques be so adamant that the Fool's brand of folly
should be so efficacious? Why should wit burn out rage, why should
fooling cauterize pretensions, why should jibes and saws in the mouth
of a true Fool be capable of making the mentally blind see and those
near to madness come nearer to sanity? Why should the folly of Lear's
Fool be so much more a kind of wisdom than any words uttered by
anyone else in the infected world of the King? We know his words are
more wise because our instincts tell us so as we listen to them—but why?

Simply because no true Fool is completely committed to the world
within which the actions of the plays are placed. The Fool, in a way, is an
ideal 'us'; he represents that part of us which does not identify with

characters or situations, but sits back and is able to see behind illusion. But it is the uncommitted part of us in an idealized form which the Fool represents. His is the wisdom we would like to have, and if we had it not only would we be able to deal clearly with the 'truth' that lies behind the actions of a great play but, perhaps more pertinently, we would be able to deal more certainly with our own real infected world, and purge ourselves of our own folly. It is often said that if you look in a glass you see a fool. What Shakespeare does is to make us look into the glass of the world of his play—but the Fool we see there wears not our motley in his brain. The Fool, then, is able to purge folly and be seen to do so because this is, ideally, what we would wish to be wise enough to do—'give *me* leave to prove a fool' is unconsciously echoed by every member of the audience.

The Fool is capable of this purging process also because his licence is always at hazard. Yet there is a paradox here. Although at hazard, he is still more free than anyone else to speak because he is relatively uncommitted to any close association with anything or anyone, as has been noted above. He is almost as free to speak about the world of the play as we are in the audience, but the best kind of critic, like the best kind of Fool, is always at hazard because both are more likely to speak a truth that no-one wishes to hear unless they speak it themselves.

VI

Yet a further question arises from this consideration of the wisdom and status of the Fool within the play. If he has these antecedents with the audience and this distance from the rest of the *dramatis personae*, what kind of dramatic figure is he? He simply refuses to be categorized as we can categorize the other characters in a Shakespeare play; and yet we know him to be based on reality.

The Fool, in effect, as he is developed in Shakespeare's plays—a brain-child shared, we have assumed, with Armin—is like any real actor; his professional function is not to be himself. Like any true actor, the Fool's job is to wear the mask of jester or folly. He is, in his function in the social environment of the play's world, a purveyor of illusion— yet we know that beneath whatever mask he is wearing something very far from illusion is being communicated to us. We are experiencing what seems to be the impossible process by which a dramatic character whose function in the very play itself is virtually that of shadow is, nevertheless, the repository of the most important truths that the play has to communicate; it is like that curious form of (to mutate the original meaning) negative capability by which an actor who, off-stage, is completely negative, evanescent, lacking in personality can ascend into the highest embodiment of historic invention when he steps into the limelight on stage. As Willeford says 'the fool on stage strikes us as radiant with a life that transcends his stylized attributes and often inconsequential jokes'.

The Fool's sudden quips, one line jokes, odd staccato sentences, often hide or contain a significance beyond their apparent meaning, and their jingles, like nursery rhymes, reverberate in the head and heart:

> The hedge-sparrow fed the cuckoo so long,
> That it had its head bit off by its young.

There is an uncanny resemblance, although of course the form and usage is different, between the dramatic effect of the Fool's interpolations (for this is where the meaningful trivia often occur) and that employed by another poet of the theatre—Harold Pinter. Those famous pauses of his, sometimes sudden and unexpected, sometimes 'telegraphed', have an equivalent importance to the Fool's utterances. Like the words of the Fools, the pauses are often more important than what, verbally, lies on each side of them. In the case of the Fools what is entirely misunderstood or only partially understood by others is important; in Pinter's case, what is unsaid—significantly unsaid—between people is important. Somewhere, we may fancy, a Fool lurks inside a Pinter play giving silence a wise language; and, curiously, we may apprehend that inside a Fool's mouth, when he speaks, in Shakespeare, what only *he* really understands, there is an aspiration for silence.

Fool: If a man's brains were in's heels, were't not in danger of kibes?

Lear: Ay, boy.

Fool: Then, I prithee, be merry; thy wit shall not go slipshod.

Lear: Ha, ha, ha!

Fool: Shalt see thy other daughter will use thee kindly; for though she's as like this as a crab's like an apple, yet I can tell what I can tell.

Lear: What canst tell, boy?

Fool: She will taste as like this as a crab does to a crab. Thou canst tell why one's nose stands i'th' middle on's face?

Lear: No.

Fool: Why to keep one's eyes of either side's nose, that what a man cannot smell out, he may spy into.

Lear: I did her wrong.

Fool: Canst tell how an oyster makes his shell?

Lear: No.

Fool: Nor I neither; but I can tell why a snail has a house.

Lear: Why?

Fool: Why, to put's head in; not to give it away to his daughters, and leave his horns without a case.

Lear: I will forget my nature. So kind a father!—Be my horses ready?   (*King Lear*, I. v. 7–32)

Mick: I'm very impressed with what you've just said.

[Pause]

Yes that's impressive, that is.

[Pause]

I'm impressed, anyway.

Davies: You know what I'm talking about, then?

Mick: Yes, I know. I think we understand one another.

Davies: Uh? Well . . . I'll tell you . . . I'd . . . I'd like to think that. You been playing me about, you know, I don't know why. I never done you no harm.

Mick: No, you know what it was? We just got off on the wrong foot. That's all it was.

Davies: Ay, we did.

Mick: Like a sandwich?

Davies: What?

Mick [taking a sandwich from his pocket]: Have one of these.

Davies: Don't you pull anything.

Mick: No, you're still not understanding me. I can't help being interested in any friend of my brother's. I mean, you're my brother's friend, aren't you?

Davies: Well, I . . . I wouldn't put it as far as that.

Mick: Don't you find him friendly, then?

Davies: Well, I wouldn't say we was all that friends. I mean, he done me no harm, but I wouldn't say he was any particular friend of mine. What's in that sandwich, then?

Mick: Cheese.

Davies: That'll do me.

Mick: Take one.   (*The Caretaker*, II. ii.)

The pauses (implied or stated) in each case, and the quips or terse comments, accrete, because of the way they are placed, and where they are placed in the text: a body of knowledge about matters behind the apparent, behind what is being actually said. But, even more, what gives the resemblance a particular *frisson* is the atmospheric quality and effect of the experts. What lies in both dramatists, whether it be comment, judgement, irony, satire, grief, seems to come from light years away from the immediate environment of the play. Deep inside Pinter's pauses and his carefully architectured dialogue, there is a primitive, elemental source whose nature is telling us something of what man really is and what his condition is. Deep inside the Fool's language and in Shakespeare's carefully modelled use of it, there seems to lie an area of comprehension of what man is that reaches back to a kind of beginning—a time before time:

> This prophecy Merlin shall make, for I live before his time.
> (*King Lear*, III. ii. 95)

The arrival of Armin gave Shakespeare the opportunity, which he took, of inserting into his plays an agency quite different from those other created characters of his plays written up to this time. We may say that, before 1599 and indeed basically, Shakespeare's normal method of characterization is realistic—that is, his characters have a high degree of fidelity to the actualities of real life. The Fools do not. They are, so to say, wild cards in the pack, errant strange jokers. They are neither realistic nor, indeed, may they confidently be asserted to be symbolic. William Willeford comments that 'The Fool is neither the player nor the audience, but both and something else', and he adds that 'The Fool is, in a unique way, both the actor and the thing he enacts.'[12]

One can sense how the critics and scholars strain as they try to come to terms with this figure. At the moment when it appears that one has grasped it, it slips away. At times the Fool seems to represent us, the audience—through his eyes and in his mouth we see and hear intimations of what might be beneath the play's obvious activities. At other times the Fool can be identified with the actor, any actor, who plays him (this is particularly true of Feste) and there is a wry poignancy in observing a superb purveyor of illusions (like Max Adrian) wandering through Illyria not, so to say, as a character but as his lonely vulnerable self.

Yet, in the long run, perhaps, in a certain sense, the Fool-figure is Shakespeare himself. The Fool was entertainer—so was Shakespeare.

[12] Willeford, *op. cit.*, p. 49.

The Fool, as part of his professional function, lived in and helped to sustain a world of illusion—so did Shakespeare. The Fool used the mask of folly to hide his lonely apprehension of the truth behind illusion—Shakespeare, as dramatist, is the highest exemplar of the way in which the artist uses illusion to communicate reality.

The new element that entered into Shakespeare's plays with the coming of Armin was a full realization that the conventions of characterization and of drama itself are not final forms. Through Armin and the Fool he learned that character does not have to depend on that impersonative factor which ties it to the appearances of so-called real life, and that there is another country of drama in which the metaphorical and the allusive are as effective for the communication of character and meaning as what is actual and explicit.

VIII

'As You Like It' and 'Twelfth Night': Shakespeare's Sense of an Ending

ANNE BARTON

I

HENRI FOCILLON has argued that the word *classicism*, rightly under-stood, has nothing to do with academicism nor even necessarily with our formal legacy from Greece and Rome. Correctly, it refers to a condition of poise: 'a brief, perfectly balanced instant of complete possession of forms' occurring at certain crucial moments in artistic styles which may otherwise have nothing in common.

> Classicism consists of the greatest propriety of the parts one to the other. It is stability, security, following upon experimental unrest. It confers, so to speak, a solidity on the unstable aspects of experi-mentation (because of which it is also, in its way, a renunciation) ... But classicism is not the result of a conformist attitude. On the con-trary, it has been created out of one final, ultimate experiment, the audacity and vitality of which it has never lost. . . . Classicism: a brief, perfectly balanced instant of complete possession of forms; not a slow and monotonous application of 'rules', but a pure, quick delight, like the ἀκμή of the Greeks, so delicate that the pointer of the scale scarcely trembles. I look at this scale not to see whether the pointer will presently dip down again, or even come to a moment of absolute rest. I look at it instead to see, within the miracle of that hesitant immobility, the slight, inappreciable tremor that indicates life.[1]

Focillon was writing about the visual arts, but there is surely a *classicism* of the kind he describes in literary styles as well. Dramatists too may achieve a 'perfectly balanced instant of complete possession of forms', the very stillness of which will, in the next moment, seem to imply limitation and invite its own destruction.

[1] Henri Focillon, *The Life of Forms in Art*, trans. Hogan and Kobler (New Haven, 1942), pp. 13–14.

1. Nicolas Poussin, '*Et in Arcadia Ego*'. (Devonshire Collection, Chatsworth. Repro-
l by permission of the Trustees of the Chatsworth Settlement.)

2. A later painting by Poussin on the same theme. (Reproduced by permission of
lusée du Louvre, Paris—*cliché des Musées*.)

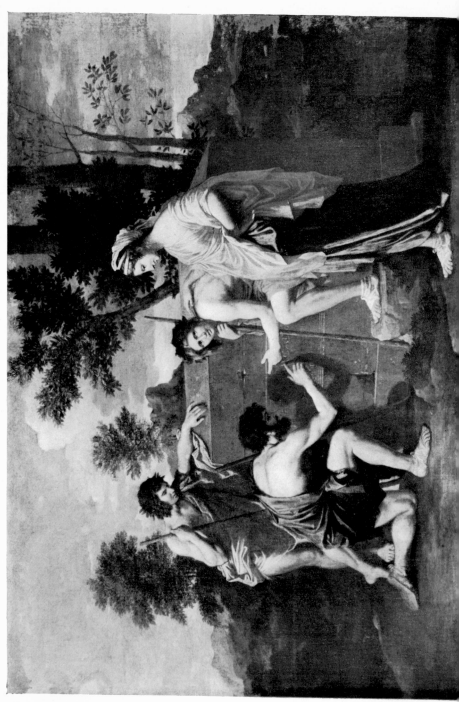

Plate 2.

As You Like It is, in Focillon's sense, Shakespeare's classical comedy. It confers solidity upon the dazzling experimentation of eight comedies written before it, stands as the fullest and most stable realization of Shakespearian comic form.[2] Critics, aware now of the 'social' nature of the comedies, of their complex structure of silently juxtaposed scenes, tend to take this form more seriously than they once did. C. L. Barber and Northrop Frye in particular have argued for the essential unity of Shakespearian comedy in ways that reach far beyond shared plot devices, or the old spotting of resemblances among the clowns and witty heroines of different plays. It has become possible to agree that the comedies, from *The Two Gentlemen of Verona* and *The Comedy of Errors* to *Twelfth Night*, are plays concerned primarily with transformation, with the clarification and renewal attained, paradoxically, through a submission to some kind of disorder, whether festive or not. We have learned to notice as typically Shakespearian the way characters move between two contrasted locales—one of them heightened and more spacious than the other—and we regard that 'new society' which makes its way back to the normal world at the end of the play as a subtler and more consequential achievement than older critics did.

The exceptionally full participation of *As You Like It* in this (after all) startlingly innovatory comic form built up through preceding plays is obvious. The comedy opposes its two environments, Arden and the court of Duke Frederick, with particular clarity and richness. This greenwood, even more strikingly than the ones in *The Two Gentlemen of Verona* and *A Midsummer Night's Dream*, is a place where people yield themselves for a time to the extraordinary, and emerge transformed. Realism is interwoven with romance, truth to life with certain fairy-tale conventions frankly exploited as such. To a greater extent than Julia and Portia, Rosaline and Beatrice before her, Rosalind in her boy's disguise is the central consciousness of it all: a heroine both involved and dispassionate who seems largely responsible for the structure of that new social order which leaves Arden so hopefully at the end. Most important of all, *As You Like It* tests against each other a great variety of love relationships and possible attitudes towards experience, by means of a technique of contrast and parallel which Shakespeare may have learned originally from Lyly, but which he had refined in the course of writing his earlier comedies to the point where it could, here, actually take the place of plot.

[2] I am assuming that *The Merry Wives of Windsor* preceded *As You Like It*.

Except as a convenient excuse for getting characters into Arden, and out again at the end, intrigue scarcely seems to matter in this play. *As You Like It* derives much of its classical stability and poise from the fact that its plot barely exists. The comedy moves forward, not through a complex story line of the kind Shakespeare had spun out in *The Comedy of Errors*, or in the Hero/Claudio plot of *Much Ado About Nothing*, but simply through shifts in the grouping of characters. Their verbal encounters, their varying assessments of each other assume the status of events in this pastoral landscape where the gifts of Fortune are bestowed so equally as to throw a new and searching light on what people really are. Shakespeare's customary generosity to his characters, his reluctance to legislate, his faith in romantic love and in the ability of human beings to transform their own natures make *As You Like It* a richer and far more dramatic play than Jonson's *Every Man Out of His Humour* (1599). These two comedies, written perhaps in the same year, are nevertheless alike in their subordination of plot in the traditional sense to an intricate structure of meetings between characters, a concentration upon attitudes rather than action. The normal functions of plot are fulfilled almost entirely by form and, in both cases, a curious stillness at the heart of the play is the result.

Shakespeare had once before composed a comedy singularly devoid of intrigue. *Love's Labour's Lost*, too, unfolds principally by way of echo and antithesis, through thematic juxtapositions suggesting relationships and judgements which Shakespeare often does not care to make explicit in his text. There is a sense in which the only thing that 'happens' in *Love's Labour's Lost*, after the arrival in Navarre of the Princess and her ladies in Act II, is the death of the King of France as reported in the fifth act by Mercade. Yet the effect produced by this second event, geographically distant though it is, is nothing less than the annihilation of the entire world of the comedy. In the moments following the entrance of Mercade, the sheltered, uneventful and thoughtlessly cruel life of the royal park comes in retrospect to seem not only frivolous but unnatural and false. The comedy turns and rends its own former preoccupation with words and attitudes as opposed to actions. Sadly, Navarre and his companions prepare to leave their retreat for an altogether less comfortable, if ultimately more rewarding, world in which things happen and death and time cannot be sidestepped. Only by deeds as opposed to vows, by dearly-bought and tangible 'deserts' (V. ii. 793), can love's labours, grossly misconceived by the men for most of the play, at last be won.

The plotlessness of *As You Like It* is not like this. In no sense does it represent a criticism of the characters who flee into Arden, nor of the life they lead there. Although it will be necessary for most of them to return to an urban civilization at the end, to leave the greenwood, this return does not imply a rejection of the values of the forest. They have not been idle, nor is death a fact which the inhabitants of Arden have ever tried, fraudulently, to evade. *Love's Labour's Lost* is extreme in the suddenness with which it introduces its reminder of mortality in Act V. Yet it is surely significant that all but two of the comedies Shakespeare wrote before *As You Like It* achieve their comic catharsis by way of some kind of confrontation with the idea of death. *The Comedy of Errors* unfolds feverishly under the shadow of the fate threatening old Aegeon at the setting of the sun. It achieves recognition and pardon in the last act after a virtual massing of images of destruction, many of them clustered around the skeletal figure of Pinch, that 'mere anatomy . . . a living dead man' (V. i. 238–41). *The Two Gentlemen of Verona* seems to disintegrate, never really to recover, when it introduces the murderous attack of the outlaws and Proteus' attempted rape in Act V. In *A Midsummer Night's Dream*, the death sentence which sends the lovers into the forest is caught up and forcibly transmuted into laughter by the Pyramus and Thisbe interlude at the end. Bottom and his friends may render the tragedy ridiculous; they remind us all the same that this is the way Hermia's story might in all seriousness have ended: with blood and deprivation. As it is, Lysander's dismissal of Pyramus, 'He is dead; he is nothing', rings disturbingly in the ear (V. i. 300). *Much Ado About Nothing* goes so far as apparently to kill and ceremonially inter Hero before a comic resolution can be reached. Antonio must be rescued, narrowly, from Shylock's knife before *The Merchant of Venice* can permit a consummation of the marriages made at Belmont. Only *The Taming of the Shrew* and *The Merry Wives of Windsor* are devoid of any genuinely dark tones, and this perhaps is one reason why critics have persistently felt that these plays are closer to farce than to true comedy.

Even as Shakespearian tragedy usually makes some delusive gesture towards a happy ending just before the catastrophe, providing us with a tantalizing glimpse of Lear re-united with Cordelia, Antony successful, or Hamlet reprieved, so the comedies tend to win through to their happy endings by way of some kind of victory over the opposite possibility. In doing so, they assure the theatre audience that the facts of the world as it is have not been forgotten. Like the moment of false hope which animates the fourth acts of tragedy, the encounter with death which precedes the comedy resolution demonstrates a saving awareness that this story might well have ended differently. Comedy pauses to look disaster squarely in the face, but is still able to proceed honestly towards a conclusion flattering to our optimism. The manœuvre is designed to shore up the happy ending, to allow us to surrender ourselves, at least temporarily, to a pleasing fiction.

II

In all the comedies which Shakespeare wrote before *As You Like It* (*The Taming of the Shrew* and *The Merry Wives of Windsor* excepted) this emphasis upon death towards the end of the play is strident and momentarily disorientating. The effect produced is not unlike the one achieved by Nicolas Poussin in the earlier of his two paintings on the theme 'Et in Arcadia Ego'. In the version at Chatsworth (Plate 1), painted about 1630, two shepherds and a shepherdess discover, in a pastoral landscape, a tomb which is the spokesman of death: 'I am here, even in Arcadia.' Poussin was influenced at the time by Titian (and also, as Erwin Panofsky has pointed out, by Guercino's treatment of the same subject[3]), but it is not simply an interest in Baroque diagonals which governs the rush of the three figures towards the sarcophagus. The movement contains within itself a sense of recoil: of sudden horror and dismay. Neither emotionally nor in terms of the composition do the two shepherds and the girl accept the object before them. They react against it with gestures full of disorder. Some twenty years after the Chatsworth *Et in Arcadia Ego*, Poussin returned to the subject. The painting he produced, now in the Louvre (Plate 2), is classical both in terms of specific stylistic indebtedness and, more importantly, in the sense of Focillon's definition. It stands in something of the same relationship to the Chatsworth painting as does *As You Like It* to Shakespeare's earlier comedies. Here, the tomb stands solidly and uncompromisingly in the midst of a sunlit landscape. The words carved on it now seem to emanate both from Death personified and from the regret of the dead man himself that he too once lived in Arcadia but does so no longer. The three shepherds and the shepherdess

[3] Erwin Panofsky, '*Et in Arcadia Ego*: Poussin and the Elegiac Tradition', in *Meaning in the Visual Arts* (London, 1970), pp. 357–8.

grouped about the monument are serious, but they are in no way discomposed by this reminder of their own mortality which they have come upon so suddenly in the midst of the Golden World, in no way frightened or thrown off balance. Indeed, they have contrived to use the rectangular mass of the tomb in the centre of the composition as a kind of support, or focal point, for the achieved harmony of their own attitudes and gestures. They have made it part of their own order, accommodated it perfectly within a pattern of line and movement which both emotionally and technically has been able to accept this potentially awkward fact of death and even to build upon it.

In *As You Like It* too, death is something faced steadily and with due consideration, but it has almost no power whatever over the balance, the poise of a comedy which has quietly assimilated this factor from the start. A comparison between *As You Like It* and its source, Thomas Lodge's *Rosalynde* (1590), reveals Shakespeare's desire at almost every point to mitigate the violence inherent in the original story. Lodge had moved from one explosive moment of time, one crisis, to another. Shakespeare refuses to do this. In his re-working of the tale, Charles the wrestler injures the old man's sons but does not kill them, and he himself is not killed. The episode of the robbers in *Rosalynde*, their attempt to abduct the heroine and her companion, is omitted and so is the battle at the end in which Lodge's usurping prince had been defeated and slain. Instead, Shakespeare's Duke Frederick is peacefully converted to goodness through the agency of an old religious man palpably invented for that purpose. The protracted scenes of enmity and struggle between Lodge's hero and his elder brother are made perfunctory, almost abstract, in the comedy. It is true that both Rosalind and Orlando incur a threat of death early in the comedy, but this threat is in both cases a transparent device for sending them into the forest rather than a possibility seriously explored. The wrestling match, Oliver's intention to burn the lodging where Orlando lies, the spite of Duke Frederick, are all treated in the manner of fairy-tale. Not for an instant do they endanger the comic tone. Lodge had described his hero's rescue of his unworthy brother in rousing and basically realistic terms. Shakespeare distances it into the most static and heraldic of pictures: an emblem of lioness and serpent sketched at secondhand. Old Adam may imagine that he is going to die in Arden for lack of food; Orlando rushes into the banquet with drawn sword. These images are no sooner presented than they are corrected. The crisis was false. Calmly, even a little mockingly, the play rights itself. It assimilates the intrusion. Harmonious, balanced, and tonally even, *As You Like It* harbours a stillness at the centre which no turn of the plot, apparently, can affect.

Although a consciousness that 'men have died, from time to time, and worms have eaten them' (IV. i. 92–4), that human life is 'but a flower' (V. iii. 26) is spread throughout the comedy, this consciousness is never allowed to sharpen into a dramatic or even into a genuine emotional climax. Reminders of mortality flicker everywhere through the language of the play. Most of the characters seem to carry with them, as visibly as the shepherds painted by Poussin, an awareness of death and time. Rosalind's high spirits, Orlando's love, Duke Senior's contentment in adversity, and Touchstone's wit all flower out of it. Yet when the melancholy Jaques, in his meditation on the wounded deer, his delighted account of Touchstone's platitudes—'from hour to hour we ripe and ripe, / And then from hour to hour we rot and rot' (II. vii. 26–7)—or in his dismal chronology of the ages of man, tries to argue that life must necessarily be trivial and pointless because it ends in the grave, his attitude is amended or put aside. It is as important to the classical equilibrium of the play that Jaques' pessimism should be qualified in this fashion, firmly displaced from the centre of the composition, as it is that the violence built into the story as Lodge had told it should be smoothed away.

In his encounters with the Duke and Touchstone, with Orlando and (above all) with Rosalind, Jaques fares badly. He stumbles from one discomfiture to another. Only in the closing moments of the play when Shakespeare, without warning, allows him to speak the valediction of the entire comedy does his voice go uncontradicted. Formally, in a speech which considerations of rank ought to have assigned to Duke Senior, and symbolism to the god Hymen, Jaques estimates the futures and, by the way, the basic natures of all the other main characters. He puts the seal on the weddings, sets in motion the dance he himself declines to join. As he does so, he becomes something that he was not when he wished for a suit of motley, when he destroyed the harmony of Amiens' song, begged Orlando to rail with him against the world, or when he sentimentalized over the herd-abandoned deer. A figure of sudden dignity, his judgements are both generous and just. Although his decision to seek out Duke Frederick, separating himself firmly from that new society embodied in the dance, may be regretted, it cannot really be criticized. Moreover, his absence from the dance sets up reverberations, asks questions more disturbing than any that were aroused earlier by his twice-told tales of transience and decay. This new attitude towards Jaques is important in determining the character of *As You Like It* at its ending. It represents, in Focillon's terms, that 'slight, inappreciable tremor' within the immobility of the classical moment, a tremor which guarantees the vitality of the moment itself but which also prefigures its imminent destruction.

III

It is notoriously difficult for endings in fiction not to seem false.[4] They are likely to declare their own artificiality, reminding us that although plays and novels necessarily reach a more or less tidy conclusion, real events and relationships do not. For Fortinbras, the death of Prince Hamlet was a beginning; even for Horatio, it is only an event occurring near the middle of another play. This continuum, this extension of the story into an infinity of contiguous persons and episodes is something that Shakespeare, in shaping his fifth act, was forced to indicate only slightly, or to ignore. To a certain extent, tragedy as a form aids the dramatist in overcoming the problem of conclusions. Although tragedy endings abbreviate and distort reality, they can nonetheless afford to suggest a finality which the chronicle history for instance cannot, precisely because we recognize in the death of the tragic protagonist an image of our own future extinction. Every member of the theatre audience feels that he stands, like Hamlet or Othello, in the centre of his play, surrounded by minor characters who for their part are equally convinced of their centrality in a performance which is both the same as ours and different. An objective awareness that the play will continue without us does not conflict with our private sense that it stops as soon as we cease to be a part of it. In terms of the individual consciousness, tragedy fifth acts are true.

Artistic forms which dismiss their characters into happiness, often through the solemnization or promise of marriage, are far more problematic. Such endings are not real conclusions, even in the qualified sense that tragic obsequies are. They are a kind of arbitrary arrest. By means of art, the flux of life has been stilled. Satiety, death, the erosion

---

[4] I am indebted here, and indeed throughout this essay, to Frank Kermode's discussion of the problem of beginnings and endings in fiction in *The Sense of an Ending* (Oxford, 1967).

of personality by time have all been denied or else indefinitely post-
poned in order that an ephemeral moment of happiness may pose as a
permanent state. Fairy-tale accepts and indeed flaunts this implausibi-
lity. Formulaic concluding sentences like the familiar 'And so they all
lived happily ever after', the more evasive 'And for all I know, they are
reigning there yet', or 'If they have not left off their merry-making,
they must be at it still' are really signal-flares of impossibility. They are
the appropriate finish for stories about beggars who become kings,
benevolent frog-princes who rescue maidens in distress, or sea-nymphs
who keep open house for mistreated younger sons in halls of crystal
drowned forty fathoms deep. Fairy-tales are like Christian allegories of
salvation, in that both ask the reader to accept on faith the idea of an
eternity of bliss which is deliberately at odds with the way of the world
as we know it. As such, they stand at a remove from those comic forms
which are determined both to gratify our longing for a golden world
and to realize it in what, for lack of a better phrase, one must call
"realistic terms'.

Anthony Trollope, adept though he was at happy endings designed
to please his feminine readers, was too honest an artist not to question
them. At the end of *Barchester Towers*, he complained wryly of the
difficulty of composing last chapters that were both cheerful and
genuinely satisfying:

> Promises of two children and superhuman happiness are of no
> avail, nor assurance of extreme respectability carried to an age far
> exceeding that usually allotted to mortals. . . . I can only say that if
> some critic, who thoroughly knows his work, and has laboured on it
> till experience has made him perfect, will write the last fifty pages of
> a novel in the way they should be written, I, for one, will in future
> do my best to copy the example. Guided by my own lights only, I
> confess that I despair of success.[5]

If comedy endings pose problems for the novelist, they are even more
tricky for the dramatist who, deprived as he is of the novelist's weapons
of digression and objective comment, wishes to leave us with the
image of a world transfigured but to make it credible as fairy-tales are
not. Shakespeare's handling of the end of *As You Like It* is masterful
in the way it welds together realism and romance. The play releases its
audience cheered and consoled, conscious of having participated

[5] Anthony Trollope, *Barchester Towers*, chapter LI.

briefly in an existence which, although heightened and more harmonious than its own, cannot be dismissed as a mere 'improbable fiction'.

It is important to the ending of *As You Like It* that Arden has never, unlike the wood in *A Midsummer Night's Dream*, been presented as magical. This is not quite an ordinary Warwickshire forest. References to palm trees and lionesses, to Duke Senior and his followers as reincarnations of 'the old Robin Hood of England', men who 'fleet the time carelessly as they did in the golden world' (I.i. 107–9), ensure that this is to some extent Arcadia. It is, however, an Arcadia touched by the older, pre-Virgilian tradition: a place where the seasons alter, where the wind can be cold and the underbrush tangled, where food is hard to come by and Corin's master is of churlish disposition. Touchstone's initial reaction to the forest: 'Ay, now am I in Arden; the more fool I; when I was at home I was in a better place' (II. iv. 13–14) is exactly that of the disgruntled traveller arriving, after much effort, at Venice in the rain.

Essentially Arden is enchanted only in the sense that it is a place where, miraculously, Fortune does not oppress Nature. In the forest, people are free to be themselves as they are not in the court of Duke Frederick. There, Le Beau needs to adopt a foppish false countenance in public and can only whisper nervously to Orlando, when he finds him alone, of that 'better world than this' in which it might be possible to drop the mask and to 'desire more love and knowledge of you' (I. ii. 263–4). Although Le Beau himself never reaches it, Arden is indeed this 'better world'. The freedom it offers, however, is not unlimited and dizzying like that of fairy-tale. At the end of the comedy as at the beginning, William will be a clod and Audrey awkward and ill-favoured. Frogs remain frogs and ugly ducklings stay ugly; they do not change into princes or into swans. The changes which do occur in characters like Rosalind and Orlando, Duke Senior, Phebe, Celia and even Oliver, are really self-discoveries, a deepening and development of personality. For the most part, these people earn their own happy endings. Their destinies are not imposed upon them arbitrarily, as they are upon Hermia and Lysander, Helena and Demetrius, by a supernatural world.

Four pairs of lovers marry at the end of *As You Like It*, a number so great that Jaques can pretend to fear another Flood is toward, as they range themselves two by two. Four weddings agreed upon in the final scene of a comedy is daring, a test of audience credulity. In his previous plays, Shakespeare had never attempted more than three (leaving aside the deferred nuptials of *Love's Labour's Lost*), and he preferred to space them through the course of the comedy. The conclusion of *As You Like It* veers towards the implausible in asking us to accept four marriages, two lightning conversions, and the inexplicable appearance of the god Hymen among the cast of characters. At the same time it insists that although fairy-tale elements are undeniably present here, as indeed they have been in varying intensities through the play, this ending still presents an image of reality. The classicism of the comedy declares itself both in the assurance with which it exacts belief for improbabilities so considerable, and in the unprecedented generosity and inclusiveness of the society which finally emerges from Arden. The cynicism of Touchstone, the unseemly postures of Audrey, may disturb the symmetry of the dance at the end. No society, not even this one, is perfect. Nevertheless, the fact that the fool and the goat-girl can form part of the pattern testifies to the flexibility of the new social order, its ability to accommodate deviation. More than any of its predecessors, *As You Like It* demonstrates Shakespeare's faith in comedy resolutions. It is a triumph of form.

Of the characters whom one would expect to find in the final scene, only two do not participate in the dance. Adam is too old to take part in the establishment of the new order. Quietly, he has vanished from the play. His absence defines one kind of limitation admitted by the comic society. Jaques, who is present when the revels begin, but refuses either to join or to watch them, defines another that is more important. Unlike Shylock or Don John, this man has never menaced the lives or happiness of other characters in the play. His exile at the end is voluntary, a reasoned decision against which the Duke protests in vain: it is not in any sense a punishment or ritual casting out. That 'better world' created in Arden which prepares now to reinvigorate the court would gladly assimilate Jaques, if only he were willing. The fact that he is not willing suggests that there are certain kinds of experience after all, certain questions, which lie outside the scope of the happy ending, generous and convincing though that is.

Jaques' pessimism has hitherto been blunted by characters who, although fully aware themselves of the facts of death and time, have wisely refused to be crippled by such knowledge. His despair has functioned as a useful test of Rosalind and Orlando's sanity and sense of proportion. A seeming threat to the classical equilibrium of the comedy, Jaques has in fact provided it with needful opportunities to demonstrate its own strength and poise. His withdrawal at the end impoverishes the comic society about to leave Arden. Like a ship which has suddenly jettisoned its ballast, the play no longer rides quite evenly in the waves. Jaques' departure does more than simply imply that 'there is a world elsewhere'. It accentuates that slight inclination towards fantasy already present in this final scene, a tendency signalized by the abrupt entrance of Jaques de Boys, his extraordinary account of Duke Frederick's conversion, and by Hymen's affirmation of something we should all wistfully like to believe: that the gods themselves delight in happy endings:

> Then is there mirth in heaven,
> When earthly things made even
> Atone together.
>
> (V. iv. 102-4)

A tremor appears in the balance of the comedy.

Yet the balance holds. It would be wrong to over-stress the fairy-tale elements in the conclusion, even as it would be inaccurate to see its joyousness as impaired by Jaques' decision to seek a kind of experience unavailable within the comic dance. Essentially *As You Like It* remains whole and complete at its ending, displaying only a flicker of qualification and unease. In associating Jaques' self-banishment with the dreamlike figure of the old religious man, the fabulous quality of Duke Frederick's decision to embrace an ascetic life, Shakespeare deliberately minimizes its impact. Although he may choose to separate himself from the comic society, Jaques remains within a heightened world. The journey he is about to undertake will not conduct him to a reality serving, by its contrast, to diminish and render fictional the world centred upon Rosalind, Orlando and Duke Senior. Such a distinction would destroy the play's classical poise. The moment of classical stasis must always, however, be brief. In *Twelfth Night*, the next of the comedies, the fragmentation only hinted at in the last scene of *As You Like It* became actual, as Shakespeare began to unbuild his own comic form at its point of greatest vulnerability: the ending.

IV

All of *Twelfth Night*, up to the final scene, takes place in a heightened world. There is no contrasting environment, no Athens or Duke Frederick's court, to set against Illyria. Messaline, the place from which

Viola and Sebastian have come, is even more shadowy than Syracuse
in *The Comedy of Errors*, or those wars from which Don Pedro,
Claudio and Benedick find release in Messina. Messaline has no character whatever, and certainly no claim to be regarded as that normal
world to which characters have so often returned at the end of a Shakespearian comedy. Illyria itself, on the other hand, has a very distinct
character and declares it from the opening moments of the play. The
sea-captain, appealed to by Viola for information about the country in
which she has so unexpectedly arrived, might just as well have said to
her what the Cheshire Cat says to Alice: 'They're all mad here.' Even
before the unsettling appearance of twin Cesarios, both the ruler of
Illyria and his reluctant mistress have manœuvred themselves into
unbalanced states of mind. They are surrounded, moreover, by characters even madder than they: Sir Toby Belch, Sir Andrew Aguecheek,
or Feste, the man whose profession is folly. Malvolio in his dark room
may seem to present the play's most extreme image of insanity, yet
Olivia can confess that 'I am as mad as he, / If sad and merry madness
equal be' (III. iv. 14–15). Sebastian, bewildered by Olivia's passionate
claims upon him, will earnestly debate the question of his own sanity.
Antonio, already bewitched as he sees it by Sebastian, is accused of
madness by Orsino's officer when he tries to explain his situation.

The eruption onto the stage of identical twins is calculated to make
people distrust the evidence of their own senses. *The Comedy of Errors*,
which plays the same game of mistaken identity in a doubled form, had
also made use of images of madness. Yet the lunacy of *Twelfth Night* is
both more widespread and more various. It is part of the whole atmosphere of the Feast of Fools suggested by the play's title, not simply a
product of the failure to understand that there are two Cesarios and not
just one. For Elizabethans this title would have stirred immemorial
and continuing associations with a period of time in which normal
rules were suspended, in which the world turned ritually upside down,
allowing the plain man to become king and pleasure to transform itself
into a species of obligation. Certainly the spirit of holiday reigns in
Illyria, particularly in the household of the mourning Olivia. The
countess herself may disapprove from a distance of the nightly chaos
presided over by Sir Toby: only Malvolio tries in earnest to repress it. As
soon as he does so, he places himself in danger. He becomes the churl
at the banquet, the sobersides at the carnival. The revellers, forgetting
their own private dissensions, recognize him at once for the common

enemy and hunt him from their midst. As feasters, men living in a celebratory world that, temporarily at least, is larger than life, they instinctively protect themselves against the niggard who refuses to yield himself to the extraordinary.

As members of the *Twelfth Night* audience, we too are sharers in the extraordinary, a fact which perhaps explains why Malvolio has found tender-hearted apologists in the study but very few sympathizers in the playhouse. His humiliation at the hands of Feste, Maria, Fabian and Sir Toby removes a threat to our own equilibrium, to the holiday mood induced by the comedy in its early stages. We make common cause with Sir Toby and the Fool against Malvolio because we do not want him to spoil fun which in a sense is ours as well as that of characters actually on the stage. By means of laughter, we too cast Malvolio out. As soon as the steward has pieced together the meaning of the mock letter to his own satisfaction, as soon as he has swallowed the bait, he ceases to be a threat. Yellow-stockinged and cross-gartered, trying to produce some rusty approximation to a smile, Malvolio has become part of precisely that heightened world of play-acting, revelry and lack of control which he so despised. Festivity has made him its unwilling prey. Thereafter, it will do with him what it likes, until the moment of awakening.

This moment of awakening is in some ways the most distinctive feature of *Twelfth Night*. Sir Toby is the first to scent the morning air. At the end of Act IV, he is wishing that 'we were well rid of this knavery', that some means of releasing Malvolio 'conveniently' might be devised before the mood of holiday inconsequence breaks (IV. ii. 65–8). Act V displays a marked harshening of tone. It begins by massing together images of death in a fashion that harks back to Shakespeare's preferred comic practice in the plays written before *As You Like It*. In this respect, as in its renewed emphasis on plot, *Twelfth Night* breaks away from the classicism of its predecessor. Orsino, confronting Antonio in his fetters, remembers that when last he saw this face 'it was besmeared / As black as Vulcan in the smoke of war' (V. i. 46–7). To the grim realities of combat and mutilation now recalled there is added the agony of Antonio's account of his friend's treachery. The appearance of Olivia only makes matters worse. Orsino, half-crazed with jealousy of Cesario, threatens publicly to 'kill what I love' (V. i. 113):

> Him will I tear out of that cruel eye
> Where he sits crowned in his master's spite.

> Come, boy, with me; my thoughts are ripe in mischief:
> I'll sacrifice the lamb that I do love
> To spite a raven's heart within a dove.
>
> (V. i. 121-5)

The situation is further complicated by the priest's confirmation of Olivia's marriage, a marriage so recent that since its solemnization 'my watch hath told me, towards my grave, / I have travell'd but two hours' (V. i. 156-7). Between sincere and passionate affirmation on the one side and, on the other, equally sincere and passionate denial, the deadlock is complete. Only Sebastian can untangle this knot. The next character to enter is not, however, Sebastian but the wretched Sir Andrew Aguecheek. He comes, surprisingly, as the victim of real violence:

> For the love of God, a surgeon! Send one presently to Sir Toby. . . .
> Has broke my head across, and has given Sir Toby a bloody coxcomb too. For the love of God, your help! I had rather than forty pound I were at home.
>
> (V. i. 166-71)

Sebastian has levelled precisely those inequalities upon which Sir Toby battened. Predator and prey have been used alike despite the considerable difference in their swordsmanship and general efficiency. And indeed something more than a pair of coxcombs has been broken.

Surgeons, after all, belong to a sober reality of sickness and disease outside the limits of festivity. This, at least, ought to be their territory. Feste's reply to Sir Toby's question, 'didst see Dick Surgeon, sot?', is less than consoling: 'O, he's drunk, Sir Toby, an hour agone; his eyes were set at eight i' th' morning' (V. i. 189-91). Sir Toby himself has hitherto turned day into night and night into day. He has argued in Falstaffian terms that 'to be up after midnight and to go to bed then is early; so that to go to bed after midnight is to go to bed betimes' (II. ii. 7-9). For the reveller, the only meaningful chronicity is the one Prince Hal attributed to Falstaff, one in which hours are 'cups of sack, and minutes capons, and clocks the tongues of bawds, and dials the signs of leaping houses' (1 Henry IV, I. ii. 5-11). Bleeding and in pain, forced to recognize another and harsher kind of time, Sir Toby demands the services of the surgeon, only to discover that this functionary, like himself in happier state, has sat up all night revelling and is now blissfully asleep in just those daylight hours when he is wanted. It is bad enough to be jolted unceremoniously into reality, but even more bitter to find that the surgeon you urgently require is still, in an unregenerate fashion, disporting himself at the carnival. Condemned to suffer pain without relief, Sir Toby gives vent to the uncharacteristic utterance, 'I hate a drunken rogue' (V. i. 193).

In the next moment, he turns savagely on Sir Andrew's well-meant offer of assistance and companionship in misery. 'Will you help—an asshead and a coxcomb and a knave, a thin-fac'd knave, a gull?' (V. i. 196–9). Only a moment before, Sir Andrew had wished 'for forty pound' that he was safely at home again. It was the genuine accent of the reveller for whom the party has suddenly become poisonous, who wishes now that he had never set out from the familiar, homely world to the masked ball; the man for whom day breaks after a night of abandon and fruitless pursuit of profit in a garish and essentially shaming way. On top of all this comes the sudden treachery, the revelation in his true colours of a supposed friend. Sir Andrew does not reply to Sir Toby's abuse. He simply vanishes, never to reappear in the comedy. Sir Toby leaves the stage too, not to be seen again. Subsequently it will be revealed that he has married Maria, as a recompense for her plot against the steward. For him, as for Sir Andrew creeping back to his depleted lands, holiday has been paid for in ways that have real-life consequences.

At precisely this point, as the two broken revellers are being helped away in a state of debility and antagonism, Shakespeare exchanges prose for verse and radically alters the mood of the scene. He allows Sebastian, that comedy resolution personified, at last to confront his twin sister, to assure Olivia of his faith, to renew his friendship with Antonio and to enlighten Orsino. There will be a happy ending. It is, however, a happy ending of an extraordinarily schematized and 'playlike' kind. Viola has already had virtual proof, in Act III, that her brother has survived the wreck. They have been separated for only three months. Yet the two of them put each other through a formal, intensely conventional question and answer test that comes straight out of Greek New Comedy:

> *Viola:* My father had a mole upon his brow.
> *Sebastian:* And so had mine.
> *Viola:* And died that day when Viola from her birth
> Had numb'red thirteen years.
> *Sebastian:* O, that record is lively in my soul!

> He finished indeed his mortal act
> That day that made my sister thirteen years.
>
> (V. i. 234–40)

This recognition scene is intensely moving. Its emotional force and purity derive, however, from consonances that are recognizably fictional. In the theatre, the fact that an audience will always be more struck by the *dissimilarity* in appearance of the actors playing Viola and Sebastian than by that marvellous identity hailed so ecstatically by the other characters, also serves to drive a wedge between fact and literary invention.[6] We are dealing here, Shakespeare seems to announce, with a heightened, an essentially implausible world.

For Olivia and Sebastian, Viola and Orsino, this heightened world perpetuates itself. For them, there will be no return from holiday, no need to leave Illyria. Yet the little society which they form at the end of the play is far more fragmentary and insubstantial than the one that had been consolidated in Arden. The final pairings-off are perfunctory. Olivia accepts Sebastian for himself. Orsino, rather more surprisingly, accepts a Viola he has never seen as a woman. Rosalind had returned in her own guise as a girl at the end of *As You Like It*, uniting Ganymede with the lady Orlando loved first at Duke Frederick's court. Considering the abruptness of Orsino's resolve to substitute Viola for Olivia in his affections, an unknown Viola only guessed at beneath her 'masculine usurp'd attire' (V. i. 242), Shakespeare might well have done something similar here. Instead, he treats this joining of hands summarily, and turns away at once to the very different issue of Malvolio.

In the final act of *Twelfth Night*, a world of revelry, of comic festivity, fights a kind of desperate rearguard action against the cold light of day. It survives only in part, and then by insisting upon an exclusiveness that is poles apart from the various and crowded dance at the end of *As You Like It*. Viola and Orsino, Olivia and Sebastian may no longer be deluded, yet it is still Illyria in which they live: an improbable world of hair's-breadth rescues at sea, romantic disguises, idealistic friendships and sudden, irrational loves. This is not quite the

---

[6] Jonson claimed, according to Drummond (*Works*, ed. C. H. Herford and P. Simpson (Oxford, 1925), vol. I, p. 144), that he had never undertaken any adaptation of the *Amphitruo* of Plautus because it was impossible to find actors who were identical twins. Shakespeare, writing a different kind of comedy, one concerned to explore the relationship between illusion and reality, accepted and indeed built upon the obstacle which Jonson found insuperable, here and in *The Comedy of Errors*.

country behind the North Wind, but it approaches those latitudes. The two romantic couples stand on the far side of a line dividing fiction from something we recognize as our own reality, and the society they epitomize is too small to initiate a dance.[7] Of the other main characters, no fewer than four are conspicuous by their absence. Maria, Sir Toby and Sir Andrew are not present to witness the revelations and accords of the closing moments. Malvolio intrudes upon them briefly, but entirely uncomprehendingly. Like Sir Toby and Sir Andrew, he comes as a figure of violence and leaves unreconciled, meditating a futile revenge. For him too, the dream is over and the moment of awakening bitter. Jacques had walked with dignity out of the new society; Malvolio in effect is flung.

There is only one character who can restore some sense of unity to *Twelfth Night* at its ending, mediating between the world of the romantic lovers and our own world, which is (or is about to be) that of the chastened Sir Andrew, the sobered Belch and the unbending Malvolio. In a sense, he has been doing just this all along in preparation for some such ultimate necessity. Throughout *Twelfth Night*, Feste has served as commentator and Chorus, mocking the extravagance of Orsino, the wasteful idealism of Olivia's grief, Viola's poor showing as a man. He has joined in the revels of Sir Toby and Sir Andrew while remaining essentially apart from them, aware of their limitations. Most important of all, he has kept us continually aware of the realities of death and time: that 'pleasure will be paid one time or another' (II. iv. 70), that 'beauty's a flower' (I. v. 37) and youth 'a stuff will not endure' (II. iii. 51). Two contradictory kinds of time have run parallel through the comedy, diverging only at its end. One is the time of holiday and of fiction, measureless and essentially beneficent, to which Viola trusts when she remains passive and permits the happy ending to work itself out with no positive assistance from her (II. ii. 38–9). The other time is remorseless and strictly counted. Although even Viola and Orsino catch glimpses of it, its chief spokesman has been Feste.

At the very end of *Twelfth Night* these two attitudes towards time distinguish two groups of characters, dividing a world of fiction

[7] It consists, in fact, only of themselves and the minor figure Fabian. There is no place for this Antonio, as there was for his namesake in the love/friendship resolution of *The Merchant of Venice*. In John Barton's 1969 Stratford production of *Twelfth Night*, Antonio made his exit alone at the end, in a direction different from that taken by the lovers.

from one of fact. The audience leaving the theatre faces its own jolt into reality, into the stern time of a world beyond holiday, but at least it is given Feste and not Malvolio as its guide. Left alone on the stage, Feste sings his song about the ages of man, a song which draws its material from the same source as Jaques' pessimistic catalogue. This time, there will be no attempt at qualification or correction. Yet the song itself is curiously consoling. It leads us gently and in a way that is aesthetically satisfying from the golden world to the age of iron which is our own. A triumph of art, it builds a bridge over the rift which has opened in the comedy at its conclusion.

Feste is tolerant as Jaques, on the whole, was not. He does not attempt to judge, or even to reason. He simply states fact. The child is allowed his fancies: a foolish thing is but a toy. When he grows up he pays for them, or else discovers that the self-deceptions in which he is tempted to take refuge are easily penetrated by the world. Marriage ultimately becomes tedious, and so do the infidelities to which it drives a man. The reality of wind and rain wins out, the monotony of the everyday. The passing of time is painful, may even seem unendurable, but there is nothing for it but resignation, the wise acceptance of the Fool. All holidays come to an end; all revels wind down at last. Only by the special dispensation of art can some people, Viola and Orsino, Olivia and Sebastian, be left in Illyria. For the rest of us, the play is done; fiction yields to fact, and we return to normality along with Sir Toby and Maria, Sir Andrew and Malvolio.

V

Endings, Frank Kermode has stated, are most satisfactory when they are not negative, in the sense of representing a mere absence of continuation, but instead 'frankly transfigure the events in which they were immanent'.[8] He cites *Anna Karenina*. Shakespeare's comedies before *Twelfth Night* are also works of art in which a retrospective view from the final scene is encouraged, and alters our understanding of the play as a whole. Essentially teleological, as *Volpone* and *The Alchemist* are not, their fifth-act marriages and revelations are designed to carry far more weight than Jonson's ultimate exposures of roguery or deflation of peccant humours. The fact that Volpone ends in prison, that Doll and Subtle flee over the back wall, or that Young Kno'well

[8] Kermode, *op. cit.*, p. 175.

marries Bridget Kitely, constitutes in each case a tidy rounding-off of plot, a convenient place for the comedy to stop. These endings do not illuminate earlier scenes in the way that Mercade's announcement both elucidates and transforms the entire previous development of *Love's Labour's Lost*, or the harmonies of *As You Like It* at its conclusion transfigure the 'broken music' (I. ii. 126) of the wrestling match at Duke Frederick's court. Even *The Taming of the Shrew* and *The Merry Wives of Windsor*, although in some respects standing apart from the other comedies, still ask to be considered afresh in the light of Katharine's final position, and of the accords worked out in Windsor Park.

Only with *Twelfth Night* did Shakespeare, apparently, lose faith in endings of this kind. The consequences of that divided fifth act, of admitting the fictional nature of the comic society, are manifest both in the ironically titled *All's Well That Ends Well* and in *Measure For Measure*. Even less than *Twelfth Night* can these be described as plays whose conclusions 'transfigure the events in which they were immanent'. Instead, realism collides painfully with romance. The world as it is submits at the end, with a calculated artificiality, to the laws of comic form. In doing so, it belittles those laws. There is no question in these comedies of some characters being excluded from the final scene, as they were in *Twelfth Night*. Everyone participates in the resolutions of *All's Well That Ends Well* and *Measure For Measure*, such as they are. These resolutions, however, float free and unattached above the comedies they supposedly crown. As admitted fairy-tale endings, they do not pretend to shadow reality. They are not even consonant with the previous development of the two plays, nor with the nature and personalities of the characters involved. It is hard not to see both these endings as confessions of the inadequacy of comedy resolutions. Certainly they stand at a remove from the damaged but poignant harmonies of *Twelfth Night*, let alone from the artistic balance and optimism of *As You Like It* in its fifth act. After *Measure For Measure* Shakespeare abandoned comedy. When he did return to the form in *Pericles*, some years later, he made it perfectly clear that he was now writing fairy-stories. The last plays as a group flaunt their own impossibilities and theatrical contrivance. They announce at the very beginning that they are only plays and insist throughout upon revealing the wires which make the puppets move. The marvellous restorations and discoveries which conclude *Pericles*, *Cymbeline* and *The Winter's Tale* are perfectly in accord with their nature as old tales: dreams before daylight, a dance of shadows. Only the emotions generated are, miraculously, real. Out of this readjustment of form Shakespeare seems to have drawn for a little while—up to the point of *The Tempest* and the incomplete symmetries of its fifth act—a renewed faith in comedy endings.

IX

Theatrical 'trompe l'oeil' in 'Measure for Measure'

JOCELYN POWELL

I

THE economy of a play is necessarily different from that of other more completely literary genres. This difference centres in the dramatist's employment of time. A poet or novelist may expect the reader to create his own dialogue with each word or sentence, to move through the complexities of the work according to an individual tempo; the rhythmic forms of poems or novels indicate units of coherence rather than precise temporal shape. But in a play time passes irretrievably; there is no going back; the performance unfolds towards its conclusion as a succession of moments exactly proportioned. They have but this one shape; it is now or never. This is easy to forget. Studying the texts of plays, one may think they possess the same opportunities for reference and recollection as a poem or a novel; in reality they occupy a different world, dependent for its proper articulation upon a nice sense of space and time.

In a play the meaning exists in the moment. What is important is what can be grasped in that moment and its connection with what can be at that moment recollected. The focus of attention is all-important and can over-ride inconsistency of detail in a greater consistency of association. When Lady Macbeth says:

> I have given suck, and know
> How tender 'tis to love the babe that milks me—
> I would while it was smiling in my face
> Have pluck'd my nipple from his boneless gums,
> And dash'd the brains out, had I so sworn
> As you have done to this,
>
> (*Macbeth*, I. vii. 54–9)

we mark the violence of her determination, its ferocity and destructive-
ness, we feel its symbolic force—we do not wonder what has become
of her children, or speculate as to whether their loss in infancy might
be the cause of her barbarity. Similarly, if Shakespeare once arranged
the decease of young Benvolio at the end of *Romeo and Juliet*, as Q1
suggests, he soon learned that out of sight meant out of mind and cut
the reference rather than stimulate irrelevant questions that might dis-
tract the audience from the real matter in hand. At both these moments
the audience's thoughts will be moving along very particular lines,
and it would be wasteful not to take advantage of the fact.

The nature of the spectator's concentration gives a drama a certain
freedom of manœuvre which is a necessary complement to the limitation of space and time. Attention may work through association
of action rather than by logic of event and so give the unfolding of
circumstances the same scope poetic diction gives to the functions of
grammar. Mallarmé said that in a poem words should be linked to
create larger fresher words that were whole lines together. In a play
actions may be linked to form larger experiences which are apprehended through the suggestiveness of their juxtaposition rather than
the circumstantial logic of their sequence. In Shakespeare's comedies
this relationship of image to event is particularly subtle. The romance
basis of the plays allows the building of a free structure in which events
carry a symbolic meaning beyond their significance as narrative, and
these meanings bear the burden of integrating the various elements
of the plot, which is thus experienced in a number of different modes.
Often the symbolic integrity has a greater importance than consistency of narrative and character elements, and we are made to forget
such difficulties, as we were made to forget Lady Macbeth's children,
by the focuses created for our attention by the imaginative strength
and richness of the symbolism. The prime example of such a play is
Measure for Measure, whose integrity and significance depend equally
on this theatrical *trompe l'œil*.

II

The technique of *Measure for Measure* is imagistic. A great variety
of dramatic means are employed: its style shifts through romance and
allegory to satirical farce and intense psychological drama; but the
organization of the play enables these contrasts not to contradict each

other. Instead they constantly shift the attention of the audience, so that now one and now another series of perceptions and associations rise out of the material of the story. Nor do they overbalance each other. Shakespeare arranges the dramatic focus so that within the pattern of the whole experience the intrigue with Mariana is no more an anticlimax to Angelo's attempted seduction of Isabel than is the latter's consent to marry the Duke a frivolous dismissal of her character. Such transitions are justified by a fundamentally theatrical logic. The dramatist creates a pattern of experience through which we may come not merely to understand, but also to apprehend, a particular problem of existence.

The technique is theatrically very simple. It is the critical intellect operating after or away from the dramatic event that makes it seem devious. The variety of the play's structure is held together by a pattern of images which move between word and action. This imagery guides the imagination through the contradictions of the play and enables us to feel its unity and significance. Its ambivalence as word and deed enables the play to be experienced as a whole; the elements of the pattern are grasped as one. The centre of the pattern is the Duke, whom Shakespeare has brought from the periphery of the story to be its mainstay. The play opens with his departure on a journey, stealthily and without ceremony; and it ends with his return from that journey, in pomp and with full public celebration at the gates of the city. The action between converts the image of the journey into the spiritual journey of the Duke himself, a voyage into the nature of his place and purpose. The play is about Vincentio's problems as a ruler and a man, indeed about the tension between the two roles. The manifold images of the action flow out from this centre, and feed back their various experiences into our understanding of it.

Shakespeare's original audience must have found the opening of the play extremely curious and striking. The Duke, we learn, has failed in his responsibilities. His lax easiness in authority has led to licence, and he acknowledges his fault:

> For we bid this be done,
> When evil deeds have their permissive pass,
> And not the punishment.
>
> (I. iii. 37–9)

To rectify this he has appointed a deputy, a 'man of stricture and firm abstinence', who may restore, by an absolute application of the law, the Duke's lost order. To watch this done the Duke remains in Vienna in the disguise of a Friar.

There are two important points here. First, we may assume the Duke's acceptance of responsibility for Angelo's judicial decisions. He has chosen him as the right man for the job, since the nature of his office demands that someone act in his place. It is above all necessary to preserve the reputation of the office he has failed in by dissociating himself (the symbol of that office in his people's eyes) from a change in judicial procedure that may appear tyrannical. The change has been made needful by his own misconduct as a man, but the stain of this wrong must not contaminate his office as a Duke:

> Therefore, indeed, my father,
> I have on Angelo impos'd the office,
> Who may, in th'ambush of my name, strike home,
> And yet my nature never in the fight
> To do in slander.
>
> (I. iii. 39–43)

The Duke's conduct here is responsible rather than selfish, but his judgement of the situation in his Dukedom, and of its remedy, does stand or fall by his choice of deputy.

Secondly, we are presented with two complementary images of authority—that of the judge, having temporal power, and that of the Friar, whose power is spiritual. This dual nature of authority is of particular relevance to a nation whose king claims also to be head of the church. In deputizing his judicial authority to Angelo and disguising himself as a friar, the Duke not only retains spiritual authority but enables the dramatist to focus our attention on this underlying aspect of temporal power. This is crucial. The opening scenes set up a sort of judicial trinity—the merciful Duke, whose mercy promulgated licence; the judicial deputy, who metes out measure for measure; and the charitable friar, who prepares the soul for the body's last agony. The spiritual responsibility of the friar is constant to both the foregoing attitudes to justice, and the significance of this is gradually revealed through the test case that forms the basis of the plot, Angelo's condemnation of Claudio:

> See that Claudio
> Be executed by nine to-morrow morning;

> Bring him his confessor; let him be prepar'd;
> For that's the utmost of his pilgrimage.
>
> (II. i. 33–6)

In fact, the opening movement of the play patterns out a hierarchy of judgement. At the bottom are those whom the law commands, the criminals, falling into two groups: the young gentlemen, who are ostensibly green in offence, and the hardened criminals to whom vice is a trade; then, the judges: the Duke's deputy, Angelo, and his assistant, Escalus, who provides us with a glimpse of the problems of the Duke's old liberal views—and also the friar, the agent of moral and spiritual judgement, as is demonstrated by the scenes the Duke plays with Juliet and with Pompey; finally, there is the Duke himself, who must judge the integrity with which his deputies have carried out his will. But it does not of course rest here: the Duke, too, has a judge beyond him. He governs by divine right, but is himself the 'deputy elected by the lord'. When Angelo answers *his* lord's accusation his words have a frightening ambivalence:

> O my dread lord,
> I should be guiltier than my guiltiness,
> To think I can be undiscernible,
> When I perceive your Grace, like pow'r divine,
> Hath look'd upon my passes.
>
> (V. i. 364–8)

The Duke's place as the Supreme Lord's deputy is that holy 'name' that has been preserved from slander by the election of Angelo; but the Duke's own actions throughout the play are coming before the throne of a higher judge who watches the use he makes of the divine office entrusted him, an office which carries with it no less than a responsibility for the ordering of man's life on earth, spiritual and temporal. The Duke, therefore, in that he stands before the throne of God, has a common relation to the lowest of his subjects. This is demonstrated in Angelo's simile. The Duke's office is 'like' that of divine power; but he is not divine, he is a man, and under judgement as all men are. Angelo is not of course telling the Duke this: it is anyway sufficiently known; but his words bring before us at the play's climax the manner in which Angelo, the deputy before his judge, is a mirror image of the Duke himself. This is already implicit in the initial decision to create a deputy to exercise a more rigorous justice, and its significance for authority is resolved, as we shall see, at the turning point of the play. The pattern of the whole follows the Duke's realization of his nature as a man holding a divine office. Such a one must sustain two roles as the deputy of God: that of the absolute voice of temporal justice, and that of the spiritual guardian of eternal life; but in neither role must he forget that he remains a man. In the last act of *Measure for Measure* the Duke achieves and sustains this strange and terrifying triple identity. The way we are made aware of this is a theatrical *tour de force*, which depends on the gradual establishment in the audience of the human and personal significance of each of these *personae*. It is brought about by involving the Duke dramatically in a number of differentiated actions which are nonetheless powerfully connected by the interaction of their imagery. Vincentio's triple identity as man, priest and ruler vests in his person a symbolic seriousness which is crucial to the whole experience.

III

As the Duke forms the source of the action, so the source of the imagery can be found in the nature of the test case over which that action is chiefly concerned, Claudio's seduction of Juliet. At bottom this act seems hardly criminal at all. As Lucio describes it it is rather part of the natural creative processes of all nature:

> Your brother and his lover have embrac'd.
> As those that feed grow full, as blossoming time,
> That from the seedness the bare fallow brings
> To teeming foison, even so her plenteous womb
> Expresseth his full tilth and husbandry.

(I. iv. 40–44)

But it is not only a matter of blossoms and harvest: the image of creation and abundance is linked with an image of appetite. This is the problem. There is a necessary relationship between creation and pleasure, but they are troublesome partners. Angelo has a very different view of the matter:

> Ha! Fie, these filthy vices! It were as good
> To pardon him that hath from nature stol'n
> A man already made, as to remit
> Their saucy sweetness that do coin heaven's image

> In stamps that are forbid; 'tis all as easy
> Falsely to take away a life true made,
> As to put metal in restrained means
> To make a false one.
>
> (II. iv. 42–9)

The equation of lust with murder seems to modern ears somewhat
excessive, and yet it is not merely a function of the puritanical Angelo;
it is part of a dialectic of images that analyses the very subtle difference
of inflection that turns creation to destruction in human actions.
False coining is a common enough image, in Shakespeare's time, for
illicit sexuality; but in this play the connection between interest and
increase are made germane to the argument in all parts of the story,
while the equation of false creation and willed destruction is made the
pivot of the plot.

It is the images of appetite, trade and coinage that set up the relationship of Claudio and eventually Angelo to the brothels of Vienna. In
the brothels, the creative powers of love are made the occasion for
personal gain; procreation is a form of self-interest; it is rendered sterile
and poisonous as it increases the bawd's wealth:

> Fie, sirrah, a bawd, a wicked bawd!
> The evil that thou causest to be done,
> That is thy means to live. Do thou but think
> What 'tis to cram a maw or clothe a back
> From such a filthy vice; say to thyself
> 'From their abominable and beastly touches
> I drink, I eat, array myself, and live'.
> Canst thou believe thy living is a life,
> So stinkingly depending? Go mend, go mend.
>
> (III. ii. 16–24)

Such beastliness turns profit into loss; material increase is spiritual
death, for the natural creative process is blocked for material gain. It
is not fortuitous that the bawd's name is Pompey Bum. And the des-
tructiveness of this aspect of human behaviour is taken up in the
recurrent images of venereal disease. Such gain preys upon its own
flesh:

> *Lucio:* How doth my dear morsel, thy mistress? Procures she
> still, ha?

> *Pompey:* Troth, sir, she hath eaten up all her beef, and she is herself
> in the tub.   (III. ii. 50–53)

Though there is a world of difference between this and Claudio's real
love for Juliet (a difference that is expertly conveyed by the difference
of tone between the episodes), there are none the less some sinister
connections. Such bartering with love lies behind Claudio's plight,
as he himself tells us in similar images. He is contracted to Juliet; he is
entitled to her bed by law; but he wants not her alone but also her
dowry, and this prudent and profitable consideration has led to their
lacking the denunciation of 'outward order':

>   this we came not to,
> Only for propagation of a dow'r
> Remaining in the coffer of her friends.
> From whom we thought it meet to hide our love
> Till time had made them for us. But it chances
> The stealth of our most mutual entertainment,
> With character too gross, is writ on Juliet.
> *Lucio:* With child, perhaps?
> *Claudio:*   Unhappily, even so.
>   (I. ii. 142–9)

The 'mutual entertainment' of Claudio and Juliet has 'unhappily' been
fruitful. They have created life accidentally and irresponsibly, and this
act has also become destructive. In Claudio's speech the same images
of procreation and money come together; upon one level this also was
an act of greed. And the same images characterize Angelo, too—but
by inversion. Angelo was engaged to Mariana, but broke off with her
when 'her brother Frederick was wrecked at sea, having in that same
vessel the dowry of his sister'. Angelo and Claudio are not only technically guilty of the same crime, as has been frequently noticed, but are
also mirror-images of an important moral antithesis: greed can be
active or passive, licentious or puritanical. Claudio is a prodigal: in its
context his action is a squandering of life; but Angelo is a miser: greed
can lie as much in the reservation of your powers to yourself as in the
useless squandering of them for gain or pleasure. The hidden money
in the coffers of Juliet's friends is an image of Angelo's life.[1]

In fact the Duke has pointed out the wider implications of this idea

---

[1] For further associations of this image cf. Marinell guarding the 'Rich
Strond', Spenser, *The Faerie Queene*, Bk. III, Cant. IV.

at the very beginning of the play. Appointing the reluctant Angelo as his deputy, he says:

> Heaven doth with us as we with torches do,
> Not light them for themselves; for if our virtues
> Did not go forth of us, 'twere all alike
> As if we had them not. Spirits are not finely touch'd
> But to fine issues; nor Nature never lends
> The smallest scruple of her excellence,
> But, like a thrifty goddess, she determines
> Herself the glory of a creditor,
> Both thanks and use.
>
> (I. i. 33–41)

In this speech the images of trade take on an opposite significance. Gratitude and beneficence come to the fore in considering our 'use' of the lives Nature has lent. Here we sense the presence of the final judge, who asks a reckoning on the 'talents' with which we were endowed when he returns from his journey into a far country. If Claudio and the bawds may be said to squander and abuse their powers, Angelo may be seen to bury them in the ground. This reticence, secrecy and seclusion images a lack of spiritual and physical charity, and by it Angelo is linked with both Isabella and the Duke. On one level or another all three hold themselves back, protect themselves from the challenges of life. One might almost think Milton to have had Shakespeare's play as well as Spenser's poem at the back of his mind when he wrote:

> I cannot praise a fugitive and cloistered virtue, un-exercised and unbreathed, that never sallies out and sees her adversary, but slinks out of the race, where that immortal garland is to be run for, not without dust, and heat. Assuredly we bring not innocence into the world, we bring impurity much rather; that which purifies us is trial, and trial is by what is contrary. That virtue therefore which is but a youngling in the contemplation of evil, and knows not the utmost that vice promises to her followers, and rejects it, is but a blank virtue, not a pure; her whiteness is but an excremental whiteness.[2]

The three central characters of *Measure for Measure* all partake of this 'excremental whiteness', and the progress of the action may be seen as

[2] John Milton, *Areopagitica*, in *Prose Works*, ed. K. M. Burton (London, 1958), p. 158.

a trial of their mettle 'since the knowledge and survey of vice in this world is so necessary to the constitution of human virtue'.

IV

Angelo, Isabella and the Duke are all, at one stage or another, spiritual and personal misers. Angelo 'scarce confesses that his blood flows' and takes pride in his gravity; the Duke says he 'loves the people', but he will not open himself to them, and dislikes staging himself to their eyes (this is known to be a fad of King James I. That Shakespeare does not merely intend a fulsome compliment is suggested by the elaborate 'staging' of the final scene at the city gates): perhaps it is this shyness that has kept the lion in his cave; Isabella is reluctantly persuaded to leave the very cloister of Milton's image to intercede for her brother's life. Angelo first feels 'the strong and swelling evil of my conception', and experiences the impurity he brought into the world. His trial is through overt sin, and is the simplest of the three. The Duke and Isabella, on the other hand, move through a series of experiences wherein they learn the nature of sin through the terrors of virtue.

Isabella holds the play's most powerful scenes and endures its most awkward difficulties. Initially she is treated with tremendous psychological realism. We are told she is a young lady 'skilled in reason and discourse', and we see that this is so in her scenes with Angelo, where she applies her Ciceronian training to a case she finds it hard to plead. Her language is by no means continuously incandescent. When pressed indeed she is sometimes at a loss for words and her *loci* are hardly happy:

> Tomorrow! O, that's sudden! Spare him, spare him.
> He's not prepar'd for death. Even for our kitchens
> We kill the fowl of season; shall we serve heaven
> With less respect than we do minister
> To our gross selves?

(II. ii. 83–7)

In fact her powers of persuasion are more stimulated by anger than by love. She has a textbook knowledge of virtue that Angelo's intellect can easily counter, and initially she is only kept at him by the encouragement of Lucio. By and by, however, he begins to make her angry. His inattention annoys her:

> Well, believe this:
> No ceremony that to great ones longs,
> Not the king's crown nor the deputed sword,
> The marshal's truncheon nor the judge's robe,
> Become them with one half so good a grace
> As mercy does.
>
> (II. ii. 58-63)

She harps upon his deputizing in a way that is useful to the image of the play, but scarcely tactful from one in her position; and the addition of tell-tale petulant phrases like 'Well, believe this', show her mounting irritation at him. 'So,' she says, 'you must be the first that gives this sentence.' There is a shrewishness about her phrasing that suggests that critics who suppose that the dramatist intends her for a paragon are missing the point of her style. She and Angelo are a fair match for each other, though she can, when moved enough to be unselfconscious, allow her knowledge of the nature of creation to shine suddenly through:

> Alas! alas!
> Why, all the souls that were were forfeit once;
> And He that might the vantage best have took
> Found out the remedy. How would you be,
> If He, which is the top of judgment, should
> But judge you as you are? O, think on that;
> And mercy then will breathe within your lips,
> Like man new made.
>
> (II. ii. 72-9)

Words like these counter the edge on her tongue, but we have surely been amply prepared for her scene with her brother.

The point of this encounter is too often missed by factitious moralizing. In the first place, Isabella's submission would be quite useless: Angelo orders Claudio's execution anyway. In the second place, her intellectual position is impregnable. She believes she holds her soul in trust from God as the Duke holds his dukedom. She believes that to consent to Angelo would be to defile that soul. She considers, and in this she is quite orthodox, that death is a lesser evil than eternal damnation. It is impossible to argue this: if you believe it, it is so; if not, not. What remains, and is surely intended to be the centre of our interest, is the human side of her actions. Having made her spiritual decision, she behaves with great warmth. She goes herself to prepare her brother for his death, and goes under considerable stress and fear. Initially all is well; but, when she has to struggle with his fear as well as her own, her will breaks and she releases the tension in anger. There is no suggestion that the depth of her rage is justified; but this is a different matter altogether to the justification of her original decision, and it is this former matter that is the kernel of the scene. It is the human problem, not the moral decision, that is crucial; the scene is a trial in charity—not in her consenting, but in her accepting his weakness. She fails, and she fails again when she learns that Angelo has been false to his bargain and cries:

> O, I will to him and pluck out his eyes!
>
> (IV. iii. 116)

All this is surely very understandable. The strain and the rage are failures but they are very moving failures, and in the final act she does not fail.

Both Angelo and Isabella present the audience with the ironical gap that exists between human ideas and human actions, and the dramatic manner employed is psychologically intense precisely in order to focus our experience of this problem on the difficulties of living up to abstract decisions. In the second scene with Angelo (where the deputy seems to falter continually in his path), and in the scene with Claudio, we, the audience, directly experience with the characters the implications of their attitudes. This is done expansively and persistently at this point in the play, because the great moments of resolution at the end are going to depend on our apprehension of these problems and there will be time then for only the simplest recollection of our experience. At the climax of Isabella's dialogue with her brother, when she leaves him in anger, the direction of the play changes, and the pattern that is to bring the images to a resolution takes over from the experiences in which they are based. This entails a complete change of style and focus. The characters on whom we have been concentrating become threads in a complex fabric of images.

The transition must be considered in some detail. As Isabella leaves her brother's cell, the Duke enters, in his disguise as a friar, and arrests her precipitous exit. The dialogue switches from verse to prose, the subject matter of the action from profound psychology to suggestive romance. The style of this prose has often puzzled critics, but in fact its euphuistic melody is exactly calculated to relax the extreme tension of the previous scene without losing the attention of the audience. It creates quite a new atmosphere for the unfolding action. In this action Isabella has a very different role to play, and the centre of attention is to become the Duke and his desperate twisting of human designs.

Shakespeare preserves our attention at this point first by the author-ity and calm of the Duke's appearance, and then by interesting us in a new character and thus substituting narrative for action. Now, in this new, musical prose, we first hear of Mariana, deserted by Angelo on her brother's wreck, whose love still continues while he 'a marble to her tears, is washed by them, and relents not'. The scene gradually directs us away from Isabella towards this other woman, firstly by the change of melody, which creates a dreamy, hypnotic atmosphere after the former tension; next by our interest in the new story; and finally by our projection of our own sensations on to Isabella—we feel her hypnotized as we are. Her passivity, like ours, is convincing as a natural reaction after her rage and despair; but through it we forget her. Her part is reduced to simple comment and compliance.

Instead, we are made to concentrate on the righting of two of Angelo's crimes together. Because of this, Isabella's participation in an act which permits another to do very much what she has refused her-self avoids our notice. It is perceived from quite another direction and in the light of previously established images; from this point of view it is simply not relevant. Angelo's puritanical chastity has squandered the life of Mariana. 'What a merit were it in death,' Isabella comments, chorus-like, 'to take this poor maid from the world.' Mariana's life is decaying as Angelo's is drying up, and we hear of her confined in her 'moated grange'. The solution of this problem now holds our attention, and it is presented through narrative symbols rather than by people.

The power of this image of 'the moated grange' has proved astonishing. This is probably the consequence of the complex context of associations in which it is introduced. Mariana is first heard of in the romance story of her shipwrecked brother, and is borne in upon images of water and the sea, metaphors of her grief, and associations which are echoed in her name. In contemporary poetry, water and sea are common images in a context of passion; they suggested storminess, submissiveness, or fertility, where the occasion offered; and in the image of the moated grange itself we find the fertile and the submissive combined with a subtle sense of decay, derived from Mariana's wasting grief and the heavy music of the song that accompanies her first

G

appearance. Mariana brings with her a magic world that is a function of her place in the pattern.

The power of this world is deepened with Isabella's arrival at the grange and her description of the place of tryst where Mariana and Angelo are to meet:

> He hath a garden circummur'd with brick,
> Whose western side is with a vineyard back'd;
> And to that vineyard is a planched gate
> That makes his opening with this bigger key;
> This other doth command a little door
> Which from the vineyard to the garden leads.
> There have I made my promise
> Upon the heavy middle of the night
> To call upon him.
>
> (IV. i. 26–34)

The sound and movement of this passage have a dreamy, sensual quality quite unlike the usual intellectual energy of Isabella's speech. She has become part of the atmosphere. The images of the grange and the summer-house have a suppressed but anticipated eroticism that is infectious. The description of the enclosed garden, the setting sun, the gate, the vineyard, and the heavy night, create a mood that recalls *Péléas and Mélisande*. This mood finds its centre in the still figure of Mariana herself. She makes explicit on the stage a level of experience that has all along been implicit in Isabella, Angelo, and the Duke. Here, of course, the association is particularly with the former, and we are given another mirror-image. Isabella is about to wall herself up in a convent, to cut herself off from the world. She is doing for herself what Angelo has done for Mariana. The convent and the moated grange are felt as different aspects of the same action, an antithesis that is to be resolved when convent and moated grange meet in Angelo's 'garden, circummur'd with brick,/Whose western side is with a vineyard back'd'.[3]

Technically, this antithesis is reinforced and connected to the moral predicaments of the other characters throughout the play by a musical

---

[3] The convergence of these images is interestingly paralleled by Marvell in his *Appleton House*. I find it impossible to decide the extent to which my interpretation of Mariana has been influenced by Tennyson, or the extent to which Tennyson may be said to have been influenced by the dramatic mechanisms I am describing.

undercurrent of sound. The first mention of the convent comes with
a transition from argument to melody:

> Lucio: Send after the Duke, and appeal to him.
> Claudio: I have done so, but he's not to be found.
> I prithee, Lucio, do me this kind service:
> This day my sister should the cloister enter,
> And there receive her approbation;
> Acquaint her with the danger of my state;
> Implore her, in my voice, that she make friends
> To the strict deputy.
>
> (I. ii. 167–74)

It is a delicate moment, something akin to Bassanio's mention of
Belmont, and enters the street of Vienna like a sound from another
world. The weight of the words and the sibilant flow of the line
achieve this. A sudden hope is combined with anticipation as to the
nature of this being who is so introduced, and this is sustained by
Lucio's poetic paradoxes in the first scene in which Isabella appears.
One cannot tell whether he is blaspheming or sensing some deep truth.
The same mood is caught in the narrative of the Duke (dressed as a
friar) of Mariana's life, and reaches its climax in the verse and music of
the moated grange scene. Here also it is given a visual climax. The
Friar stands between the two women, and seems almost to merge
them together into a single being:

> Duke: I pray you be acquainted with this maid;
> She comes to do you good.
> Isabella: I do desire the like.
> Duke: Do you persuade yourself that I respect you?
> Mariana: Good friar, I know you do, and have found it.
> Duke: Take, then, this your companion by the hand,
> Who hath a story ready for your ear.
> I shall attend your leisure; but make haste;
> The vaporous night approaches.
>
> (IV. i. 49–56)

They move together, and then away into the shadows of the garden.
The Duke's final line suggests both the deepening darkness and what
is to be accomplished in it. Mariana and Isabella are in a sense the same
woman, and from the moment of the Duke's narrative we have been
made to sense them as such. Our desire to circumvent Angelo is a
response to the central metaphor of the play: it will transform a

secluded, sterile action into an open and creative one; death may be transformed into new life by an acknowledgement of the primary responses of the personality. Love is a matter of both the flesh and the spirit. Marriage is a sacrament.

V

Returning again to Angelo's comment on Claudio's crime, we may now understand the function of comparing the squandering of creative power with the destruction of life: such licence is a form of spiritual murder, and the two terms of the comparison create an analogy between the processes of creation and the processes of law. The Duke's easiness encouraged vice by confirming the practice of waste. In her anger at Claudio, Isabella clinches in a startling metaphor this level of the relationship of the comic plot to the play as a whole:

> O, fie, fie, fie!
> Thy sin's not accidental, but a trade.
> Mercy to thee would prove itself a bawd;
> 'Tis best that thou diest quickly.
>
> (III. i. 149-52)

In these lines Isabella's position matches that of the Duke and that of the deputy. The brothels of Vienna and the demonstrated justice of Escalus show how vice is confirmed by mercy and further how the vicious, thus confirmed, become hardened into a state of beastliness. In countenancing this the Duke is in a sense a spiritual murderer, and to extricate himself he instigates Angelo's policy of physical retribution to protect the wronged and prevent increase of corruption in the wrongdoer. Angelo understands this well, and explains it to Isabella:

> *Isabella:*   Yet show some pity.
> *Angelo:* I show it most of all when I show justice;
> For then I pity those I do not know,
> Which a dismiss'd offence would after gall,
> And do him right that, answering one foul wrong,
> Lives not to act another.
>
> (II. ii. 99-104)

The image of this restrictive policy is the prison, and it is here that the Duke learns the reality of this puritan alternative to riot and waste.

Here, by a neat convergence of images, the bawd Pompey Bum becomes assistant to the hangman Abhorson, and the Provost remarks, on Pompey's complaining, 'Go to, you weigh equally. A feather would turn the scale.'

The Duke's realization is brought about through his exercise of his spiritual function: preparing the souls of the condemned to meet their doom. The constant references to confessional practice have given offence to critics—after all, the Duke is not a priest; but they are crucial, and an excellent example of the economy of the play. I have already suggested that in disguising the Duke as a friar Shakespeare intends to raise questions of spiritual responsibility inherent in the course of temporal power. In the Roman Catholic church the spiritual welfare of the condemned man was the care of the priest who administered the Last Sacrament: the responsibility of the secular arm reached only so far as to provide that facility. Shakespeare is not content with this, and makes the Duke's realization of his own spiritual responsibility for his subjects the means to his development. Once disguised as a friar the Duke becomes an image of this dimension of his office, and we are made to concentrate in his presence on the spiritual implications of the retributive justice which he has instigated and which Angelo is carrying out. The constant references to his priestly functions are the means to remind us of the 'reality' of the spiritual aspect of his office. This reality is not of course circumstantial: he is not in orders; but it is, on a deeper level, fundamental to his existence as Duke. The disguise enables us to perceive this dual function, it makes it palpable, and operates dramatically as a means of emphasizing now the spiritual and now the secular nature of the activity. The sustained irony of the Duke's irresponsible and Machiavellian intrigues being carried out in this guise is masterly.

In the scenes with Lucio it is the role of Duke that is emphasized. Vincentio's need to distinguish his office from himself, a need he understood from the beginning, is further developed. In these scenes we are conscious of a man's attempts to separate the truth about himself from the lies, particularly with reference to his attempts to *be* the office he holds. The disguise enables us to separate the office and the man. Both Vincentio and the audience see the Duke in the third person through Lucio's eyes. The man confronts his image.

The mood here is comic, and provides a useful release for the irony naturally inherent in a disguise situation, so enabling us to take the

Friar seriously in other situations. Indeed Lucio is used throughout the play to bridge the gap between the artificialities of the plot and its serious implications. He is a very natural character, a descendant of Mercutio (the Folio's description 'a fantastic' seems to me editorial licence), and with somewhat of the latter's dramatic function. He is a friend of Claudio, though apparently he has a taste for more devious forms of pleasure. Through him we are shown the effect of the proclamation on those who may well, but have not yet, fallen under its ban. His humour seems to become more nervous as the play proceeds, and his scenes with the Duke seem to bear the psychological burden of escape into an older and better time that provides an excuse for his conduct. He projects his own behaviour on to the Duke (who allowed it), as an act of self-justification. But this natural expression of character is at odds with the Duke's sense of his position. The scenes reflect the latter's struggle to preserve the sanctity of his office; and Lucio's slanders ironically reveal the uselessness of the Duke's purity on a level where his virtue was true but also a denial of life. The scenes are both satirical and sinister. Lucio must be condemned, both for his slander and his misbehaviour; he may be said to condemn himself; and the judgement upon him provides an ironical counterpoint to the restorative justice of the last scene.

In the Duke's scenes with the other comics, however, his role as spiritual counsellor is paramount. Through these encounters he learns the purpose of justice, which is the re-education of the soul. In Overdone, Pompey, and Barnardine he meets various degrees of that hardening of the heart through vice which is increased or promoted by licence. He discovers that the absolute solution—the ending of the vicious life—is also a form of murder; that the judge who condemns a criminal to death risks the death of the man's soul as well as of his body and thus takes for himself that ultimate judgement that belongs to God alone. This is a devilish usurpation; but there is a way out that does not refuse responsibility. Vincentio has encountered it in the prison. When he speaks with Juliet she acknowledges her fault and demonstrates the role of punishment in creating that awareness of sin that is the foundation of repentance. When asked if her sorrow does not stem merely from the shame of being condemned she replies:

> I do repent me as it is an evil,
> And take the shame with joy.

(II. iii. 35–6)

The Duke therefore works towards the same end with Pompey:

> Take him to prison, officer;
> Correction and instruction must both work
> Ere this rude beast will profit.
>
> (III. ii. 28–30)

But before he can truly understand this conception he has to experience in himself the tyranny he observes in Angelo.

On learning of his deputy's veniality, the Duke takes it upon himself to right this wrong by craft. First he arranges the substitution of Mariana for Isabella, a move which rights a further wrong, he thinks, as well as satisfying Angelo and ensuring Claudio's reprieve. During these scenes, as we have noted, the attention is concentrated poetically on the nature of Angelo's physical miserliness, and narratively on the need to circumvent him. This plot, however, fails, and on its failure Shakespeare takes full advantage of any doubts we may already feel as to the Duke's part in the affair. He now commits himself to an even more questionable substitution, that of Barnardine for Claudio. The technicalities of the case, perhaps, are soundly based. Barnardine is a convicted murderer (the reiteration of this theme is notable), and so a forfeit to the law. The very fact of his existence at all seems the result of the Duke's old laxity, since 'his friends still wrought reprieves for him'. But the almost incredible shallowness of the Duke's attitude to life and death at this point is brilliantly emphasized by his glib improvizations. 'O, death's a great disguiser,' he remarks, countering the Provost's suggestion that the head might be recognized and the substitution detected, so 'call your executioner and off with Barnardine's head. I will give him present shrift and advise him for a better place.' It all seems so wonderfully easy, this substitution of one life for another, until the Friar actually confronts the life he intends to dispose of so opportunely.

This famous scene is the turning point of the play. Before the hardened Barnardine, the Duke's authority, spiritual and temporal, is impotent. It is not so simple to prepare a soul for death, and the king of the prison, who has created a personal glory from the stuff of his imprisonment, is not to be frightened by such a creature as a friar. He has been through this before, and he's the boss. Faced with this bulk of incomprehending animal obstinacy the Duke loses self-control, and orders the prisoner's immediate execution. This, it has been rightly

observed, is singularly improper conduct in a friar; but the answer is
hardly to allot the offending line to the Provost. The point surely is
that the Duke forgets himself. His powerlessness releases itself in
violence. The wavering:

> Unfit to live or die. O gravel heart!

heralds the explosion,

> After him, fellows; bring him to the block.

> (IV. iii. 60–61)

The voice of authority, when it rings out, commands obedience. His
line would be followed by the tumultuous exit of the hangmen. Then
the quiet voice of the Provost intercedes:

> Now, sir, how do you find the prisoner?

But having ordered death the Duke has realized the central dilemma
of his position and the gravity of the deed he has just committed:

> A creature unprepar'd, unmeet for death;
> And to transport him in the mind he is
> Were damnable.

> (IV. iii. 63–5)

The beasts and men we have been dealing with have become general-
ized. There is a strange humanity in the word 'creature' in this context,
a word that levels all living things before God. The Duke has realized
that in his order he is himself a Barnardine: he too was committing
murder, murder of a soul.[4]

And now, in fact, the unseen Creator intervenes. Unprompted, the
Provost answers:

> Here in the prison, father,
> There died this morning of a cruel fever,
> One Ragozine, a most notorious pirate,
> A man of Claudio's years; his beard and head
> Just of his colour. What if we do omit
> This reprobate, till he were well inclin'd,
> And satisfy the deputy with the visage
> Of Ragozine, more like to Claudio?

> (IV. iii. 65–72)

---

[4] There is a piece of *trompe l'œil* here: the Duke's command is never recalled.
But to do so would be a waste of time. As the scene proceeds we take it for
granted.

It is a grand and magical moment. At last, as the Duke realizes the limitations of his spiritual power and the nature of his spiritual responsibility, after all his own desperate contrivance, the matter is taken out of his hands. There is no need for this trick simply as a dramatic device, and as such it could be handled better; it is the demonstration of hidden power that is crucial. The Duke acknowledges his position in the hand of God:

> O, 'tis an accident that heaven provides!
>
> (IV. iii. 73)

Relief, submission, in a sense salvation, all breathe out through that 'O' as the Duke perceives his natural dependency and acknowledges it in the face of his own struggling intrigues. He now knows that his own human fallibility, like that of Angelo, is incompatible with the idea of justice that led him to appoint his deputy.

From this moment Vincentio's voice takes on a new authority. He accepts his role now as God's instrument and begins to lay out the lines of the solution with clarity and firmness. The verse becomes sure and measured, the vocabulary latinate and mysteriously biblical in its resonances. Now, too, the Duke's many roles begin to converge as, in his Friar's gown, he refers to himself as Duke with the pronoun 'I'. The effect is electrifying in bringing this aspect to the front of our minds again and urging the play towards its conclusion:

> Now will I write letters to Angelo—
> The Provost he shall bear them—whose contents
> Shall witness to him I am near at home,
> And that, by great injunctions, I am bound
> To enter publicly. Him I'll desire
> To meet me at the consecrated fount,
> A league below the city; and from thence,
> By cold gradation and well-balanc'd form,
> We shall proceed with Angelo.
>
> (IV. iii. 89–97)

The first 'I' is ambivalent between Duke and Friar, but the second firmly introduces his royal role and is brought to a climax in the final 'we'. From now on the movement of his speech focuses attention on the Duke as the central point of a concluding pattern. The use of the personal pronoun here, on the lips of the Friar but with clear reference to the Duke, creates an objectifying effect as in the scenes with Lucio, and we are now able to observe Vincentio on all three levels of his personality, the focus changing constantly as now one and now another becomes significant. Through this means, the various levels of implication in the imagery of the plot can be grouped to present a maximum *sense* of the play's significance. This is felt by the audience from the movement of the action, and depends upon the juxtaposition of experiences, not on the circumstantial logic of action.

VI

On the first level we sense Vincentio as Duke and judge. This level of his activity is supported by the whole paraphernalia of the civic entry, and by the authoritative and declamatory style with which he speaks; and it justifies for us the way in which he behaves to Angelo and Isabella as if he had no knowledge of the matter. Shakespeare deflects our attention from Vincentio's practical problems in arranging the dénouement by interesting us in a presentation of what Isabella would really have been up against had the Duke actually been absent all the while. The opening movement of the last act is about tyranny and the frailty of justice, and about what Angelo can get away with. For much of the time it is as if the Duke really is another character.

Of course, there is yet a further dimension to this ordered judgement of the Duke's. The acknowledgement of divine aid in Act IV and the prophetic tone of his utterances make us associate this judge and his moving of the pattern of revelation with the Supreme Judge above. In this way the Duke's return is given the importance of a 'Last Judgement' in our imaginations, an importance which exists rather in our experience of the proceedings than in any direct association of them with the man, Vincentio. The image of judgement is not associated with him as a function of his personal character. It is rather of his office. And this effect is increased by the fact that when he re-enters as Friar the play does not concentrate on his intrigues, but uses him as an image of the revealer of corruption. The Friar is now an apocalyptic figure:

> Be not so hot; the Duke
> Dare no more stretch this finger of mine than he
> Dare rack his own; his subject am I not,
> Nor here provincial. My business in this state
> Made me a looker on here in Vienna,

> Where I have seen corruption boil and bubble
> Till it o'errun the stew.
>
> (V. i. 311–17)

Our sense of the truth of this as a description of what we have seen will be more important to our minds here than our awareness that the Duke *is* provincial to Vienna. We accept him as a 'looker on', and the irony of the first line becomes menacing rather than comic. It underlines the fact that there is more to this figure than appears, but does not give us an image of someone having a jolly time playing lots of parts. To all intents and purposes Duke and Friar are perceived here as different identities within the pattern.

The two roles merge as Vincentio confronts Barnardine:

> *Duke:* Which is that Barnardine?
> *Provost:*   This, my lord.
> *Duke:* There was a friar told me of this man.
>
> (V. i. 476–7)

This is another magical moment. It has that same ambivalence of circumstantial and imaginative reality as Hal's rejection of Falstaff:

> I have long dreamt of such a kind of man,
> So surfeit-swell'd, so old, and so profane;
> But, being awak'd, I do despise my dream.
>
> (*2 Henry IV*, V. v. 50–52)

As the Duke speaks, we are again aware of the levels of Vincentio's being and of his knowledge. We have seen him ordering Barnardine's death; we have seen him recognize that to kill him would be damnable; we see him now in the place of judge. And we also see Barnardine, the obstinate, bestial, triumphant king of the prison, his rags now in the light of day seen for what they are, cringing before the glittering assembly like Caliban before Prospero or the soul before the throne of God. We are aware of the Supreme Judge, and of the responsibilities of the man, his deputy. The deputy pronounces:

> *Duke:* Sirrah, thou art said to have a stubborn soul,
>   That apprehends no further than this world,
>   And squar'st thy life according. Thou'rt condemn'd;
>   But, for those earthly faults, I quit them all,
>   And pray thee take this mercy to provide
>   For better times to come. Friar, advise him;
>   I leave him to your hand.
>
> (V. i. 478–84)

The Duke will not touch the man's life, but offers him time to rebuild his soul. He is taken by the Friar. This is not, as the recent Stratford-on-Avon production played it, a foolish piece of impracticality. It is an image of a principle of creative justice. It is the purpose of authority Shakespeare wishes us to consider, and as the bewildered creature is handed over to his ascetic spiritual governor we should feel more than a touch of the fear of the soul who sees the reality of itself for the first time. In such a theatrical context we can be made to sense Barnardine's discovery of his own sin. We feel his shame. It is not the convent that is reserved for Isabella, but the Friar's rules for him. He exchanges physical imprisonment for the spiritual restraint of apprehended guilt. The image is viable, but not as a statement of fact so much as a metaphor of that self awareness which alone makes malleable the hardened heart.

The moment marks the resting point in the Duke's journey from the extremes of licence and retribution towards re-creative justice. Now the other judgements can be patterned out on the same principle: restitution through acknowledgement of guilt. They flow with a simple inevitability out of the established imagery of the play. Even the punishment of the egregious Lucio projects the same principles in a comic (or perhaps sarcastic) mode. He, like Claudio, is made to acknowledge the product of his deeds. Of this justice, of course, Vincentio is himself a part, and the *trompe l'œil*, which enables us to separate the functions of man, priest and king incarnate in the same figure, now becomes invaluable as a technical device by which this figure can function—in his role as Duke—as a touchstone for the feelings of the other characters, including his human self. This trick has caused difficulty, since at the moment of absolute command the detail of the Duke's conduct does not seem to match his judgements. He appears not only to intend the death of Angelo, but to be encouraging Isabella to a bloody revenge. He conceals from her her brother's survival.

> To make her heavenly comforts of despair,
> When it is least expected.
>
> (IV. iii. 106-7)

and having primed her to the exposure of Angelo, suggests she 'command those fretting waters' from her eyes 'with a light heart'. On the face of it such words are worse than tactless, and such behaviour, in any personal context, unpardonable. He motivates her to accusation and vengeance, and in the final scene plays shamelessly on that desire. The difficulty is, however, a formal one. It is necessary above all at this point in the play to arouse in the audience exactly that desire for vengeance that the play itself is to overturn. (Just how well Shakespeare manages this may be seen, perhaps, in the writings of those critics—they number Coleridge among them—who complain at the grave miscarriage of justice implicit in Angelo's reprieve.) The audience must be made to experience the difficulty of mercy. They have, by now, realized the *problem* of justice—that condemning the body may mean the abrogation of the judgement of God through the murder of the unprepared spirit; but they are not aware of the pain of the solution, the workings of which the final act is to untangle. The Duke is therefore used ambivalently once more—as the godlike instrument of resolution, and as a means to articulate the dark emotions implicit in Isabella's situation, which she herself has only one opportunity to demonstrate in her angry outburst on hearing of Angelo's treachery. The Duke's action and diction present the form of his control, while elements of his dialogue plant in our minds the undercurrents of the situation. Since we are aware of the existence of the feelings he is suggesting, it is these that catch our attention rather than his right as a man to articulate them or to behave in this manner.

This technique has been used before. While the Duke is explaining to the Friar his reasons for departure, the nature of which has already been discussed, he is made to add another, apparently quite inconsistent:

> Lord Angelo is precise;
> Stands at a guard with envy; scarce confesses
> That his blood flows, or that his appetite
> Is more to bread than stone. Hence shall we see
> If power change purpose, what our seemers be.
>
> (I. iii. 50–54)

This would seem to justify completely the Friar's doubts as to the advisability of making restitution in this manner for the ills of the past years; and the dubious nature of the decision becomes yet more apparent when we learn in Act III that the Duke is aware of Angelo's betrayal of Mariana. But to argue this is to fail to take into account the nature of the theatrical experience. When the Duke appoints Angelo, the audience does not know of this affair, nor do they know the Duke has any such suspicions; this can therefore have no effect on their initial attitude. When they do discover it, the rights and wrongs of the appointment are a thing of the past: it is the trapping of the corrupt judge that concerns them. In a real person such inconsistency might well suggest serious mental aberration; but this will not be the case with a fictitious dramatic personage, so long as the two awkward matters are not directly juxtaposed. Similarly with the remark about Angelo. It comes at the end of the scene. The Duke's attitude has already been fully expounded and we now take it for granted. These lines do not therefore seem a contradiction; they merely suggest to the audience further important possibilities in the forthcoming action. This is emphasized by the structure of the final couplet, which sounds like the tag to a moral parable and is thus effectively removed from the personal context. The lines have the effect of the 'cliff-hanger' of the modern serial, as do the lines of comfort in Act IV. From the Barnardine scene on, the Duke becomes in effect a catalyst to the action, almost an abstract force. He becomes so by right of his power as a ruler, by the authority of his speech rhythms and vocabulary, and by our new awareness of a ruler's function created by that scene. It is in fact necessary to elevate him into abstraction at this point, so that our psychological interest and human sympathy can return to Isabella. It is through her that we are to experience the difficult act of mercy, and it was as a basis for this experience that she was treated with such human precision in the first half of the play.

Three times, as we have seen, Isabella has given way to anger: with Angelo, with Claudio, and with the Duke. At last the accomplishment of vengeance is in her power, and this time she controls it. As Mariana pleads, the Duke, like the impersonal instrument reiterating a major theme in a symphonic coda, declaims the justice of vengeance. The arguments for revenge and mercy are piled up on either side creating a desperate tension; but after a climax of indecision Isabella kneels and pleads for Angelo's life. It must be said she does not plead very well, as she did not earlier plead well for her brother; but she does kneel, and her intercession shows us the meaning of that spiritual charity which comes from a real awareness of the ambiguous fabric of existence which renders the pure idea invalid in the face of the human act. Her intercession goes beyond words. In the judicial context in which her act is framed there is nothing to be said—but she knows what must be *done*, and finds words, some words, to do it.

VII

This extraordinary moment may give us a final insight into the significance of the devious organization of this play. Shakespeare has been employing *trompe l'œil* for a double purpose: firstly, to create juxtapositions of action and image within the economy of a play; but secondly, to project the necessary ambivalence of human perception. This matrix of inconsistencies resolved within a wider dramatic pattern is an image of a basic human predicament. The forms of thought are inadequate for the interpretation of the world of actions. A deed may be differently defined by word or by act. This has nothing to do with ends justifying means: it is rather a comment on the problems of grasping *either* accurately in terms of human experience. Shakespeare is attempting the resolution of a paradox of existence (a paradox created by warring elements—thought and feeling—both flawed by man's original sin) in terms of intuition. The tools of the intellect, language and logic, give way again and again before the force of feeling, but feeling in its turn can overwhelm and destroy. Man is not by nature integrated, and actions governed by thought or feeling alone are shown to be the forerunners of spiritual and physical violence. Precision of thought and looseness of feeling find analogies in avarice and licence. The forms through which man apprehends life must be revived so that he may pretend no longer to absolute rightness, to absolute authority. Isabella and Angelo are both wrecked on this reef. They are made to feel the pull between logic and experience. The Duke may bring all the powers of language to bear on his sermon in dispraise of life, and yet its whole rationale may be overturned by a moment of vibrant feeling. The sheer vitality of his sister's presence can overwhelm in Claudio all his ideal resolution by its simple promise of life. Absolute knowledge is out of man's reach, and the pretence to it is as harmful as ignorant licence. Right can only be grasped through grace, which cannot be commanded. Grace is given freely and comes from without; only when directed outwards by a love that looks to the pattern beyond itself and seeks to incorporate with others can the mind and body act as one.

The final acknowledgement of this is the Duke's marriage with Isabella, a marriage which resolves the inwardness of their natures in terms of the outgoing images of the play. Their virtues must go forth of them. The new openness is already heralded by the manner of

Vincentio's return to his city. Now he does 'stage' himself to the eyes of men, despite his reticence; but he does so not to show himself off but as a duty, a gift of himself to his place and people, and against his personal inclinations. It is very important that the public nature of this final scene is clear to an audience. The open shame and confession the scene entails is an act of great courage on the part of the protagonists. Only Lucio thrusts himself too much into the public eye, with unfortunate consequences. (He is of course extremely useful in releasing the tensions of the scene and so preserving its seriousness.) The effect of this public trial is to show the main characters gradually letting themselves go, gradually being taken, as the spectators are, by the tide of resolution. The final chord of that resolution brings the Duke and Isabella together.

It is charming to note how the Duke does try to manipulate matters one last time. As he restores her brother to her, he proposes to Isabella —an act that brings him dangerously near to repeating Angelo's original bribery: the restoration of her brother to life is again to be paid for by her virginity. The timing of this is disastrous. Isabella is preoccupied and does not answer. She is probably not even listening. In front of his people the Duke must withdraw. His business is elsewhere and his own case must be the last to be resolved. The unfolding pattern resolves it finally for him.

Isabella's lack of comment, even to the Duke's final proposal, has puzzled some critics; but surely no reply is needed here. The solution is absolute, and must be accepted by her: it has been revealed as her place in the pattern of life. So clear is it that no words are necessary. They would indeed detract. This marriage is the resolution of the charity inherent in both their natures, at first withdrawn but now released by the experiences they have undergone. It is this image that is primary. It cannot be argued, but it must be *felt* to be right. The formal proposition and the silent acquiescence is the sign of a new understanding which the play has struggled to bring about in the audience also. Strindberg describes its significance well. As the Confessor says to the Stranger towards the end of the trilogy *To Damascus*:

> You are a child who has been living in a child's world, where you have been playing with thoughts and words. You have laboured under the fallacious belief that anything so mundane as language could be a cloak for anything as subtle as feelings and thoughts. We, who have discerned this solution, therefore give voice to our

thoughts as little as possible, for we apprehend and perceive one another's thoughts.[5]

It is a sign of strength in the Ciceronian novice to *say* nothing. What she has to say she says with her whole self.

The *finale* of *Measure for Measure* is astonishing in its pace and complexity. It sweeps you forward in the grip of pure plot to the great climaxes—the discovery of the Duke, the plea for Angelo, the pardon of Barnardine, the discovery of Claudio, and finally the union of the Duke and Isabella. But these moments are all great pauses—moments of silence and revelation where the meaning may be sensed but not voiced. The characters and the spectators with them are swept onto an eminence from which the integrity of the surrounding landscape may be apprehended. The effect of the interweaving images here is powerfully exciting and by no means merely theatrical. It is a function of the play's meaning. In its excitement we sense that abandonment of the soul to the will of God, a will and purpose too deep for thought, that the events of the play have promulgated in its characters. Humanity no longer struggles to wrest God's meaning from him, but simply to live out its proper life:

> They know and do not know what it is to act or suffer.
> They know and do not know that action is suffering
> And suffering action. Neither does the agent suffer
> Nor the patient act. But both are fixed
> In an eternal action, an eternal patience
> To which all must consent that it may be willed
> And that all must suffer that they may will it,
> That the pattern may subsist, for the pattern is the
> action
> And the suffering. That the wheel may turn and still
> Be forever still.[6]

[5] *Eight Expressionist Plays*, trans. Arvid Paulson (New York, 1965), Pt. III, IV. i.

[6] T. S. Eliot, *Murder in the Cathedral* (London, 1938), Act I.

X

Two Unassimilable Men

A. D. NUTTALL

I

WE do not naturally associate Jaques with Caliban; yet a form of association exists, and is demonstrable. Edward A. Armstrong expounded it in his book, *Shakespeare's Imagination* (1946): the same distinctive 'cluster' of images is used for both Jaques and Caliban. For both of them we have a reference to an infected body (*As You Like It*, II. vii. 60; *The Tempest*, I. ii. 370), to food (*AYLI*, II. vii. 14; *Tempest*, I. ii. 330), to music (*AYLI*, II. vii. 5; *Tempest*, III. ii. 130–35, 146). Moreover, there are what may be called coincidences of thought: Duke Senior says of Jaques,

> I think he be transform'd into a beast;
> For I can nowhere find him like a man.
>
> (*AYLI*, II. vii. 1–2)

And Prospero calls Caliban,

> A freckl'd whelp, hag-born—not honour'd with
> A human shape.
>
> (*Tempest*, I. ii. 283–4)

Duke Senior calls Jaques,

> a libertine
> As sensual as the brutish sting itself.
>
> (*AYLI*, II. vii. 65–6)

And Prospero calls Caliban,

> A thing most brutish.
>
> (*Tempest*, I. ii. 357)

Note: All references to Shakespeare are to the text of Peter Alexander, 1951, except for the reference on page [238] to *The Tempest*, II. i. 119, where the line-numbering is Alexander's but the Folio reading is preferred. The translations, except where otherwise attributed, are my own.

There is nothing about a sting in the quotation from *The Tempest*, nor does the word appear elsewhere in the play; but hedgehogs mount their pricks at Caliban's footfall (II. ii. 11–12) and he is constantly threatened with or fearful of pinches (I. ii. 329, II. ii. 4, IV. i. 232, V. i. 276).

Our first inference from all this is psychological. Shakespeare wrote the parts of Jaques and Caliban from the same quarter of his mind, so to speak. Some will say that no further inference is possible; that the coincidence of imagery is a freak of the poet's psychology which is proved already to be critically irrelevant by our very surprise at the association. That surprise, after all, arises from our sense of each character in his proper setting: from our knowledge that Caliban is uncivilized, natural and earthy while Jaques is cultured, neurotic and austere. This is what the plays teach us, as long as they are read or watched as plays, and such teaching is in a manner invulnerable. For criticism must always concern itself with the work as apprehended, rather than with the material conditions of that apprehension. Statistical analysis may one day show us that Gray is more alliterative than Collins, but if we cannot hear the difference between the two poets we have, as critics, learned nothing; if, on the other hand, we can hear the difference, two things follow: first that the difference is relevant to criticism, and, second, that we had no need of the statistical analyst to tell us what our ears had already picked up. The 'scientific' investigator of poetry is therefore unhappily placed; he is either irrelevant or superfluous.

But this dismissal is much too slick. There are sounds we might never have heard, if we had never been invited to listen for them. And indeed if it were otherwise, it is criticism which would find itself superfluous. Good literature is usually indefinitely rich; we never know what more is to be found in it. The claim that criticism must concern itself with the work as apprehended is correct, but apprehension itself is commonly not instantaneous but progressive. Certainly if we cannot hear the stronger alliteration of Gray the analytic information is critically useless, but we must listen *after* we have read the analysis. Only if it obstinately remains inaudible should we (now of course it becomes an obligation) reject the statistical findings. Thus 'scientific' analysis of literature provides us with no critical imperatives; but we must not conclude too briskly that it therefore offers us nothing. In fact it issues invitations.

So with Jaques and Caliban: we are invited to do what we might not otherwise have done; to put these two together in our minds. Other Shakespearian characters with whom the Caliban 'image-cluster' is associated—Aaron the Moor, say, or Thersites—easily connect themselves thematically with their image-cousin of *The Tempest*. There the poet's psychology correlates well enough with certain palpable continuities in the *œuvre*. With Jaques and Caliban it would appear that some effort is required. But this must never become an effort to suppress. We need never deny the manifest differences as we hunt for latent similarities. After all, the differences are not such as logically to preclude any connection. Shakespeare is full of recurrence which is never mere repetition. Always there is variation, often outright reversal. His imagination was shamelessly promiscuous. Prince Hal himself speaks with the accents of Iago,[1] and the echo is, critically, no accident.

In terms of plot the connection between Jaques and Caliban is indeed tenuous. Jaques, like Antonio in *The Merchant of Venice* and Malvolio in *Twelfth Night*, is excluded from the ritual of coming together which marks the end of the comedy; Caliban, on the other hand, is filled with good resolutions and taken back to Milan. Jaques, it seems, could not be assimilated by the festive world, but Caliban could be domesticated. The best we can say is that they are both outsiders, opposed in some way to the proper harmony of society, which is to say very little.

One is sometimes tempted to assume that the notion of the outsider as a source of discord and possible evil begins with Shakespeare and ends with the decline of the Comic World-picture, say, with Miss Wade of *Little Dorrit* (for Miss Wade is already assuming the modern ambiguity). But this is too definite. Homer's Thersites is a social outsider, and Aeschylus' Aegisthus, with his illegitimacy and distinguishing 'low' style, is almost Shakespearian. Grendel is excluded from the mead-hall, *dreamum bedæled*, and even the Green Knight, before the bathetic dénouement, is noticeably *outré*. Nevertheless, it is in Shakespeare that the use of an outsider-figure becomes insistent, and in Milton an inherited cosmology is altered in such a way as to accommodate the consequent change in ethical imagination. The universe of *Paradise Lost* is geocentric; so far Milton follows Dante. But Dante's universe is, strictly speaking, not so much geocentric as diabolocentric.

---

[1] See W. H. Auden, *The Dyer's Hand and Other Essays* (London, 1963), pp. 205–6.

At the centre of the earth, where Down becomes Up,[2] is the Devil; he is Hamlet's Old Mole, deeper than bedrock, the ultimate insider. But Milton's Satan comes from outside; the drop of light he sees suspended from the ramparts of Heaven at the end of Book II is not the Terrestrial Globe but the entire Ptolemaic universe, and he must penetrate the spheres before he can touch the top of Mount Niphates. To be sure, there may be a technical theological reason for this, and the curious reader can turn it up in *De Doctrina Christiana* (i. 33, The Columbia Milton (New York, 1934), vol. XVI, pp. 374–5). But whatever the motive of the change, the imaginative consequence is manifest: Satan comes from the other side of Chaos. Evil no longer threatens the soul from inside.

But the genre which pre-eminently concerns itself with people as composing a society is comedy; tragedy is about individuals as they fall away from the grand composition. Arguments about the comparative truth-value of tragedy and comedy are, so far, futile, for the following two sentences are both true. 1. People do fall in love, marry, and their children marry; life goes on. 2. Each of us, you who read and I who write, will die.[3] Hence comedy is an art of profile, of the third person, whereas in tragedy we are face to face. In Shakespeare we sometimes find a tragedy of individual(s) superimposed on a comic plot of social continuity. The thing is most clinically obvious in *Romeo and Juliet*, where the story of the families is comedy (at times almost farce) and only the lovers are tragic.

Because of the 'impurity' of Shakespearian genre, then, we need not be surprised to find that meditation on the idea of the outsider is possible even in a technical tragedy. The exotic Othello, who is honoured in the state of Venice for his soldiership, finds when he leaves the public, martial sphere for the private that he is not accepted, is not understood and cannot understand. The Venetian colour bar is sexual, not professional. Othello, coal-black among the glittering Venetians, is visibly the outsider, and in his bewilderment he looks for the man who is visibly the insider, the man who knows the ropes, the 'good chap' (or, as they said then, 'honest'). And he finds him.

But Iago has no friends, no loves, no positive desires. He, and not Othello, proves to be the true outsider in the play, for he is foreign to

[2] *Inferno*, XXXIV, 74–81.
[3] On this way of distinguishing tragedy from comedy, see Helen Gardner, '*As You Like It*', in *More Talking of Shakespeare*, ed. J. Garrett (London, 1959), p. 21.

humanity itself. Othello comes from a remote clime, but Iago, in his simpler darkness, comes from the far side of chaos. Hence the pathos of Shakespeare's best departure from his source. In Cinthio's novel the Ensign, with a cunning affectation of reluctance, suggests that Desdemona is false and then, seeing his chance, remarks, 'Your blackness already displeases her.'⁴ In Shakespeare we have instead a note of barroom, masculine intimacy, an assumed complicity of sentiment; in effect, Iago says, 'Well, she went with a black man, you know . . . so what is one to think?' (see III. iii. 232–7). Othello's need to be accepted makes him an easy victim of this style.

Moreover, it may be that *Othello* can provide us with a clue to the labyrinth of the comedies. *Othello* itself is written against, rather than with, the grain of genre. Even more than *Romeo and Juliet*, it is Shakespeare's domestic tragedy, where 'domestic' is not merely a difference added to the genus 'tragedy' but is rather a mark of paradox. Othello leaves 'the big wars' and the windy seas for a little, dim world of unimaginable horror. 'War is no strife to the dark house and the detested wife' comes not from Othello but from a comedy, yet it will serve here. *Othello*, we might say, is the tragedy of a hero who went into a house. And the essence of the hero's humiliation is sexual.

Certainly, the outsiders of the comedies are variously connected with obscure sexual distress (and this too can be applied to Milton: Satan is sexually wretched, the voyeur in Eden). In *Twelfth Night* the baiting of Malvolio is sexual; his austere pride is founded on a Narcissism which his tormentors first stimulate and then snub. He is sexually only half-alive, but eager, clumsy and capable of being hurt. At the end of the comedy he finds no bride. Antonio in *The Merchant of Venice* is probably homosexual. The great love-feat of the play is performed, not by Bassanio for Portia, but by Antonio for Bassanio. The leaden casket bore the legend,

> Who chooseth me must give and hazard all he hath.

W. H. Auden noticed that this line holds for two people in the play, neither of whom is Bassanio.⁵ The real *agon* of *The Merchant of Venice* is between Antonio and Shylock. At the end of the comedy there is no bride for Antonio. It begins to look as if the crucial unifying factor for outsiders in the comedies is exclusion from marriage. Angelo, in

⁴ See the Arden edition of M. R. Ridley (London, 1958), p. 241.
⁵ *The Dyer's Hand*, p. 235.

Measure for Measure, is an exception which proves this rule. He adds to personal asceticism an impersonalist theory of law, according to which judges are themselves subject to justice; only thus is law ethically practicable in a corrupt world. But Angelo's lust is awakened by the very purity of Isabella; the stimulation and baiting of Malvolio is re-enacted in a horribly intensified mode. At the end Angelo is presented with the bride he had previously rejected. Yet this, perhaps, is his final humiliation. He had affirmed that if ever he himself should break the law he ought in justice to suffer by the law. His precarious tenure of intellectual honour in the midst of his degradation before Isabella depends on the genuineness of his commitment to this view. But when the end comes he is not allowed to prove his honour. His importunate pleas for punishment are answered with forgiveness. Angelo has served his purpose; the Duke breathes forth again that uncharitable charity which will one day force him to hide his radiant face once more, while some detested substitute cleans up the mess. Thus, although Angelo is technically admitted to the festive conclusion of the comedy, his admission conceals an ingenious insult. By this marriage Angelo is finally emasculated. Yet forgiveness is forgiveness, and *Measure for Measure* is a real comedy.

II

The sexuality of Jaques is more problematical. It is likely that many who flinch from the association of Jaques with Caliban do so partly on the ground that Caliban is driven by undisguised lust whereas Jaques is donnish, neurotically self-frustrated—is, as we say, repressed. Yet this presentiment must be wrong since, as we have seen, the clearest connection between the two characters is at the point of sexuality. Jaques, with his mannered wretchedness, was of all things a libertine, or so says the Duke (and he must know). And, if we allow ourselves to reflect, it is even probable. It was never our sense of psychological reality that was offended, only of convention. I once met a Jaques, and he was not in a book.

Jaques, then, is in some ways a reversed Angelo. He is a tricky subject for psychoanalysis since he began with lust and ends with asceticism. His libidinal exterior concealed a rank hatred of the world. Of course, as we see him, he lacks the high principle of Angelo, and will probably never attain it, though at the end he goes to a monastery or hermitage.

We have been told by social anthropologists[6] that in earlier ages social misfits were accommodated by the monastic system, so that there was a place even for the unplaceable. We may deceive ourselves for a moment into thinking that Jaques finds a home in this way, but not for long. Jaques goes to the religious order not to join but to watch. He will be to it as he was to Arden, *spectator haud particeps*, the everlasting looker-on. But in any case all this is mere typological doodling. Jaques, however often we listen, never sounds like Angelo, never feels like him. We had better follow where the echoes lead; we had better turn to Caliban.

Every cartoonist knows that the real point about desert islands is that they offer a sexually limited environment. The tiny mound of sand, topped by two palm trees, a voluptuous blonde and one or more others (male) has become part of our popular iconography. Shakespeare, variously prophetic in his last, futuristic production, forsaw this too. Part of the tension of *The Tempest* arises from our awareness of Miranda's situation. She is the only woman on the island; she is *tabu* to Prospero because she is his daughter, and to Caliban because she is white (and possibly of another species). Ferdinand on the other hand is both socially and mythically eligible. The anachronistic term 'colour bar' was applicable to *Othello* and it is still more applicable here. We saw how the Venetian colour bar was principally confined to sexual relations: 'Ah, but would you let your daughter marry one?' In *The Tempest* (which might have been called *America*) the primary sexual fear is extended and elaborated by the various tensions of colonization. When Shakespeare pillaged the Bermuda pamphlets to write his play, he lifted not just incidental marvels but a fundamental theme. The black man (Caliban is perhaps an Indian) is now just an exotic threat but the recalcitrant and ineducable serf. Nevertheless, the crisis of the relationship between native and newcomer remains sexual. It is when Caliban attempts to violate Miranda that the attempt to civilize him is dropped and the long vilification begins. Yet the island was Caliban's if it was anyone's.

But the clairvoyance of *The Tempest* is not exercised on the future only; is also audaciously retrospective. In the last phase of his writing life, Shakespeare seems to have been groping towards a kind of drama which was attained by Ancient Greece in the period which followed the age of the great tragedians. Some of the later tragedies of Euripides

---

[6] See e.g. David Riesman, Reuel Denney and Nathan Glazer, *The Lonely Crowd* (New Haven, Conn., 1950), p. 12.

are almost comedies—the *Helena*, the *Iphigenia in Tauris* and, most vividly, the *Ion*. The idea of Shakespeare reaching out for a Euripides he cannot read and of whom he has scarcely heard may seem a subject for compassionate silence, but if we watch him at work any pity we may have felt is quickly forgotten. He had a nose for this business.

As early as *The Comedy of Errors* Shakespeare had known that what we may call the Stories of the Children Lost and Found were Greek, and that (because Menander still lay buried in the Egyptian sand) he must get what he needed from Plautus. It is instructive to compare Shakespeare's use of Roman Comedy with Jonson's. Jonson catches the ferocious energy, the intrigue, the cruel mirth—in a word the Roman-ness. Shakespeare catches the mythic resonance, the Greek behind the Roman. Already he was on the right path. The Greek Old Comedy we read at school—Aristophanes[7]—has nothing to do with Shakespeare. But in the fragments of that transitional and New Comedy which lie behind Plautus we find far more 'pre-echoes' of Shakespeare than we could ever have hoped for: Falstaff and sack in Theopompus's *Nemeas*,[8] the minuscule fauna and flora, elves (σατυρίδια) and country dancing of *A Midsummer Night's Dream* in Strattis,[9] the awe-struck religious-tourist atmosphere of the Delphic scene in *The Winter's Tale* in Lysippus,[10] a meditative Duke Senior in Amphis,[11] and perhaps most striking of all, the Chorus of *Henry V* conjuring the vasty fields of France from a wooden O in Heniochus.[12] Less striking, but relevant, is the *Dyskolos* of Menander, which opens with the invitation, so foreign to the preceding age, to 'imagine that this place is Phylae in

[7] With the exception of the *Ecclesiazusae* and the *Plutus*, which belong to a later genre.

[8] Fr. 32, in *The Fragments of Greek Comedy*, ed. and trans. John Maxwell Edmonds, (Leiden, 1957), vol. I, p. 860.

[9] Fr. 66, Edmonds, *op. cit.*, vol. I, p. 834. Norwood translates σατυρίδια 'elves' (in his *Greek Comedy* (London, 1931), p. 35) and has the backing of Liddell and Scott. Edmonds however suggests (*loc. cit.*) that the word may be either the name of a plant or of a kind of scarecrow, made in the shape of a little satyr. If Edmonds is right, the parallel with *A Midsummer Night's Dream* is not so close.

[10] See Augustus Meineke, *Fragmenta Poetarum Comoediae Antiquae* (Berlin, 1840), vol. II, p. 746. This passage is excluded both from Kock's *Comicorum Atticorum Fragmenta* and from Edmonds.

[11] Fr. 17, Edmonds, *op. cit.*, vol. II (1959), p. 320.

[12] Fr. 5, Edmonds, *op. cit.*, vol. I, p. 916. Edmonds' free translation disguises the point at issue.

Attica'. It is sometimes assumed by historians of drama that a free allusion to the fact that something is being represented belongs naturally to the primitive phase. In Greek drama it comes late. In any case, the 'logical atmosphere' of a Menandrian prologue is subtle. The speaker does not say, 'I am acting the part of Pan'; he rather implies, 'I, the god Pan, have come down to tell you that this place is Phylae'. None of this material will be found in any textbook account of Shakespeare's sources, and it is quite proper that it should not, since (dare we say it?) he could not possibly have read it. It therefore stands as an uncanny example of mere likeness, of a latent reciprocity between Shakespearian drama and the Greek at the very period when it begins to slip from our knowledge. If it be unprofessional to entertain such analogies, then we must presumably censure Gilbert Norwood, who in his *Greek Comedy* (1931) noticed almost all the points of resemblance. But the myth was Shakespeare's proper quarry, and this directs us to Menander, the prince of New Comedy, the poet, above all, of ἀναγνώρισις of the Recognition Scene (and now we should begin to think, not of *The Comedy of Errors*, but of *Pericles, Cymbeline* and *The Winter's Tale*).

Yet even Menander is not the true source. Though he has much more grace than Plautus or Terence he has only a little more enchantment. His world is not only socially exclusive; it is, as R. B. Braithwaite used to say, 'demythologized'. The nature of the New Comedy has been well summarized by T. B. L. Webster: 'Mythological comedy has little place; mythology travestied in the old way would be discordant, mythology untravestied belonged to tragedy.'[13] Thus in one respect Menander's historical position is the reverse of Shakespeare's. Menander was falling from myth into naturalism; but Shakespeare was aspiring from naturalism to myth. The English poet, it will be noticed, had the harder task. Nature is simply given; it is there to be observed. Myth is handed down, and in the process is subject to loss or diminution. Shakespeare knew that the real source was Greek and that the goods as they reached him had been damaged in passage. He could no longer trust the facile excesses of Renaissance iconography—

> Come, thou monarch of the vine,
> Plumpy Bacchus with pink eyne:
> (*Antony and Cleopatra*, II. vii. 111–12)

[13] *Studies in Later Greek Comedy* (Manchester, 1953), p. 115.

—but hungered for a deity more severe, more beautiful, more Greek:

> The gods themselves,
> Humbling their deities to love, have taken
> The shapes of beasts upon them: Jupiter
> Became a bull and bellow'd; the green Neptune
> A ram and bleated; and the fire-rob'd god,
> Golden Apollo, a poor humble swain,
> As I seem now.
>
> (*The Winter's Tale*, IV, iv. 25-30)

Shakespeare tracked his myth as far as the Roman imitator of Menander and then went on alone. We, who know more than he could know, can judge how straight he ran.

Properly speaking, myth deals with the significant actions of gods and men, but Menander's gods are faded. The true object of Shakespeare's stylistic search therefore lies one stage further back. Now New Comedy is derived not, as many people think, from Old Comedy but from tragedy. The dramatist most parodied, most quoted and most revered by the poets of transitional and New Comedy is, of course, Euripides.[14] Satyrus wrote in his *Life* of Euripides:

> . . . The quarrels that we remark in comedy between husband and wife, father and son, master and slave, or the climaxes brought about by rapes, suppositious children, recognitions by rings and necklaces . . . these of course are the framework of New Comedy, and were brought to perfection by Euripides.[15]

We must remember that it was not just any body of Greek myth that Shakespeare was seeking but one only: the Stories of the Children Lost and Found. The pattern of the story is comic as we have come to

[14] Axionicus wrote a play called *Phileuripides* (*The Lover of Euripides*); a character in Philemon (fr. 130) says that if he believed in immortality he would hang himself to meet Euripides. Strattis (who, incidentally, wrote a play which sounds oddly like *The Winter's Tale*—about a man who fell in love with a picture—fr. 40) wrote a burlesque of Euripides called the *Phoenissae*. Quintilian (*Institutio Oratoria*, X. i. 69) says that Euripides' plays were greatly loved by Menander. See G. Norwood, *op. cit.*, pp. 50f.; Katharine Lever, *The Art of Greek Comedy* (London, 1956), p. 189; A. S. Owen's edn. of Euripides' *Ion* (Oxford, 1939), p. xvii.

[15] *Oxyrhynchus Papyri*, 1176, ed A. S. Hunt, Part IX (London, 1912), p. 149. See also Satiro, *Vita di Euripide*, ed. G. Arrhigetti (Pisa, 1964), p. 63. The translation is Norwood's.

understand the term; but the divine dimension, which Shakespeare also needed, was, as the Greeks understood matters, tragic. It is likely that there was never more than one dramatist who fulfilled both these requirements, and that was Euripides. In the preface to his translation of the *Ion* Gilbert Murray wrote:

> The *Ion* belongs to a particular class of tragedy in which the hero is the Son of a God and a mortal princess. The birth is concealed, the babe is cast out or hidden and in danger of death from a cruel king, but in the end is recognised as a son of god and established as founder of a New Kingdom and ancestor of a royal house.[16]

Between Plautus and Shakespeare there is a demonstrable relation of influence; between Euripides and Shakespeare there is only the most tenuous and speculative historical connection. In the Temple Shakespeare of 1894 Sir Israel Gollancz suggested that Shakespeare read the *Alcestis*, perhaps in Pettie's Latin translation, and used his reading when he wrote *The Winter's Tale*. Today some scholars feel that the correspondences between the two plays are close enough to justify our naming *Alcestis* as an actual source. But the idea has never obtained universal assent. On the other hand, the objective similarity of certain passages (especially *Alcestis*, 1121–50, and *The Winter's Tale*, V. ii. 18–132) is beyond dispute. The *Alcestis* is early Euripides (438 B.C.) but, with its comic episodes and solemn-happy ending it anticipates the manner of the late romantic tragedies. And it is the manner which is important. There is a sense in which the correspondences between the *Alcestis* and *The Winter's Tale* are in any case the *less* striking in virtue of the fact that the story of the *Alcestis* *is* the story of *The Winter's Tale*. But the congruity of atmosphere between late Shakespeare and late Euripides has a more persistent, if less tangible, interest. If we read, not as source-hunters but as critics, we shall see that late Euripides is *like* Shakespeare as no other dramatist is. We enter the world of the *Ion* and—as we watch an εγγενὴς φόνος ('an in-the-family-murder') narrowly averted, the mutual recognition of mother and son in the sacred city, perhaps most of all as we listen to Creusa likening her fortune to that of a vessel lost in a storm (1502–7)—we feel that we have been here before. The reader who surveys the evolution of Greek tragedy from Aeschylus to Euripides and then turns to the parallel development of Shakespeare's work may begin to feel that some inner dialectical necessity is involved.

[16] (London, 1954), p. 5.

After the abrupt catastrophes of tragedy the sweet intricacies of romantic comedy grow strong.

We are suggesting, then, that Shakespeare in seeking his myth recognized instinctively that the tradition was, precisely, a tradition, and not a set of terminal authorities. Plautus to him was not so much a model as a perspective glass through which he discerned new lands.

He seems in *The Tempest* to have used Virgil in exactly this way. This play is of course strewn with Virigilian allusions, ranging from mere names like Carthage, Dido and the Harpy to turns of phrase (e.g. 'lie there, my art', I. ii. 25, *artemque repono*, *Aeneid*, V. 484). Perhaps the most effective of these reminiscences occurs at I. ii. 421–7, where Ferdinand meets Miranda. These lines, the commentaries tell us, echo *Aeneid*, I. 328–9, *O quam te memorem, virgo?* Yet even here Shakespeare's true kinship is with the Greek behind the Roman. Virgil's lines describe the meeting of Aeneas and Venus, so that Aeneas' extravagant cry proves merely accurate; the woman before him is truly divine. Miranda, on the other hand, is the mortal daughter of the king of the island. This turns the sentiment into a mixture of erotic vision, lover's hyperbole and well-judged compliment. None of this is present in Virgil but all of it is present in Virgil's Greek source, Homer's description of the meeting of Odysseus and Nausicaa (*Odyssey*, VI. 149–52). Moreover, Nausicaa and her father, the King of the Phaeacians, live

> ἀπάνευθε πολυκλύστῳ ἐνὶ πόντῳ,
>
> ἔσχατοι apart, on the many-sounding sea, far away . . .
>
> (VI. 204–5)

And so did Miranda and Prospero. Think of the island, the magic, of Sycorax (the 'swine-raven'); this is the world of Calypso in her sea-girt isle, of Circe and her victims, of enchantment, sea-sorrow and bewilderment. Why do we pause on the *Aeneid* and the laborious exodus from Troy when all this lies only a little further on? Shakespeare's play belongs far more firmly than does the *Aeneid* to the Odyssean genre of the νόστος, the 'journey home'.[17] It is the *Aeneid* which gets into the commentaries; the larger relevancies are more easily missed.

But what exactly are we claiming here? Not clairvoyance, this time. The correspondences are too close. Some of them, indeed, are fairly specific. Odysseus, just before his speech to Nausicaa, is worried about

17 Nevill Coghill wrote, 'It is a play about going home' in his 'The Basis of Shakespearean Comedy', *Essays and Studies*, New Series, III (1950), p. 24.

etiquette (VI. 142-4) and Ferdinand, within his speech, hopes to be instructed 'how I may bear me here' (I. ii. 425). Gonzalo's amazement that their clothes are not discoloured by the sea (II. i. 58-60) recalls the happiness of Odysseus when he washes away the sea-stains from his body and is made beautiful by Athene (VI. 224-37). No, Shakespeare has probably read a translation of at least the sixth book of the *Odyssey*. Homer was available to him in Latin, French or Italian, even if Chapman had not yet got so far with his English. But, in any case, with a source so celebrated it is in a manner idle to cite editions and translators; half an hour in a tavern with a learned friend could have supplied him with all he needed. The *Odyssey* has left fewer traces than the *Aeneid* in the verbal texture of the drama (perhaps it was read long before), but it is the Greek and not the Roman source which controls the *ethos* of the play.

III

One other channel of transmission remains: the Greek erotic romances. This has of course been dealt with pretty exhaustively by scholars.[18] The principal source of *The Winter's Tale* is Greene's *Pandosto*. In *Pandosto* Greene drew heavily on the *Daphnis and Chloe* of Longus, and less heavily on his more habitual favourite, Achilles Tatius. If we ask what element in Shakespeare's late plays was the peculiar contribution of this literature we might guess: the special sexual accent. Both Achilles Tatius and Longus are, what Shakespeare is not, mildly pornographic. Only the rhetorical brilliance of the one and the lyric sweetness of the other remain to mark the contrast, in this sphere, between their age and ours. Most obviously, this sexual accent appears in Shakespeare in the preoccupation with virginity at risk which we find in all four of the late plays. But perhaps the most pervasively important of all the romance sources for Shakespeare's final period is the one he used for *Pericles*, namely the story of Apollonius of Tyre. *Pericles* was the first of the 'late plays' and set the new style. It is therefore not improbable that the story which gave Shakespeare the idea for *Pericles* also gave him the idea of a new kind of romance-comedy. But the sexual element in *Apollonius of Tyre* is very sinister.

[18] See especially S. L. Wolff, *The Greek Romances in Elizabethan Prose Fiction* (New York, 1912); F. W. Moorman's Arden edition of *The Winter's Tale* (London, 1922), esp. pp. xixf.

We do not have the Greek original of the story of Apollonius. A Latin version exists, but Shakespeare used the medieval verse redaction of Gower. When Shakespeare had first essayed a Greek story, in *The Comedy of Errors*, he worked, as we saw, through Plautus. But he also made some use even then of Gower's version of the Apollonius story. When towards the end of his career, he returned to Romance, Plautus was forgotten and *Apollonius* filled his mind.

Leslie Fiedler has argued in an unpublished paper that the motif of incest, which is strong in *Apollonius*, is importantly, if less obviously, present in other late plays. We begin to see that the root from which the late plays grew is older even than Euripides. Riddles, babies left to die in wild country, oracles, incest, royal children found and reared by shepherds—all these elements are present in the myth of Oedipus. Of course Sophocles is unequivocally the tragedian, and his plotting is centripetal whereas Shakespeare's (except for *The Tempest*) is romantically centrifugal. A summary of Sophocles' play does not sound in the least like a Shakespearian romance. But the article on Oedipus in any classical dictionary—which gives us, not the plot of a particular drama, but the prior myth—immediately suggests the story-pattern of *Pericles*, *Cymbeline*, *The Winter's Tale* and *The Tempest*.

In *Pericles*, of course, the incest motif is explicit. In *The Winter's Tale* Leontes is attracted to his own daughter (V. i. 223–8), a theatrically powerful moment based on a much longer incestuous episode in *Pandosto*. But it is only a moment; Leontes swiftly tells us that it was only because she reminded him of his lost wife, and we breath easily again. And when the lost wife is restored, and given by Shakespeare an emphasis which tends to eclipse the restoration of Perdita, we may feel that the demons are safely under lock and key.

Thus, while the epilogue of *Pericles* sets the Prince of Tyre and Thaisa in antithesis to Antiochus and his incestuous paramour, in *The Winter's Tale* the incest motif occurs in the subject of redemption, Leontes. But the conclusion of either comedy provides the father figure with a lawful wife. In *The Tempest* this is not so. And yet we feel some need of it. There is of course no mention of possible incest between Prospero and Miranda, but the thought may be there. Prospero's rage at Caliban's attempted rape of Miranda is natural enough. It explains itself on political, social, ethnical and perhaps even biological grounds. But his attitude to Ferdinand, the ideal son-in-law, is less perspicuous. Prospero's moments of real verbal energy are devoted to the prohibition of pre-marital sex. It is no good saying that in this he is merely the good father, protecting his daughter. It is not so much the presence of the paternal prohibition that is significant, but its violence, and together with its violence the absence of any other strong emotion. There is something deeply amiss in that final movement of The Tempest towards love and fruition. The very Masque breaks up in discord. Prospero has no real blessing to give. Further, his language to Ferdinand is edged with an excessive hostility, which Ferdinand can allay only by professing that long virginity has reduced his appetite (IV. i. 54–6)! Three men and a girl together on a desert island. The tensions are not really so obscure. The old Freudian myth revives in our minds; Prospero is not gaining a son but losing a female.

I have felt the need to explore the 'Greekness' of Shakespearian romance at some length partly to undermine the excessively Christian predisposition of many readers. Prospero belongs not in the ethically warm universe of Christianity but in the hard, bright, far-off world of Greek legend, with its demons, sun, sea and mortality.

After his strangely chill forgiveness of his enemies, Prospero goes home, not to marriage, nor even to resume the reins of government, but to think about death (V. i. 311). The ending of The Tempest is sick with ambiguity. Even the ostensibly idyllic discovery of the lovers playing chess is a discovery of possible cheating and proffered complicity (V. i. 172–4). Prospero's most memorable speech in the play ('Be cheerful, sir. Our revels now are ended . . .', IV. i. 147–8) begins as a word of comfort to Ferdinand and ends as an intuition of annihilation. We are told that in Jacobean times the old were encouraged to meditate on imminent death and that Prospero's resolve is healthy and proper to his circumstances. But Prospero is no saint out of Izaak Walton; we have small ground for confidence about his undiscovered country. The very epilogue of the play curiously combines the conventional appeal for applause at the end of a comedy with a plea for prayers to help one who is in danger of despair.

We are getting to know Prospero. Now look back at his relations with Caliban. Is there no residual, excessive anger there? When we imagine how a good duke should behave, and then listen to Prospero, do we feel no surprise? The abuse which Prospero pours out on Caliban is strangely copious; it implies an efficient rather than a final cause. Shakespeare's figures of authority, Henry V, the Lord Chief Justice, do not speak thus. Prospero's fierceness is not purely functional; it exceeds the object; it is pretty obviously epiphenomenal, the consequence of Prospero's psychological state rather than the instrument of his reasoned indignation.

But Caliban had really tried to ravish Miranda. What a rape was there! Glass-house innocence corrupted by—its shadow or its prototype?—outdoor ignorance. Prospero had arrived on Caliban's Eden and forthwith begun to act like God. In particular, he produced a marriageable girl, a kind of Eve. Remember Adamastor, the African giant in the fifth canto of the *Lusiads* (another epic of sea-sorrow) who poured out curses when he remembered how he had been promised a white bride, and found instead that he had lost his human nature.[19] It was Miranda, who, hour by hour, took pains to teach Caliban language (I. ii. 353–8). The speech in which Miranda tells the story of this ill-advised tutorship has been ascribed by many editors to Prospero, but without warrant. It may seem curious that it was Dryden who began this dubious tradition—curious, because we might think that the author of *The Enchanted Island* knew well what *The Tempest* was about at the level of sex; indeed he laid on extra kicks. To meet the girl who had never seen a man he procured a man who had never seen a girl. But no, Dryden's instinct was coarse after all. There is already in *The Tempest* a man who has never seen a girl. His name is Caliban.

Perhaps Miranda found it easy to think of Caliban as a child. Not only is he taught to talk, but he is shown the man in the moon, and cries to dream again. Prospero let his daughter bring Caliban out of this dark infancy and yet professes to be astonished at the result. Diderot would not have been, for he wrote,

> Si le petit sauvage était abandonné à lui-même, qu'il conservât toute son imbécillité et qu'il réunît au peu de raison de l'enfant au berceau la violence des passions de l'homme de trente ans, il tordrait le col à son père et coucherait avec sa mère.[20]

The context of these famous words is a discussion of education. Moreover, it is the 'sound' *Moi* of the dialogue who speaks here, not the subversive *Lui*.

[19] Luis Vaz de Camoens, *Os Lusíadas*, V. xxxix–lx, in the edition of J. D. M. Ford (Cambridge, Mass., 1946), pp. 153–9; in Richard Burton's translation, 1880, vol. I, pp. 192–9.
[20] From *Le Neveu de Rameau*, in Diderot, *Oeuvres Romanesques*, ed. H. Bénac (Paris, 1959), p. 479.

H

The Tempest, then, is about the complexities of innocence and civility. Foreigners come to an island, bringing science and a stronger magic, law and politics, courtesy and vulgarity, temperance and drunkenness—God-Prospero with his staff, God-Stefano with his bottle. Shakespeare's mind, nearing the end of its course, begins to race. His reach exceeds his grasp. In the story of Apollonius he glimpsed an antique literature still inaccessible; in the Bermuda pamphlets a continent still to be discovered. The genre of the play is not easily determined. It is surprisingly close to science-fiction (Ariel, unlike Puck, is a consistently imagined possibility for which no concept is already available) and is still closer to that Utopian fiction which is science-fiction's rich relation (one of the most famous in this line has, appropriately, a title taken from *The Tempest*). When, in our own century, men reached the moon, the most beautiful thing they saw was earth-rise. The moon is blank, but from it can be seen something marvellous, huge, coloured, infinitely various and changing, and that is our own earth; so that if *per impossibile* a man had grown up on the moon there would be one place above all that he would long to reach. And we are already there. Remember Milton's Satan, looking in from outside. In a manner, Prospero too inhabits an island in the moon. Milan is home: corrupt, desirable, live. Hence Miranda's visionary cry, 'O brave new world, that has such people in it!' in part survives the undercutting cynicism of Prospero's reply, "Tis new to thee' (V. i. 183–184).

The play looks forward, as I have hinted, to the idea of America (O brave new world!) and backward to the idea of Pastoral. The island is the green refuge, where wounds heal far from court or city, and it is the place of unredeemed brutality. Who then are the corruptors and who the corrupted? Prospero and Caliban live together in undissembled hatred. While Ferdinand and Miranda get on with the business of getting married, the real war is between master and slave. But the relationship, until Stefano and Trinculo come, is stable by its very asymmetry. Prospero is stronger than Caliban. He vilifies him for not working, but seems to need the vilification (and hence the idleness) more than he needs the work. Prospero is Caliban's keeper, and Caliban is Prospero's whipping-boy. Caliban is devoured by lust and Prospero is strangely shaken by his daughter's marriage. Neither gets a bride in the end (it will be said that Prospero is of the wrong generation, but Leontes got his Hermione and Pericles his Thaisa).

IV

Now that we have sketched in Caliban's setting, let us try to do the same for Jaques. *As You Like It* is true pastoral and an unequivocally happy play. But it is not serene. There is anti-pastoral scepticism, local unhappiness and, in the bloody napkin, the momentary thought of what death could do if it ever entered Arden.[21] Falstaff, old apple-John, the Silenus of the Histories, who died smiling on his fingers' ends and babbling of green fields, found himself in the middle of a real battle at Shrewsbury, and suddenly spoke like a small child: 'I would it were bed-time, Hal, and all well' (*1 Henry IV*, V. i. 125). Rosalind echoes him, 'I would I were at home' (*AYLI*, IV. iii. 159). But Rosalind is love triumphant, full of intelligence and sanity. Erotic security has made her strong. Only once does she mistake her path. Ardent herself, she sees Phebe frigid, and mistakes masochism (not, of course, the extreme variety) for narcissism (III. v. 35–63). By a delicious stroke of comedy, her joyous indignation, intended to arouse love for Silvius, draws an undesired devotion on Rosalind herself. But there is no satire on complacency here. Rosalind only wants for others the happiness she has attained herself, and the comedy plot finally ratifies her wish with power. Similarly, the down-to-earth scepticism which Rosalind loves to express—'But these are all lies, men have died from time to time and worms have eaten them, but not for love, not for love' (IV. i. 92–4)— holds no destructive force, since it springs from a well-founded belief in the reality of Orlando's love.

Where loving health is joined with power, as it is in Rosalind, we might suppose that no shadow of perversion could ever cross the stage. But that is not quite true. First the very mechanism of the plot involves a sort of echo of sexual deviance. The lovers both look like boys. Further, the mere name 'Ganymede' is a homosexual allusion. Remember Marlowe's lines:

> Jove slily stealing from his sister's bed
> To dally with Idalian Ganymed[22]

Marlowe haunts this play as the 'dead shepherd' of III. v. 84 and

21 This observation is Laurence Lerner's. See his 'An Essay on Pastoral', *Essays in Criticism*, XX (1970), p. 292.

22 *Hero and Leander*, First Sestyad, 147–8, in *Marlowe's Poems*, ed. L. C. Martin (London, 1931), p. 35.

perhaps as the source of the phrase 'a great reckoning in a little room' (III. iii. 11–12). But, in any case, what 'Ganymede' meant to the Elizabethan is clear in Richard Barnfield's *The Affectionate Shepherd, containing the Complaint of Daphnis for the love of Ganymede* (1593). All this, to be sure, is only there to be contradicted. Much of the comedy arises from the incongruity between Rosalind's appearance and her true sex. Nevertheless, we should concede that the joke is a little risqué (or even risky).

One can see very well why Shakespeare sustains this productive incongruity. But why does Rosalind sustain it? Why, in short, when she reaches Arden, does she not change her clothes? Her costume was chosen for its power to protect her from sexual importunity and was useful to her on her journey. But now that she has found her lover why does she continue to wear it?

Various answers can be given. Rosalind's disguise confers liberty. In a sense it permits her to be herself, in that it allows her natural energy to express itself in unrestricted movement. This release extends from the purely physical—skirts are cumbersome—to the psychological—women are conventionally expected to be passive. There is an irony here which goes a step beyond Miss Betty Friedan. Rosalind has found the conventional feminine *persona* restrictive, not just of her individuality as a human being, but of her very femaleness, of her proper sexual role. It is not Rosalind but convention which is awry.

Again, perhaps we were wrong a moment ago to distinguish so sharply between Shakespeare and Rosalind. Rosalind manipulates the rest, much as Shakespeare manipulates them all. She is the creator's ally in the camp of the creatures. She does the dramatist's work of coaxing the different strands of the plot to a proper solution. It is easy to feel that Prospero is an ectype of the poet himself, and the same is true, in a lesser degree, of Rosalind. Both of them have magical powers, and there is an old analogy between poetry and magic. It is with us still in Auden's epigraph to his *Collected Shorter Poems*:

> Although you be as I am, one of those
> Who feel a Christian ought to write in prose,
> For poetry is magic . . .

There is a related reason why Rosalind keeps her doublet and hose. Our earlier question was too banausically utilitarian in spirit. Of course, in the real business of life, she wishes to attract and marry Orlando.

There will be a time for that. But now she is in Arden, and there is no clock in the forest, and she wants to *play*. The structure of the drama mirrors this suspension of the practical, for all the 'plot' is bundled into the first and last moments and the greater part of the play is a timeless meditation on the pastoral.

Lastly, Rosalind's disguise guarantees a certain objectivity in her relations with Orlando. If she were wearing her own clothes, he would recognize her and she could never afterwards quite trust a word he said. It would all be lover's rhetoric. But, as things are, she can eavesdrop on his thoughts. And yet, by a reversal of the usual routine, she hears nothing but good of herself—it is lover's rhetoric still (and she can afford to puncture it as often as she likes), but lover's rhetoric in the absence of the beloved has a different status. It is no longer tainted by a special hunger for results. Prince Hal was less lucky in his eavesdropping. No wonder Rosalind wants to prolong hers.

Yet there is something disquieting in this fission of erotic identity. There is a certain impropriety in any act of eavesdropping (and eavesdropping in an erotic stituation can easily approach voyeurism) and the impropriety is not wholly cured if our own happiness forms the object of our surreptitious curiosity. Furthermore, this disquiet, almost imperceptible as long as we confine our attention to Rosalind, grows when we look elsewhere. The notion of a love which disregards the physical presence and prefers to feed on images recurs in the play. 'Am not I your Rosalind?' says Rosalind-Ganymede, and Orlando answers, 'I take some joy to say you are, because I would be talking of her' (IV. i. 79–80). Here, of course, the comedy lies in the buried propriety of the situation. But at III. v. 92–5 the situation is more perverse. There Phebe tells the suffering Silvius that since she has fallen in love herself she enjoys listening to his ardent language. In Arden we find everywhere a felicitously controlled promiscuity of the eye: 'The sight of lovers feedeth those in love' (III. iv. 52). But note the difference between Orlando and Phebe. Phebe, listening to Silvius, immediately attaches the emotion to Ganymede; Orlando listening to Ganymede cannot help seeing Rosalind—who is really there. But even the 'buried propriety' formula can generate a certain tension. In III. ii. 371–88 Rosalind-Ganymede says that she can cure love and replace it with monastic longings. Orlando replies that he does not want to be cured, but Rosalind-Ganymede insists that she will cure him nevertheless. Then comes the moment of strangeness: Orlando replies, 'Now, by the faith of my love, I will . . .' (III. ii. 392). Orlando, whose comradely kisses were too 'full of sanctity', of 'the very ice of chastity' for Rosalind-Ganymede (II. iv. 12–16) is now sexually attracted by that same Ganymede, and attracted moreover by an offer of *monastic instruction.* Yet all remains well. It is Rosalind who is attracting Orlando. But this time the propriety is more deeply buried. Orlando is not neglecting Ganymede and mooning after Rosalind; he is pursuing a Rosalind his conscious mind has temporarily forgotten in a youth he knows as Ganymede.

This, then, is the world of Arden, a place of love misplaced yet true. The chain of unrequited love so fundamental in ordinary comic suspense is here reserved for the lesser lovers. The truest love is reciprocal and the sort of plotting that normally turns on frustrated desire is supplied instead by disguise and ragging.

Thus far Arden would appear to be a kind of Eden, and the strongest kind too, for it can accommodate and absorb scepticism and psychological tension. Yet it cannot finally find a place for Jaques. Rosalind rejects hyperbole but is happy in the fact of love. Touchstone rejects the fact of love but is happy with its material accidents. But Jaques has rejected happiness itself. Because he is radically wretched he is a walking affront to the felicity of Arden. The Duke attempts to give him the secondary status of a player within the play by treating his eloquent acidity as if it were the performance of a professional fool. And, in a fashion, Jaques is content to let it be so. Yet it is a precarious complaisance. We know that Jaques himself views the Duke as an excessively extroverted, disputatious bore (II. v. 29–32). In any case, Jaques has his own way of spoiling the show.

The ideal pattern of the scene in which Orlando happens upon Duke Senior and the rest in the forest is clear enough. Orlando's drawing of his sword is to appear as a gesture of utterly misplaced aggression. Instead of the barbarous hostility he associates with wild regions he is to meet with nothing but civility and high courtesy. Such is the ideal of the scene, but what is the reality? It is no idyll of fellowship that Orlando interrupts but a peculiarly ugly quarrel between a highborn self-deluder and a sick spirit.

The scene is II. vii. It opens with the Duke musing, in terms which may seem excessive, on the subhuman nature of Jaques:

> I think he be transform'd into a beast;
> For I can nowhere find him like a man.
>
> (II. vii. 1–2)

His meditation is broken by the arrival of Jaques himself, in a mood of strange exhilaration. He has met Touchstone in the forest and is fired (though we feel no warmth) by the true fool's grave pronouncement on time and decay. 'Oh that I were a fool!' cries Jaques, 'I am ambitious for a motley coat' (II. vii. 42–3). The Duke, who ought to be delighted by this change in Jaques, is less than convivial: 'Thou shalt have one.' The tone of this, though muted, is strictly comparable with that of Hal's answer to Falstaff's 'Banish plump Jack and banish all the world'—' I do, I will' (1 Henry IV, II. iv. 464). In both episodes a prince is addressing his dog; in both we find an exuberance from the 'butt' which is not reciprocated, in both a cunning manipulation of tempo whereby the naked encounter of two radically opposed natures is muffled by the sudden entry of another person. In Henry IV it all goes very fast. The interruption cuts across the crisis of understanding and Falstaff tries desperately to 'play out the play' over the heads of the interrupters. The result is an overlapping of plot-movements, an overlapping which crackles with life. In As You Like It we find instead a tamer consecutiveness, but otherwise the effect is similar. Jaques and the Duke have space for a brief exchange before Orlando runs in with drawn sword. Jaques pronounces himself content with the rank of fool, so long as he is given the full liberty of his wit; he asks that he be given leave to physic vice. Strangely, the Duke is enraged by this answer, and cries out that Jaques, being himself infected with the grossest lust, can never give physic to any man, but only 'embossed sores and headed evils' (II. vii. 67). Jaques has claimed fool's licence and the mere assertion of the claim has shaken Duke Senior. That the fool's freedom is a test of aristocratic confidence can be seen if we compare a moment in Twelfth Night with a parallel moment in King Lear. In Twelfth Night Feste offers to prove Olivia a fool. He completes his Erasmian catechism, convicts her of folly, and she turns, smiling, to her neighbour: 'What think you of this fool, Malvolio? Doth he not mend?' (I. v. 68–9). The fool in King Lear runs through the same basic routine with the King, but, at the point where Olivia smiled, Lear cries out, 'Oh, let me not be mad, sweet heaven, not mad' (I. v. 43). Duke Senior is far from Lear's situation, yet Jaques has the power to enrage him.

What sort of man is the Duke? He has a genius for happiness, a genius which involves a hint of mendacity. Translated to the forest, he preaches a pastoral sermon. As we listen to the lulling music of his lines we may imagine that we are being entertained with what Lovejoy and Boas called 'soft primitivism'.[23] It will be remembered that soft primitivism commends leisure and play—

> Tityre tu patulo recubans sub tegmine fagi

—whereas hard primitivism commends work. But if we attend to the meaning of Duke Senior's words we shall find that he is, after all, no soft primitive. Nor, on the other hand, is he proposing the hard primitivism of the *Georgics*. Strangely, and ironically, his pastoralism is epistemological. The life in Arden is better, he says, because it replaces illusion with reality. Truth-telling pain is better than mendacious ease. It is a startling doctrine but on the Duke's lips it never causes us a moment's surprise—because we do not begin to believe him. Amiens speaks for everyone when he compliments the Duke at the end of his speech:

> Happy is your Grace,
> That can translate the stubbornness of fortune
> Into so quiet and so sweet a style.
>
> (II. i. 18-20)

The irony is intricate. The Duke preaches realism and is praised for his power to transmute reality. Yet it does not occur to him to be annoyed at Amiens' remark; he knows perfectly well that their situation is bad—after all, he remarks at II. vii. 136 that he and his companions are not the only people in the world who are unfortunate, and having affirmed that he would not change his pastoral life,[24] he does just that at the first opportunity. No, it is not Amiens who irritates the Duke, but Jaques. And that is because the Duke is a fantasist ineffectively disguised as a realist, whereas Jaques is a realist very effectively disguised as a fantasist.

Shakespeare's control of the ironies in this scene is breathtakingly sure and shows, amongst other things, how he has matured since he wrote *Love's Labour's Lost*. The earlier comedy was polemically intended. In

[23] A. O. Lovejoy and G. Boas, *Primitivism and Related Ideas in Antiquity* (Baltimore, 1935), esp. pp. 9-11. This book was presented as the first volume of *A Documentary History of Primitivism and Related Ideas*, but no more volumes appeared.

[24] The Folio gives II. i. 18, 'I would not change it', to Amiens. Dyce transferred it to the Duke, and has been followed by most editors. If Amiens is to deliver the speech he should cough politely, and assume an 'It-goes-without-saying' expression, as if he were merely completing the Duke's thought for him (Jeeves supplying Bertie Wooster with the needed phrase).

it, if Frances Yates was right[25], Shakespeare backed the literary party of the realists, Eliot and Nashe, against the conscious artists, Harvey, Chapman, Florio and Vives; yet the play was pragmatically self-refuting, since it is itself a brilliant specimen of artifice and stylistic virtuosity. In *Love's Labour's Lost* Shakespeare struggles with his own facility, is as little believed as Duke Senior and is driven at the end to mortify the comic eucatastrophe with sudden death and marriages deferred. It is interesting that Shakespeare's problem, at the beginning of his career, was his very fluency. But in *As You Like It* he has made the technical problem of *Love's Labour's Lost* into the stuff of human characterization, in the figure of Duke Senior.

The contrast between the Duke and Jaques is pointed for us in a single scene. II. i. opens, as we have seen, with the Duke's sermon, where the style betrays the sentiment, but it continues with Jaques on the stricken deer. Jaque's moralizing is presented in *oratio obliqua* and we therefore see it first as the Duke sees it—as a delicious performance. No doubt this does no great disservice to Jaques, who would have presented it himself in exactly that style. But now the relation between style and matter is reversed. With Jaques, the lightness of the style is betrayed by the importance of what is said. The Duke, according to Jaques, is no pilgrim at the shrine of the Real. He is instead a kind of criminal against the order of nature. He has usurped the place of the wild creatures just as surely as his brother had usurped *his* place. Against all the stylistic signals, we find that we must respect what Jaques says, and that is because the play as a whole confirms his words, just as it makes a mockery of Duke Senior's. For the play shows us, not a court made simple, but a simple place made courtly. Shakespeare makes sure that we feel the real degradation of rusticity in the opening scene, where Orlando complains, 'he keeps me rustically at home', and, lest we forget, includes in the opening part of his country pastoral the grim observation of Corin on the shepherd's continuing bond of villeinage (II. iv. 71–82).

Having noted the usurpation of the forest, Jaques turned his attention to one deer, singled out from the rest because it had been shot by the hunters. This passage is one of the strangest in the play. It is written as a specimen of preposterousness, as if it has to be either false sentiment or a deliberate parody of true feeling, yet it haunts the imagination with a strange directness. No doubt it is partly because we sense that

[25]*A Study of Love's Labour's Lost*, (London, 1936).

Jaques' proclaimed kinship with the deer is not altogether playful. He, no less than Cowper, was a stricken deer that left the herd. Amiens left Jaques sobbing with the deer and we cannot tell (perhaps Jaques could not tell) whether the tears were real or feigned. At the heart of the Duke's pastoral idyll is the serio-comic killing of a wild creature—

> The wanton Troopers riding by
> Have shot my Faun and it will dye.

Thus Marvell's nymph; Shakespeare plays it as a brief ritual, to the tune of 'Who Killed Cock Robin?' Jaques, of course, is for the prosecution:

> *Jacques:* Which is he that killed the deer?
> *First Lord:* Sir it was I.

> (IV. ii. 1–2)

But the slayer is not punished; instead he is honoured with the dubious coronal of the deer's antlers. Jaques calls it a Roman triumph and indeed, where scurrility is mingled thus with celebration, the analogy is close. Did not Julius Caesar's soldiers sing at his triumph,

> Gallias Caesar subegit, Nicomedes Caesarem:
> Ecce Caesar nunc triumphat qui subegit Gallias
> Nicomedes non triumphat qui subegit Caesarem.[26]

> Caesar put down all of France
> (Nicomedes put down Caesar)
> Caesar, now in pride advance!
> As for Nicomedes, he's a
> Loser (though he put down Caesar).

But Jaques is dangerous only to the Duke, never to the pastoral idyll itself. All health and love is on its side, all the sickness on his. For pastoral is the most 'tough-minded' of genres, far tougher than tragedy. It achieves its strength by the paradoxical strategy of conceding, at the outset, the falsehood of its myth. The palpably artificial style of pastoral is a necessary element in the genre. Tragedy really pretends that death ennobles and suffering refines. Pastoral, by proclaiming itself a dream, rises above pretence. It says to us: learn the beauty, and hence the pathos, of this delusion. This is the third and last way in which the stylistic problem of *Love's Labour's Lost* is transcended. When pastoral

---

[26] Suetonius, *De Vita Caesarum*, 'Divus Iulius', XLIX, ed. H. E. Butler and M. Carey (Oxford, 1927), p. 23. The reference is of course to the rumoured seduction of Caesar by Nicomedes of Bithynia.

drops its ostentatious artifice we find a poetry in which the highest
lyric power is united with a kind of factual bleakness. Pastoral, even
more than tragedy, is the genre of privacy. Bruno Snell accurately
described the world of Virgil's *Eclogues* as a 'landscape of the mind.'[27]
Truth and friendship fall away, leaving only a kind of joy in the kinship
between wild nature and the interior mind:

> Blow, blow, thou winter wind,
> Thou art not so unkind
>   As man's ingratitude;
> Thy tooth is not so keen,
> Because thou art not seen,
>   Although thy breath be rude.
> Heigh-ho! sing heigh-ho! unto the green holly.
> Most friendship is feigning, most loving mere folly.
>   Then heigh-ho, the holly!
>   This life is most jolly.
>
> (*AYLI*, II. vii. 174–82)

Or, in the more gentlemanly accents of Horace:

> Scis Lebedus quid sit; Gabiis desertior atque
> Fidenis vicus; tamen illic vivere vellem,
> Oblitusque meorum obliviscendus et illis
> Neptunum procul e terra spectare furentem
>
> You know what *Lebedus* is like, I guess;
> A place more Godforsaken than *Caithness*.
> And yet, forgetting Friends, by them forgot
> I'd live there gladly; and from my snug Plot
> Survey the wind-vex'd Sea in billows rise,
> While *Neptune* raves, and *Jove* occludes the skies.
>
> (*Epistles*, I. xi. 7–10)

Jaques can have no quarrel with Amiens' song. The first line echoes and
transcends the Duke's thought and in its lyric impersonality exposes
the too personal frailty of his affectation better than Jaques ever could.

As You Like It, though pastoral, is not Greek in character; at least
it is not Greek as the late Romances are. Its immediate source is Lodge,
not Greene, and, as S. L. Wolff wrote, 'Lodge's prose fiction on the
whole is mediaeval, Euphuistic and Italianate rather than Hellenistic'.[28]
In *As You Like It* we find no profound evocation of the pain of loss or

[27] Bruno Snell, *The Discovery of Mind*, trans. T. G. Rosemeyer (Oxford, 1953).
[28] *The Greek Romances in Elizabethan Prose Fiction*, p. 460.

the sweetness of restoration, no recognition-scene of power, no pre-moral impetus in the story (again it was Wolff who observed that the writers of Greek Romance seem positively to have avoided human causation and responsibility in the conduct of their plots[29]—in short, no resonant myth. It might be said that Caliban is no more Greek than Jaques: but he is more fundamentally conceived. He is that of which Jaques is the social sophistication. And it may be that the Greek legends encourage such fundamentalism of mind, not just because they license us to explore the nature of such things as incest and lust (though it is important that they do that) but more importantly because they are themselves psychologically radical.

For example, it is curious that pastoral in post-classical times has seldom included sexual freedom in the catalogue of pleasures offered by the simple life. To be sure, this happens in the celebrated chorus in Tasso's *Aminta*, 'O bella età de l'oro' (656)[30]. But the speech is not only untypical of Renaissance pastoral (it swiftly drew an answer from Guarini); it is also in a sense untypical of *Aminta*, since its function is to evoke an antithesis to what we see in the play, which is frustration and misunderstanding. It has been suggested[31] that the comparative chastity of Arcadia arises from the fact that the true, latent subject of all pastoral is childhood. It is easy to imagine the psychoanalyst's reaction to this insight: 'If you wish to delude yourself into believing that child-hood is pre-sexual, please do.' But ancient pastoral was never so deluded. We might add, neither was the absurd hypothesis of a latency period ever among its illusions. The shepherd in Virgil was twelve when the sight of a little girl picking apples with her mother struck him to the heart (*Eclogues* viii. 37–41). And, if we turn to the Greek pastoral of Longus we find, instead of the indefinite metaphor-mongering of the Renaissance, a hard clarity of vision; for *Daphnis and Chloe* is, quite simply, *about* immature sexuality. The differing instincts of later thinkers, some of whom have dwelt on the innocence of childhood, others of whom have stressed its passion, are all in a manner admitted. Daphnis and Chloe are innocent in that they know nothing of sexual behaviour; but they are full of desperate desires. Sexual behaviour, says Longus,

[29] *The Greek Romances in Elizabethan Prose Fiction*, pp. 111f.

[30] Torquato Tasso, *Gerusalemme Liberata, Aminta, Rime Scelte*, a cura di Luigi De Vendittis, ed. Giulio Einaudi, Parnaso Italiano, VI (Turin, 1961), p. 686.

[31] By Laurence Lerner in his *The Uses of Nostalgia* (not yet published at the time of writing).

is not instinctive but learned (and here, I understand, he has some support from quite recent research). *That* is why his Arcadia is chaste. And, as we have seen, *Daphnis* plays an important part in the source-material of the Romances (affecting *The Winter's Tale* through Greene's *Pandosto*).

Now: has this nothing to do with Caliban? Caliban, as we have seen, resembles the *petit sauvage* of Diderot, in that he joins the passions of a grown man to the ignorance of a child. It may be that Greek Romance showed Shakespeare a way to resolve the main paradox of pastoral, which is that sexuality is natural, yet nature is pre-sexual. This paradox, submerged in the easy prose of Lodge, began to show again in the Hellenistic work of Greene. Caliban's lust is all his own yet he learned the use of it from the newcomers. Certainly *The Tempest* is structurally derived from unequivocally pastoral interludes in earlier comedies. But now we sense a fierce intelligence, less patient of concealment. In *The Tempest* pastoral feels curiously like a laboratory experiment.

V

But we have now assembled the materials we needed. We began with the strange coincidence of language applied to Jaques and Caliban, noted by Edward A. Armstrong. The scene of *As You Like It* in which all these anticipations of the later play occur is II. vii, the crucial scene in which the Duke quarrels with Jaques. It is the Duke, and only the Duke, who uses 'the Caliban language' to refer to Jaques. When we look at the relationship between Jaques and the Duke we can perhaps begin to see why this should be so. Both Jaques and Caliban are involved with a specifically sexual tension and sexual exclusion. But in both cases a conflict of sheer power seems to underlie the sexual conflict—the division between those who use and those who are used. Jaques, like Caliban, is kept in a situation of degrading servitude, though in Jaques' case it is largely a servitude of the spirit. Jaques, like Caliban, proves a recalcitrant serf. Highly educated as he is, he proves ineducable in the Duke's special mystery of happiness. Like Caliban, Jaques is sexually impeded, though in the case of Jaques the impediment appears to be internal. In either play, the anger of the governing figure asumes a strongly sexual form of expression. I think I know why this is so in *The Tempest* but I do not yet understand why it is so in *As You Like It*.

Moreover, the context of the quarrel, with its 'regress' of ill-usage, prefigures *The Tempest*. Duke Frederick usurped Duke Senior's place;

Duke Senior usurped the deer's; the deer themselves sweep on in 'fat and greasy' happiness, when one of their number is wounded to the death. And in *The Tempest* the usurpation of the Milanese dukedom is mirrored in the usurpation of Caliban's island. We noted before that *The Tempest* is founded on pastoral. We can now see in greater detail the significance of this foundation. The paradox of civility sequestered but unchanged is common to both plays. And in both there is one who marks the mendacity of this situation, in the one play by knowing and in the other play by being. In *As You Like It* all this is only a part of the drama, and largely exhausts itself in the relationship of two figures, Duke Senior and Jaques. In *The Tempest* it is the play's fundamental theme.

It has often been noticed that the plays of Shakespeare do not constitute a series so much as an indefinitely complex system. Each of the outside-figures we have discussed is linked in some way with the rest. For example, Othello stands behind Caliban, not just because neither is white, but also because of particular words uttered in *The Tempest*. Sebastian says angrily to Alonso that he is to blame because he would not match his daughter with a European husband, but would rather 'loose her to an African' (II. i. 119).[32] This, as Dover Wilson has noted in another context,[33] is the language of the stud farm. Plainly, the suggestion is a deliberate echo of the situation of Miranda, Caliban and Prospero. Again, Jaques' famous speech beginning 'All the world's a stage' (*AYLI*, II. vii. 139) was prefigured in Antonio's speech which ends with the words 'A stage, where every man must play a part, and mine a sad one' (*The Merchant of Venice*, I. i. 78–9). Or again, the account given by the first and second lords of Jaques moralizing the deer (*AYLI*, II. i. 44–65) is reminiscent in tone of Salerio's description of Antonio saying goodbye to Bassanio (*The Merchant of Venice*, II. viii. 45–9).

But none of these links is as strong as that which binds Jaques and Caliban. These two are held fast in the central paradox of pastoral. The coincidence of language with which we began proves, therefore, no freak of authorial psychology, but the clue to a thematic relation. I began this essay by conceding that Caliban was domesticated at the end of *The Tempest*, and this appeared to mark a difference between

[32] Have nothing to do with the reading 'lose'. It is Rowe's emendation of the superior 'loose'.

[33] See his introduction to the New Cambridge Shakespeare *Hamlet* (1936), p. lviii.

him and Jaques. But what if the process of domestication must produce, not an Amiens, but a Jaques? Perhaps this is the most remarkable instance of the pastoral paradox: the wild made courtly. Yet in Jaques courtliness never matured into true civility. Thus, if we indulge the fantasy and explore this Protean evolution which, for the fictitious character, serves instead of childhood, we shall find that if Jaques is Caliban, and Jaques is unassimilable, then Caliban too is, what we had always suspected, at bottom unredeemable. Which is why a good Shakespearian like Glynne Wickham misremembered the text and supposed that at the end of *The Tempest* Caliban was left on the island.[34]

Of course, since Shakespeare in all his reworkings never repeated himself, Jaques and Caliban are at least as different as chalk and cheese. Yet it is not a waste of imagination to consider Jaques as a Caliban who has been civilized. After all, Franz Kafka thought it worth his while to write about such another. In 'A Report to an Academy' we find, in all unconsciousness, a combination of the elements of Jaques and Caliban which is almost uncanny in its precision and suggests that the link between the two is more than accidental. Shakespeare, who led us back to Euripides, can propel us so far forward. In this story an educated ape lectures on the process of his own education. He tells how he was 'cabined and confined' in a sort of little-ease[35] (remember Malvolio's darkness—the echoes will not still themselves); he knew 'excellent mentors, good advice, applause and orchestral music'.[36] Such was Arden. He is associated with cages and biting.[37] So was Caliban. He is spellbound by the spectacle of a sailor with a bottle.[38] So was Caliban. He ends by giving public entertainments at banquets and social occasions.[39] So Jaques lived. Kafka's ape could never bear to look at the female they gave him: '. . . she has the insane look of the bewildered half-broken animal in her eyes; no-one else sees it, but I do.'[40] Did Jaques see this look in the face of his fellow creatures? Swift's Gulliver saw the Yahoo in his own wife and therefore removed himself from her proximity. Yet once more we smell difference stronger

[34] *Shakespeare's Dramatic Heritage* (London, 1969), p. 53.

[35] In *Selected Short Stories of Franz Kafka*, trans. Willa and Edwin Muir (New York, 1952), p. 171.

[36] *Ibid.*, p. 168.

[37] E.g. *ibid.*, p. 175.

[38] *Ibid.*, p. 176.

[39] *Ibid.*, p. 180.

[40] *Ibid.*, p. 180.

than similarity. Perhaps Touchstone is in the end closer than the Manichaean Jaques to Shakespeare himself. He could meet the gaze of Audrey—a half-bewildered animal if ever there was one—mock it, understand it and marry it.

Bibliographical Note

(A selective reading list with particular reference to those comedies given detailed discussion in the foregoing chapters.)

Editions. Among single-volume editions of the Complete Works, those edited by Peter Alexander (London, 1951) and by C. J. Sisson (London, 1954) are in standard use: quotations throughout this volume are from the Alexander text. *The Complete Pelican Shakespeare* (London, 1969: General Editor, Alfred Harbage) also provides a good text, an excellent critical essay on each of the plays and some explanatory notes to the text. Fuller introductory material and commentary are contained in the separate volumes of the new Arden Shakespeare (London, General Editors, H. F. Brooks and H. Jenkins): *The Two Gentlemen of Verona*, edited by Clifford Leech (1969); *Love's Labour's Lost*, edited by Richard David (1951); *The Merchant of Venice*, edited by John Russell Brown (1955); *Measure for Measure*, edited by J. W. Lever (1965); *The Tempest*, edited by Frank Kermode (1954). Among the comedies available in the New Penguin Shakespeare (General Editor, T. J. B. Spencer) are: *The Two Gentlemen of Verona*, edited by Norman Sanders (1968); *A Midsummer Night's Dream*, edited by Stanley Wells (1967); *The Merchant of Venice*, edited by W. Moelwyn Merchant (1967); *As You Like It*, edited by H. J. Oliver (1968); *Twelfth Night*, edited by M. M. Mahood (1968); *Measure for Measure*, edited by J. M. Nosworthy (1969); *The Tempest*, edited by Anne Righter (Anne Barton) (1968). Each of these editions contains an informative and critical introduction to the play and a comprehensive commentary on the text. Also useful are the volumes of the New Cambridge Shakespeare, edited by Sir Arthur Quiller-Couch, J. Dover Wilson, and others (1921–), and those of the Signet Shakespeare (New York, 1963– : General Editor, Sylvan Barnet); the latter series includes extracts from the source material and from standard critical studies of each play.

Critical Studies. Modern interest in the comedies as a genre begins with H. B. Charlton's *Shakespearian Comedy* (London, 1938), the first book-length attempt to trace the development of Shakespeare's comic art, in terms of a distinction between 'classical' and 'romantic' kinds of comedy. E. C. Pettet's *Shakespeare and the Romance Tradition* (London, 1949) further explores the relationship between the comedies and the conventions of non-dramatic romance literature. Nevill Coghill's essay, 'The Basis of Shakespearian

Comedy' (*Essays and Studies*, N.S. III, 1950) also emphasizes the relevance of medieval, as opposed to classical, tradition (leading too far, perhaps, in the direction of Christian allegorizing). Northrop Frye's essay, 'The Argument of Comedy' (*English Institute Essays 1948*, New York, 1949) is a brilliantly reductive analysis of Shakespeare's comic form, not in its historical context, but in terms of archetypal patterns that associate comedy with ritual celebration. C. L. Barber's *Shakespeare's Festive Comedy* (Princeton, 1959) turns away from the study of narrative and literary conventions to find in the comedies the influence of traditional holiday games and pastimes, courtly and popular. Courtly wit and stylistic artifice receive attention in M. C. Bradbrook's *Shakespeare and Elizabethan Poetry* (London, 1951); John Russell Brown discusses the imagery of the love-themes in *Shakespeare and his Comedies* (London, 1957); and Bertrand Evans, in *Shakespeare's Comedies* (Oxford, 1960), focuses upon the dramatic use of different levels of awareness between characters and audience. Frank Kermode's chapter on 'The Mature Comedies' in *Early Shakespeare* (Stratford-upon-Avon Studies 3, edited by J. R. Brown and B. Harris, London, 1961) is an excellent epitome of the modern approach to the comedies as sophisticated, complex plays with serious themes. *Shakespeare Survey* 8 (1955) and 22 (1969) take the comedies as their principal theme, and the former contains a survey by John Russell Brown of twentieth-century criticism. The main sources and analogues of the comedies are reprinted in the first two volumes of Geoffrey Bullough's invaluable *Narrative and Dramatic Sources of Shakespeare* (London, 1957–   ).

Among studies of individual plays, Granville-Barker's theatrically oriented *Prefaces to Shakespeare* contain commentaries on *Love's Labour's Lost* (First Series, London, 1927) and on *The Merchant of Venice* (Second Series, London, 1930). This is criticism which respects the spirit of the plays without over-intellectualizing them, and the same might be said of Mark Van Doren's perceptive essays in his *Shakespeare* (London, 1939). Two of the best essays on *The Two Gentlemen of Verona* are H. F. Brooks' analysis of the dramatic function of the clowns (*Essays and Studies*, N.S. XIII, 1963) and Stanley Wells' exploration of its structural defects (*Shakespeare Jahrbuch* 99, 1963). Bobbyann Roesen (Anne Barton) and Cyrus Hoy have each written critical interpretations of *Love's Labour's Lost*, in *Shakespeare Quarterly* IV (1953) and XIII (1962) respectively, while E. A. Strathmann, in examining 'The Textual Evidence for "The School of Night"' (*Modern Language Notes* LVI, 1941) undermines some of the hypotheses about contemporary allusions in the play. *A Midsummer Night's Dream* is the subject of David P. Young's admirable *Something of Great Constancy* (London, 1966), and the theme of imagination in the play has been discussed by R. W. Dent in an essay (*Shakespeare Quarterly* XV, 1964) that is usefully supplemented by the wider context of W. Rossky's article on 'Imagination in the English Renaissance' (*Studies in the Renaissance* V, 1958). Much of the best criticism on *The Merchant of Venice* is contained in the Casebook on the play edited by John Wilders (London, 1969). *As You Like It* is delightfully treated by Harold Jenkins in *Shakespeare Survey* 8 (1955), and there is an illuminating essay on Fortune and Nature in the play by John Shaw (*Shakespeare Quarterly* VI, 1955). There is a Casebook of critical essays on *Twelfth Night* (edited by D. J. Palmer, London, 1972) which however does not include L. G. Salingar's valuable analysis of the play's design in relation to its sources and analogues (*Shakespeare Quarterly* IX, 1958). *Measure for Measure* has attracted much critical attention in the twentieth century, perhaps to greatest effect in G. Wilson Knight's Christian interpretation, *The Wheel of Fire* (London, 1930), F. R. Leavis' essay in *The Common Pursuit* (London, 1952), Mary Lascelles' careful study of the play and its sources in *Shakespeare's 'Measure for Measure'* (London, 1953), Ernest Schanzer's judicious chapter in *The Problem Plays of Shakespeare* (London, 1963), and David Lloyd Stevenson's *The Achievement of Shakespeare's 'Measure for Measure'* (New York, 1966). Criticism on *The Tempest* is equally voluminous: a selection of essays on the play is reprinted in the Casebook edited by D. J. Palmer (London, 1968); there is also a difficult but rewarding study in A. D. Nuttall's *Two Concepts of Allegory* (London, 1967). Finally, of obvious relevance to the comedies are three books on the fools: Enid Welsford's standard social and literary history, *The Fool* (London, 1935), R. H. Goldsmith's *Wise Fools in Shakespeare* (Michigan, 1955; Liverpool, 1958), and William Willeford's *The Fool and His Sceptre* (Nebraska and London, 1969). Robert Armin's association with Shakespeare is discussed in M. C. Bradbrook's, *Shakespeare the Craftsman* (London, 1969).

Index